Praise for *Honest to God Preaching*

"Honesty is not always homiletical policy, but faithful biblical exegete and preacher Brent Strawn offers the church's pulpiteers a chance to change their course. Strawn is one of the key Old Testament scholars that I'd recommend as a hermeneutical and homiletical guide about sin, suffering, and violence. This thoughtful book attempts to redeem the testimony of Israel from the rampant history of anti-Semitism and reveal their ancient story as a fruitful way forward to honest preaching for today. If you want to be honest before, about, and to God, not only in preaching, but in your entire life, this is the book for you. Strawn is not only a world-class biblical theologian; he is a truth-teller. And if we follow his wisdom, the Christian pulpit will eventually be set free to tell the honest-to-God truth and nothing but the truth."

—**Luke Powery**, dean of Duke University Chapel and associate professor of homiletics at Duke Divinity School

"Brent Strawn brings his singular gifts to the reality and crisis of preaching. These include his deep, wide attention to Scripture, his deep reading in collateral disciplines, and his passion for the church. The outcome of his work is a serious, sobering summons to the church and its preachers to reconsider the burden and the wonder of preaching. The church has spent too much energy being 'the friendliest place in town' and too much time being 'the happiest place in town.' And now, says Strawn, it is called to be 'the most honest place in town.' I judge his book to be an urgent must-read invitation to the church, for none but the church (and the synagogue) has the resource for the deep pathologies of our society that can only be overcome by truth-telling. Strawn has written a singularly important book to which acute attention must be paid."

—**Walter Brueggemann**, professor of Old Testament (emeritus), Columbia Theological Seminary

"Preachers: Look no farther for your next sermon series (I won't). Professors: Look no farther for your next homiletics text (I won't). Brent Strawn has long been known in Old Testament circles for his careful scholarship and his deft writing. He's becoming known in our guilds for his inspiring and challenging work. This is no book to sit back and passively consume. It is an invitation to the courage necessary to risk ecclesial confession and restoration. Who's with me?"

—**Jason Byassee**, Vancouver School of Theology in British Columbia, pastor at Vancouver Chinese Presbyterian Church, and coauthor of *Following: Embodied Discipleship in a Digital Age*

"We complain that the Old Testament is archaic, violent, dour, and judgmental, yet Brent Strawn asserts that Scripture is simply honest. Strawn is one of our most fruitful, astute, *honest* interpreters of Scripture. Preachers will be given sermon-instigating insights on every page of Strawn's wonderful book. All Christians are sure to have a fresh, faith-renewing encounter with some of the most controversial and contested parts of Scripture as Strawn and his Old Testament friends shake our preconceptions, rattle our cages, and boldly speak to subjects that often dumbfound the contemporary church."

—**Will Willimon**, professor of the practice of ministry, Duke Divinity School; United Methodist bishop, retired; and author of *Preachers Dare: Speaking for God*

"Brent Strawn's bracing call for honesty about sin, suffering, and violence offers an important challenge to contemporary preaching. But what really sets this book apart is its close reading of some of the most difficult texts in the Old Testament. Strawn joins thoughtful exegesis with an integrative vision that illumines the whole."

—**Ted A. Smith**, A. H. Shatford Professor of Preaching and Ethics, Candler School of Theology

HONEST TO GOD PREACHING

HONEST TO GOD
PREACHING

Talking Sin, Suffering, and Violence

BRENT A. STRAWN

Fortress Press
Minneapolis

HONEST TO GOD PREACHING
Talking Sin, Suffering, and Violence

Copyright © 2021 Fortress Press, an imprint of 1517 Media. All rights reserved. Except for brief quotations in critical articles or reviews, no part of this book may be reproduced in any manner without prior written permission from the publisher. Email copyright@1517.media or write to Permissions, Fortress Press, PO Box 1209, Minneapolis, MN 55440-1209.

Unless otherwise noted, Scripture quotations are from the COMMON ENGLISH BIBLE. © Copyright 2011 COMMON ENGLISH BIBLE. All rights reserved. Used by permission. (www.CommonEnglishBible.com).

Scripture quotations marked (NRSV) are taken from the New Revised Standard Version Bible, copyright © 1989 National Council of the Churches of Christ in the United States of America. Used by permission. All rights reserved worldwide.

Scripture quotations marked (NJPSV) are taken from the New Jewish Publication Society Version. ©1985 by the Jewish Publication Society.

Scripture quotations marked (NASB) are taken from the New American Standard Bible®, Copyright © 1960, 1971, 1977, 1995, 2020 by The Lockman Foundation. Used by permission. All rights reserved. www.lockman.org

Scripture quotations marked (NIV) are taken from the Holy Bible, New International Version®, NIV®. Copyright © 1973, 1978, 1984, 2011 by Biblica, Inc.™ Used by permission of Zondervan. All rights reserved worldwide. www.zondervan.com The "NIV" and "New International Version" are trademarks registered in the United States Patent and Trademark Office by Biblica, Inc.™

Scripture quotations marked (KJV) are from the King James Version.

Print ISBN: 978-1-5064-6126-7
eBook ISBN: 978-1-5064-6127-4

Cover design: Emily Harris Designs and Tory Herman

To great preachers everywhere—usually honest to a fault—especially a few of my all-time favorites:

Reuben Welch

†David Miles

Thomas G. Long

Jon Stallsmith

CONTENTS

Preface   *ix*

Chapter 1: Only as Sick as Our Secrets   1

Chapter 2: Honest about Sin   29

Chapter 3: Honest about Suffering   59

Chapter 4: Honest about Violence   99

Chapter 5: The Importance of Being Earnest—or, Rather, of Preaching Honestly   139

Notes   *181*
Author Index   *217*
Scripture Index   *223*

PREFACE

My debts around this book are several. I thank Rolf Jacobson, who first invited me to write this little volume, for his collegiality and friendship over many years, long before Working Preacher was ever a gleam in his (and others') creative eye. I'm honored he has thought to include me in several of his many endeavors along the way, with this volume just the latest installment. I also thank Scott Tunseth of Fortress Press for his assistance and patience as I worked on the volume with many other plates spinning (more accurately, wobbling). Scott's help and encouragement got the book over the finish line.

I gratefully acknowledge the good people at Westminster John Knox Press for their permission to adapt and reuse some earlier material of mine, most especially in chapter 1. (Other parts of the book also build out from work I have published elsewhere; see further the appropriate endnotes.) I am equally grateful to several friends who read portions of my manuscript in draft form, listened to my ideas along the way, and/or made helpful suggestions of whatever sort, at least some of which (!) I followed: Will Willimon, Ryan Bonfiglio, Jon Stallsmith, and Collin Cornell deserve special mention. I am grateful, too, to my colleagues Warren Kinghorn and Luke Bretherton for some helpful bibliographical suggestions.

PREFACE

As always, I am most indebted to my family: my children, Caleb, Annie, and Micah, and especially and above all my wife, Holly (a.k.a. Sweetie), who makes everything—*all* aspects of our life together—easy. How could I ever repay that? The obvious, honest answer: never. In this project as in all others, Sweetie not only makes our common life easier, she also accompanies me, buoyantly and encouragingly, through the ups and downs of writing (mostly downs, in my case).

Finally, after recently authoring a book entitled *Lies My Preacher Told Me*,[1] I'd like to make up for any offense I caused—well, *try to*, anyway—by dedicating the present volume to all great preachers everywhere. If I am being honest, which seems important given the subject matter of the present book (and the previous one), I worry that there are fewer and fewer of these types of preachers around; but it is also my honest assessment that they are desperately needed, now more than ever. As I hope the present volume makes clear, I am speaking at this point of the kind of preachers who know the full import and dread weight of Israel's (and belatedly, the Great Church's) honesty and how to emulate that in the best of ways. May their tribe increase! I would be delighted if this little book helped toward that end.

I would be remiss, in this regard, if I didn't explicitly flag a few members of this illustrious group who have made a great impact on me: Reuben Welch was my first Bible professor, but long before that (and, in biblical idiom, "to this day"), he was a preaching legend in the denomination I grew up in (Church of the Nazarene). Reuben's penchant for honest preaching was as prophetic as it was pathos-filled, both usually physically presaged by the way his nose would turn bright red before his most intense, tear-ridden remarks. †David Miles was taken from his family and his ministry all too soon but modeled how good truly

PREFACE

good preaching can be, week in and week out, in the smallest of country churches in rural New Jersey. I have never forgotten his ways at Lamington Presbyterian Church, where I was honored to hear him in the pulpit and even more honored, occasionally, to fill in. I was privileged to join the faculty at Emory University a semester after Tom Long had, which meant we went through new faculty orientation together—a hoot for me in my first tenure track appointment but probably beyond tedious for him (yet another junior colleague!). But he was, as always, characteristically generous, patient, and kind. Of course, I admired Tom's preaching and teaching of preaching long before my arrival in Atlanta and have ever since. I've never heard Tom drop a syllable (the word "Chrysostom," Greek for "golden-mouthed," comes to mind)—except, that is, when it was preplanned! Team teaching a course on preaching the Pentateuch at the Candler School of Theology remains one of the highlights of my career. Finally—last but proverbially not least—is Jon Stallsmith, who was my pastor for many years when I lived in Atlanta. I'm deeply thankful for Stalls's ministry of preaching, which has repeatedly stunned me in terms of its intellectual honesty and deep faithfulness and which has changed many lives, including my own.

bas
Easter 2021
Durham, NC

The random, the chaotic, the unintelligible, the contingent, are dimensions of reality as we know it, dimensions that the Bible knows also and whose fissures it does not . . . try to smooth over. Indeed, the Bible's uncompromising portrayal of reality as embracing dissolution and despair as well as resolution and repair is the source of its extraordinary narrative range and power. Any less expansive, multifaceted, and honest representation of accumulated experience and wisdom would be inadequate and inauthentic.

—J. Cheryl Exum, *Tragedy and Biblical Narrative*

The task [of biblical interpretation] is far from easy. It may try the strength of hosts of labourers, and it requires a lifelong devotion to many branches of criticism, literature, archaeology, language, and history. But more is required than even this inexhaustible capacity for labour. The perfect Expositor needs further to be endowed with a genius cognate with that of the sacred writer. He [or she] must above all be a man [or woman] of dauntless independence and perfect candour. In the course of our inquiry we shall see again and again that even a translator has need of invincible honesty if he [or she] would avoid the misleading influences of his [or her] own *a priori* convictions.

—Frederic W. Farrar, *History of Interpretation*

He [or she] would be a poor Bible reader indeed, who would not be fascinated by this incomparable picture book of undisguised humanity. Everything is represented there, the lofty and the low, the terrible and the pure. These kings and soldiers, princes and bankrupts, men of God and unforgettable women—they all bustle about on the most human of all stages. What composure in describing even the darkest matters! To see [hu]man[kind] in this way means, you must know, that God has seen him beforehand. In this long conversation of a people with God—think of the Psalter!—not only is God revealed, [hu]man[kind] too is revealed to himself, more clearly than he could have seen himself by himself. Only in God's light does [hu]man[kind] come into his true size . . . here only does he release all the possibilities of his own self-understanding. In the Old Testament he becomes known to himself as a creature, who . . . is in partnership with God; a creature who is drawn into a vast divine story and who . . . needs to be addressed by God in the events of his life under all circumstances. By that word he lives, with it he stands, and without it he falls.

—**Gerhard von Rad,** *God at Work in Israel*

Alleluia.
Christ, our Passover has been sacrificed;
    therefore let us keep the feast,
Not with the old leaven, the leaven of malice and evil,
    but with the unleavened bread of sincerity and
        truth. Alleluia.

—**1 Corinthians 5:7a–8,** *Book of Common Prayer*

1

Only as Sick as Our Secrets

Two Troubling Memories

I will never forget a particular moment when my wife, Holly, and I sat in a small church in central New Jersey, listening to a sermon in my first or second year of seminary. Given the subject matter of the present book, it seems imperative for me to be honest and say that, in my judgment, the sermon was a rather bad one. I don't recall much of it now, years later, but I recall the gist of it because it produced an exchange in the pews that is forever burned into my long-term memory. The sermon was riffing on out-of-date, worn-out, and inaccurate presumptions regarding differences between the Old and New Testaments. The text being "preached" (I use that verb generously for the moment) was from the Sermon on the Mount, specifically from the so-called antitheses, where Jesus says, "You have heard that it was said . . . but I say to you" (see Matt 5:21–22, 27–28, 31–32, 33–34, 38–39, 43–44). If memory serves, we had just heard the bit about loving one's neighbor but hating one's enemy (5:43)[1] when the dreadful interaction took place.

Directly in the pew in front of us sat a family from the church, as they always did. They were committed members and very involved; the father frequently led music during the services. Right after the part about hating one's enemies in Matthew, the mother of this faithful church family leaned over to one of her children and whispered, loudly enough that Holly and I at least could hear it, "That's what the Jews do." According to this mother, Jews, whether ancient or modern, hated their enemies—apparently invariably and always.

Flash backward to a different memory from many years prior: I'm in high school, on a church youth group service project in Southern California. A few of us are on a brief break from painting the local church and are at the pastor's house next door. He starts cracking anti–Old Testament jokes . . . well, no, correction: he starts cracking jokes about Jews. I was evidently uncomfortable (rightly so!) because, as I recall, my high school self said something. I asked the pastor, probably sheepishly, if such jokes should be made about God's chosen people. His response was cavalier, I thought, even back then, but of course even more so now. It was, in effect, "They aren't God's chosen people anymore. They had their chance."

Two Crucial Points

A great deal could be said about these disturbing vignettes and on many fronts. Obviously, the things the mother from New Jersey and the pastor from California said are racist, more generally, and anti-Semitic, more specifically—not to mention deserving of swift and thorough condemnation. The main thing I want to say about these two troubling memories, however, is that each, in their own way, is effectively countered by the two major points I aim to make in this book:

1. We *only* know of Israel's failures because *Israel was honest enough to share them* with us in the first place—within the pages of Holy Scripture.
2. We would do well, in our preaching and teaching—but also more generally, in our religious experience, practice, spirituality, devotion, and so forth[2]—*to emulate Israel's honesty*, not misuse and abuse it, because *honesty provides a way forward*, perhaps even the *only* way forward, *to reconciliation, health, and recovery*.[3]

Both of the antagonists in the vignettes described above failed—massively—to grasp these two rather basic points. With regard to the first point, the mother from New Jersey mistook Israel's stunning candor in Scripture as some sort of moral (if not genetic) flaw that extended to the present day rather than see it for what it was and still is: a full baring of the soul before God and a public witness to all who will listen. Of course, it didn't help that the preacher that day was not particularly sharp about such matters, and so his sermon actually enabled if not produced the mother's profound misunderstanding.[4] For his part, the California pastor mistook ancient Israel's honesty as a track record of failure that disqualified Israel from God's favor rather than realizing nothing could be further from the truth—as is clear from the New Testament itself (see, e.g., Rom 11:29).[5]

John 5, where Christ asks a man at the pool of Bethsaida if he wants to be healed, is worth contemplating at this point. In his response, the man dissembles a good bit by *not* answering the question in a straightforward manner:

> Sir, I don't have anyone who can put me in the water when it is stirred up. When I'm trying to get to it, someone else has gotten in ahead of me. (John 5:7)[6]

To his credit, the man says he's *trying to get there*, but most of what he says doesn't answer Jesus's rather simple inquiry for a truth to be told: Does he want to get better or not? A famous saying from Alcoholics Anonymous, which I will return to more extensively below, asserts that "we're only as sick as our secrets." How could God forgive what is not candidly expressed, what isn't acknowledged as wrongdoing? Or even if God *could* (and one expects and hopes God *can*),[7] how can we be reconciled with God and with one another or find healing if we live in a stage of constant cover-up and denial? If, that is, we actually somehow *prefer* our secrecy and sickness and sin. Both the mom from New Jersey and the pastor from California missed how candid Israel is in Scripture; instead, they evidently preferred that Israel deny, cover up, and grow sick on their (not always) secret sins. When God asks Israel, "Do you want to be healed?" there is precious little dissembling. Quite to the contrary, the Old Testament frequently manifests full and at times disturbing disclosure. If nothing else, that disclosure indicates that Israel wants to be healed.

With regard to the second point, both the mother and the minister failed to emulate Israel's humble and, one might add, humbling (if not downright humiliating) honesty in their own religious practice. Instead, both of these individuals appear to have assumed that they were somehow *above* or *beyond* what they deemed Israel's deficient ways. Once again, nothing could be further from the truth, as evidenced in the prejudice and bias in both the mother's comment and the pastor's jokes: neither comes across as more virtuous than Israel's candor—not in the least and quite to the contrary. Psychologists would no doubt identify both statements as classic instances of *projection*: blaming some problem or fault of our own on someone else, as if it didn't equally (if not more so) apply to us.[8] Projection might make us feel better temporarily, but since it isn't true, it doesn't make us healthier, only sicker. The god-awful truth is that the history of the Christian church is pockmarked with failures every bit as egregious as those mentioned in the Old Testament (and the New): the terrible history of Christian persecution of Jews is only one particularly horrific example in a far-from-stellar track record.[9] Contrary to the California pastor's arrogant self-confidence, one might well worry—and with very good reason—that it is perhaps we who call ourselves Christians who have "had our chance."

I do not imagine that either of the two central points I argue in this book are particularly novel. The first one—about *Israel's honesty*—is patently obvious (or *should be*) to anyone who has cared to read the Bible closely at all or with any degree of empathy. Surely preachers and pastors should be among the closest and most empathetic of readers, but sadly, that isn't always the case.[10] In my judgment, an empathetic reading automatically and in turn leads (or *should*) to the second point about *emulating Israel's honesty*.[11] But poor practice continues on both of these fronts, and so this book seems necessary if only to remind us of things that we already know (or *should*) if we took Scripture more seriously and approached our preaching and religious practices more carefully.

Three Points of Connection

In the three chapters that follow, I will explore Israel's honesty in the Old Testament with reference to three primary subjects: sin, suffering, and violence.[12] In each chapter, I will focus on a few primary texts or textual units, at least one from a narrative book and one from the Psalms. The latter repository should come as no surprise: the Psalms are famous for their candor, and the Psalter's honesty about sin, suffering, and violence—while perhaps disconcerting to some readers—is no doubt a major reason why it has been treasured for centuries. It is with good reason that Ellen Davis has described the Psalter as "a kind of First Amendment for the faithful."[13] The texts I have selected from nonpoetic books are equally important, however; they reflect a kind of "storied" or "narrativized" honesty that can accompany, exemplify, or concretize the more liturgical and "spiritual" honesty of the Psalms.[14] In fact, when read in concert with the Psalter, it is easy to see how the narrative texts, too, are equally liturgical and devotional (spiritual) in their candor. As such, the narratives Scripture so candidly preserves, and that are themselves so candid, do not reflect simply Israel's "poor track record" or "rap sheet"—one limited to some persons or period, event or moment, *only back there and only back then*. Instead, these stories, no less than one of the great penitential psalms, are fundamentally and at root *confessions*, confessions that resonate *right here and right now*.

There is much more to say, since it will be my contention in this book that *Israel's honesty corresponds to and also facilitates crucial, indispensable aspects of faithful belief and practice*:

* *honesty about sin* facilitates *reconciliation*,
* *honesty about suffering* facilitates *healing*, and
* *honesty about violence* facilitates *recovery*.

Underlying this contention is yet another—namely, that

preaching about these subjects is a primary means of belief and practice by which these facilitations happen.

Since it is so important, let me underscore the last point by rephrasing it: Honest preaching in the wake of Israel's own honesty is a way—a central, indispensable way—Christians can move toward better, healthier, more peaceful ways of being in the world and with God. Honesty, including honest preaching, is a way—maybe even the primary way—we can experience reconciliation, healing, and recovery.

To be sure, more "honest topics" could be added to my list of three. The Old Testament is a large anthology of texts that reveals Israel to be brutally honest about a whole range of matters. I considered, for instance, a triad that was more alliterative: sin, suffering, and struggle, with the last item standing in for and including skepticism (another alliterative *s*!) among other things. Skepticism is definitely worth considering, but readers and preachers can surely do that work on their own—whether the topic is doubt or some other manifestation of uncertainty. In the present moment, when violence is such an area of concern among well-meaning (if not also psychologically projecting) Christians, not to mention a ubiquitous companion on our news and entertainment streams, it seemed important to address that issue here, especially since the general idea of "struggle" is present to some degree in *all* three of the topics discussed here.

In any event, readers and preachers will be quick to see connections between what is said in the present volume and many other topics that could use a good dose of honesty. Readers and preachers will also be able to make connections with other passages of Scripture—because, of course, many other biblical texts could be mentioned in addition to the examples I discuss here. In sum, attentive readers and creative preachers will sense the deep interconnections between the topics and texts that I have selected and a whole host of comparable items, biblical and/or otherwise.

Since this is a short book, not only are the selected texts and topics finite in number, so also is the range of interlocutors limited. It is important to engage some extrabiblical resources, however, since much excellent work has been done on honesty—especially honesty about wrongdoing, suffering, and violence.[15] I refer to some of this work along the way, as it fits with the biblical materials. While I offer reflections on preaching throughout, many of the ramifications for homiletics proper are left implicit in chapters 2 through 4. I make the implicit more explicit in the fifth and final chapter of the book, which summarizes the important benefits of being honest—in the pulpit and the pew but also outside and beyond each. After all, according to Alcoholics Anonymous, "we're only as sick as our secrets." That truism, which captures the connection between sickness and secrecy, deserves further discussion with reference to the primary subjects of preaching—namely, God, Scripture, and us, particularly if we care about reconciliation, healing, and recovery.[16]

Sickness and Secrecy, Scripture and God

A prayer for purity prior to the Eucharist in the *Book of Common Prayer* praises God as the one "from whom no secrets are hid":

> Almighty God, unto whom all hearts are open, all desires known, and from whom no secrets are hid: Cleanse the thoughts of our hearts by the inspiration of thy Holy Spirit, that we may perfectly love thee, and worthily magnify thy holy Name; through Christ our Lord. *Amen.*[17]

There can be little doubt that this phrasing is directly indebted to the Psalms, making it a scriptural epithet, not just a liturgical one. Consider, for example, Psalm 44:

> If we had forgotten the name of our God
>   or spread out our hands to some strange deity,
> wouldn't God have discovered it?
>   *After all, God knows every secret of the heart.* (vv. 20–21; emphasis added)

Or Psalms 38, 69, and 90:

> Everything I long for is laid out before you, my Lord;
>   my sighs aren't hidden from you. (Ps 38:9)

> God, you know my foolishness;
>   my wrongdoings aren't hidden from you. (Ps 69:5)

> You put our sins right in front of you,
>   set our hidden faults in the light from your face.
>   (Ps 90:8)

The Psalter repeatedly points out that the wicked are especially prone to think God can't see their secret deeds (see Pss 10:11; 64:5; 94:7). This erroneous opinion is explicitly refuted in Psalm 10:

> But you [God] *do* see!
>   You do see troublemaking and grief, and you do
>   something about it! (v. 14a; emphasis added)

Small wonder, therefore, to learn, as Psalm 10 continues, that

> the helpless leave it all to you.
>   You are the orphan's helper. (v. 14b)

The Psalms aren't the only scriptural source for the liturgical epithet, as evidenced in this important line from the book of Hebrews:

> And there is no creature hidden from His [God's] sight, but all things are open and laid bare to the eyes of Him with whom we have to do. (Heb 4:13, NASB)

Wherever it comes from—liturgy, psalm, or epistle—the sentiment that secrets must not, indeed *cannot*, be kept hidden forever recalls the saying from Alcoholics Anonymous mentioned above: "We are only as sick as our secrets." Combining *the divine epithet* with this more *recent psychological insight* suggests that honesty before God is not simply a matter of course; *it is a matter of healing*. Honesty, in this combination, is profoundly theological and also, ultimately, therapeutic.[18] This combination of *theology* and *therapy* suggests, in turn, that honesty is central to our healing and to the healing of the world or, perhaps better, central to our healing *for* the healing of the world—and that God has a hand in all that.

Scripture is full of passages demonstrating that no secrets are hidden from God, that it is, in fact, *impossible* to hide secrets from God. The chapters that follow demonstrate this in story and poetry drawn from across the Old Testament. But more should immediately be said: Scripture does not simply *attest* to honest disclosure; it *models* honest disclosure by serving as a place—a clearinghouse, if you will—for the same. When Scripture is read and prayed, reuttered and "reperformed," it realizes and manifests in us who read it and pray it the same full disclosure.[19] We who read and pray are suddenly as honest as the Scripture we are reading and praying *because* we are reading and praying this peculiarly candid canon of Holy Writ. Proclamation, teaching, and singing are additional, more public ways that Scripture is regularly reuttered and reperformed. Whichever practice is adopted, Scripture models disclosure and its benefits but also becomes, within the chosen practice (sermon, prayer, lesson, song), a primary vehicle by which we disclose everything, even and especially our deepest secrets, to God—for our good. This should come as no surprise. This is, after all, the God "from whom no secrets are hid," and hiding secrets, we have come to learn, makes us sick.

Unlike the psychological insight of Alcoholics Anonymous, the liturgical epithet from the *Book of Common Prayer* says nothing about *us*; it simply asserts that no secret is hidden *from God.* Nor does the *Book of Common Prayer* indicate that this "full disclosure" is somehow or ultimately therapeutic. It is modern psychology, especially, that has taught us the latter bit in more recent times, but this psychological insight was long anticipated beforehand in Scripture, especially in the Psalter.

The Bible inspired the liturgical epithet, of course, but it is the special gift of Scripture that it not only reveals the accuracy of the epithet but also clarifies the agent and practice—that it is *our disclosure*—and how that is for our ultimate benefit. And so it is that both the liturgical epithet *and* the psychological insight may be traced back to Scripture and its own manifold examples of disclosure. The Secret-Knowing God is a thoroughly biblical epithet, with the healing that comes from honest disclosure also profoundly biblical.

I've already noted how Scripture's penchant for honesty, if properly known and rightly utilized, might have prevented a pastor and layperson from egregious error. It is thus highly ironic, and profoundly unfortunate, that the brutal honesty of the Old Testament—its utter candor about sin, suffering, and violence (among other things)—is apparently what makes so much of it difficult, if not unpalatable, for many modern readers.[20] The Bible's honesty often proves *too* honest for many people, slightly "too real." Aren't such things—especially sinful, sad, and violent things—best kept private to oneself, for the better of all concerned?

* *Not so*, says the divine epithet: *nothing* is private before this God, "from whom no secrets are hid."
* *Not so*, says the psychological insight: the more secretive, the more sickly.
* *Not so*, says Scripture in a whole host of ways.

A modern parallel to the power of biblical honesty showcases the therapeutic power of disclosure and may prove helpful for those who wonder at, or are offended by, the brutal and beautiful candor of Scripture.

Posting Secrets

Frank Warren started the PostSecret project in November 2004, when he randomly distributed three thousand self-addressed postcards inviting people to send him an anonymous secret. He's been collecting postcards ever since, with the total now numbering well over half a million. Warren has published thousands of these postcards on his website, www.postsecret.com, which has been visited by more than 820 million people. He has produced six printed books, and some of the cards have been used in art exhibits and traveling shows, especially on college campuses.[21]

The "PostSecrets" Warren collects are usually fascinating combinations of images and words that reveal secrets, tell stories, and/or make confessions in arresting ways that are best seen to be fully appreciated. A few examples described solely with words will not do justice to the range of the secrets Warren has collected, nor to their often eye-catching visual presentations, but the following may be taken as suggestive if not entirely representative.[22]

Many of the secrets concern relationships, like *marriage* or *children*:

* "I often wonder what it would have been like if I chose the 'other man' instead of my husband" (written on a picture of a couple holding hands)
* "If I ever win . . . the first thing I'll do—is meet with a *divorce* lawyer" (on a lotto ticket receipt)
* "My entire life has been a lie by omission" (on a picture of an ultrasound on which is written "It's not his baby").
* "I hope he doesn't turn out like me" (on a picture of a child's face with their eyes covered with writing)

Others concern *the self*:

* "Everyday on my way to work, I contemplate driving past it, and never coming back" (on a picture of a traffic jam)
* "I am a 40-year-old child" (on a picture of a child's hand)
* "I have two master's degrees and a doctorate . . . but I still feel like a Failure" (on a picture of a cap, tassel, and diploma, with a capital *F* written in red ink).

Others touch on *self-harm* and *suicide*:

* "When I write a To-Do list . . . I write 'Starve Yourself' but I abbreviate it S.Y. so no one knows" (written on a chalkboard)
* "I've wanted to die for 36 years . . . but I know I'll spend eternity in Hell" (written on a picture of flames)
* "Every day I contemplate suicide and if you knew why, you'd want me dead too."

Many of the secrets concern *God* and *religion*:

* "I don't know how to go back to God . . . And I want to more than anything else in the world . . ." (with a picture of praying hands)
* "If my family found out . . . they would disown me" (on a picture of a sheep with a tag on its ear that reads "ATHEIST")
* "I hate it when people say prayer works because it didn't when I was begging God to save my baby's life" (written on an otherwise blank white card)
* "When I was 16 I had an abortion
  When I was 33 I had a miscarriage
  I think God was punishing me"
    (on a picture with a sleeping baby)

A final example may be especially appropriate for preachers reading the present volume:

* "Some days, it feels more like a Noose!" (written on a close-up photograph of a clerical collar)

These are astounding secrets and just the tip of the iceberg of what is often truly shocking material gathered by Warren. Equally astonishing is how widely the PostSecret phenomenon has caught on, leading one to wonder about its popularity—a topic that Warren himself has considered. Several items seem particularly important.

First, there is the matter of *unity and community*: somehow, someway, people feel united by these secrets, by their revelation, and by sharing them. In Warren's own words, the confession found in these postcards "helps reveal our hidden unity."[23] The final two pages of *The Secret Lives of Men and Women* illustrate this sentiment: four images of a man are depicted—first in a suit and tie, then bare, then as an X-ray image, and then gone. On each image is written, respectively, "Separated by Routine," "We are all," "Mourning in parallel form," "The same silent tragedies." The notion of "parallel mourning" that is on display in and enacted by the PostSecret project is not lost on its observers, as revealed in the following comment from a British reader:

> Some of the secrets really cause me to sit back and say a quick prayer for whoever wrote them. . . . Some of the secrets make me think: "I wonder if so and so posted that secret," and some of the secrets make me think: "WOW! I'm not alone."[24]

Not to be missed in this remark is how the honest confession of a PostSecret can lead to *intercessory prayer*, to *wondering about the secret-teller's identity*, and to *fresh awareness of one's own deeply held secrets* and *one's connection to others*. As the present book will argue, such outcomes are not hard to imagine for the attentive reader and preacher of the honesty that is housed in the Old Testament.

Perhaps readers of PostSecrets feel unified and no longer alone because sharing secrets takes *courage* and, in turn, because telling secrets *en*courages: it can actually embolden someone else to share their own stories that so often "begin with a secret and end with hope."[25] Indeed, it may very well be the telling of a secret, in the beginning, that is what produces hope, in the end. Whatever the case, the PostSecret project is profoundly personal for Warren, and precisely at this point. "When their postcards found me," he writes, "I was able to find the courage to identify my secret and share it too."[26] And Warren is hardly the only one: "I have witnessed many times how the courage of sharing a secret can be contagious."[27] In short, PostSecrets, no less than Israel's honesty in the Bible, turn out to be acts that are "re-performable."[28] That is often the way it is with honest disclosure.

A third item to be mentioned is that *disclosing secrets can change people*—both the secret-tellers themselves and, not infrequently, others who hear, read, or see these secrets, even long after the fact. Sometimes the change brought about by means of honest disclosure is quite literally lifesaving, as evidenced by the cooperation between the PostSecret project and suicide prevention services.[29] The change that occurs is not always a matter of life and death but is no less salvific despite that. Consider the following testimonies from various observers from around the United States:

- ✴ To the person who mailed the postcard that read, "The thing I hate most about myself is that I'm too lazy to

ONLY AS SICK AS OUR SECRETS

change the things I hate," I read your secret and cried. I decided to look at myself and see what my problem was. More than being lazy, I realized it was about fear. I was afraid of trying my hardest and still not succeeding. But then I realized I was already living my worst-case scenario by not even attempting to move forward. Today, I decided fear and laziness would not rule my life. I hope knowing you helped someone will help you too. —New Mexico

* Every single person has at least one secret that would break your heart. If we could just remember this, I think there would be a lot more compassion and tolerance in the world. —Mississippi

* On Thursday, I enjoyed dropping my postcard into the post office box and watching it disappear. My secret does not own me anymore. I don't need revenge. —California[30]

These testimonies are about nothing short of *transformation*, which is also captured beautifully on a postcard showing two women dancing on a rock jutting out over a large canyon. The accompanying text reads:

i used to write my secrets on postcards
they were never posted

now i tell them to real people that know and care
  about me

  thanks, postsecret
  and goodbye.[31]

"Goodbye," because PostSecret is no longer needed. A real, life-altering change has occurred, for the good, forever.

Warren has been asked if he has a favorite secret in the collection. His response captures the potential of real change brought about by secret telling:

> Yes, but I never had a chance to see it. I learned about it in an email that read, in part, *I thought long and hard about how I wanted to word my secret and I searched for the perfect postcard to display it on. After I had created my postcard I stepped back to admire my handiwork. Instead of feeling relieved that I had finally got my secret out, I felt terrible instead. It was right then that I decided that I didn't want to be the person with that secret any longer. I ripped up my postcard and I decided to start making some changes in my life to become a new and better person.*[32]

Much more could be said about the preceding points, but the many connections between the PostSecret phenomenon and truths made known from modern psychology should be obvious. The great benefit of psychoanalysis was, after all, first described as the "talking cure," both by the patient "Anna O." (whose real name was Bertha Pappenheim) and then later by Freud himself.[33] Psychology has come a long way since Freud's days,[34] but research continues to show the real benefits to physical and mental health that are associated with honest disclosure. As I will discuss further in chapter 3, the work of James W. Pennebaker and others has demonstrated that various health benefits also (and perhaps especially) accrue when the disclosure is manifested *in writing*.[35] Freud knew that repressing things caused problems; Pennebaker and his fellow researchers have shown that opening up about things does the exact opposite—it helps in all sorts of ways. Opening up can even produce improved immune function in those who disclose. As it happens, inhibition is hard work that takes a toll on the body's defenses. Keeping secrets, that is, not only prevents one from processing them (and, in some cases, their associated traumas), it can also manifest physically, in physical maladies. The body never lies, according to Alice Miller;[36] Pennebaker's work adds further support to how the body reveals its secrets—tells its truth—one way or another, sooner or later.[37] This is not to say, of course, that all who are ill are keeping secrets. Of course not! It is only to say that keeping secrets can often result in ill health: a sickness of body to accompany the sickness of soul, as it were, because, of course, the two are profoundly interrelated. And so, according to Pennebaker, "excessive holding back of thoughts, feelings, and behaviors can place people at risk for both major and minor diseases."[38] "Confession," on the other hand, "can neutralize many of the problems of inhibition. Furthermore, writing or talking about upsetting things can influence our basic values, our daily thinking patterns, and feelings about ourselves. In short, *there appears to be something akin to an urge to confess.* Not disclosing our thoughts and feelings can be unhealthy. Divulging them can be healthy."[39]

The chapters that follow demonstrate that echoes—or, rather, anticipations—of Pennebaker's and others' important work on the healing power of honesty are found all over Holy Scripture. Here, says biblical scholar J. Cheryl Exum, one finds an "uncompromising portrayal of reality"—one that embraces "dissolution and despair as well as resolution and repair"—because "any less expansive, multifaceted, and honest representation of accumulated experience and wisdom would be inadequate and inauthentic."[40] This, Exum avers, is the very source of the Bible's "extraordinary narrative range and power."[41] Gerhard von Rad concurs, finding in Scripture an "incomparable picture book of undisguised humanity" that fascinates all but the most incompetent readers.[42] "Everything is represented here," he continues, and it takes place "on the most human of all stages," with Scripture manifesting remarkable "composure in describing even the darkest matters!"[43] Such a candid presentation is only possible, according to von Rad, because "God has seen [humanity] beforehand."[44] That is no surprise: this is the God from whom no secrets are hid, after all.

To return once more to the PostSecret project, the therapeutic aspects of truth telling are not lost on its founder, even if Warren doesn't discuss them in great detail. In the foreword to the first PostSecret book, however, psychologist Anne C. Fisher explicitly comments on the similarities between Warren's work and psychotherapy:

> The prominent themes in PostSecret mirror some of the reasons people are drawn to psychotherapy: seeking relief from suffering; sharing painful experiences (especially concerning difficulties in relationships or feelings of isolation); expressing shame and anxiety about aspects of self that are difficult to face; and admitting one's impulses, fears, and fantasies. . . . Both in psychotherapy and in PostSecret, the goal is to bring experience to conscious awareness and to express what is deepest inside and not have it be the end of the world. The goal is to make inner experience concrete by placing it outside the self. This exercise gives us the potential and the

opportunity for self-reflection, for self-acceptance, for increased understanding about the self, and for healing and personal growth."[45]

There are, to be sure, profound differences in scale between PostSecret and full-blown psychoanalysis. "PostSecret is even briefer than the briefest of psychotherapies," Fisher writes, adding that "the healing experience in PostSecret is bite-size, manageable."[46] The fundamental dynamics remain the same, regardless: "One postcard, one shared aspect of self, the secret, shared in a structured way, shared as part of an art project that may slip quietly under the radar of the psychological defenses. Release the secret onto the card, then release the card to Frank by mailing it, *and notice what happens inside.*"[47]

Warren has put the matter much more succinctly in his ultrashort epilogue to the same volume: "I like to believe that whenever a painful secret ends its trip to my mailbox, a much longer personal journey of healing is beginning—for all of us."[48]

One final observation: according to Warren, confessing secrets, telling the truth, often has the aura of the sacred about it. In *PostSecret: Confessions on Life, Death, and God*, Warren states that some of the postcards "are invested with painstaking detail and look like sacred objects, perhaps offering *a kind of prayer.*"[49] It is perhaps for this reason that he includes, in his acknowledgments, special thanks to his mail carrier, Kathy, "who has *faithfully* delivered hundreds of thousands of postcards to my mailbox with kindness and care, *as if the secrets were sacred.*"[50]

Only as Sick, *Only* as Healthy

Those attuned to the honesty of Scripture, perhaps especially the Psalms—those ancient prayers of Israel and (belatedly) the church, full of exquisite and at times painful candor—would no doubt affirm that PostSecrets are a kind of prayer. Hence, and as a result, yes, of course, they are sacred, despite the fact that most of them are not couched in the religious language of formal prayer. But does the lack of explicit religiosity even matter? The epithet from the *Book of Common Prayer* speaks only of the God who somehow sees all secrets; the religious orientation (or lack thereof) of the secret-keepers themselves goes unmentioned. Perhaps, in the end, that orientation is irrelevant. Whether the secret-teller is religious or not, the secrets are still and *nevertheless* known by the Lord.

This emphasis on the Secret-Knowing God in the liturgical epithet and in the Bible writ large is an element that goes largely unappreciated in PostSecret and in much secular psychology. But lest we be tempted to be dismissive of the latter because of its presumed theological deficiency, the words of Fisher about the psychodynamics of PostSecret are helpful:

> At the foundation of psychotherapy is relationship. . . . It is about one human being expressing authentic caring and concern for another, offering comfort, witness, acceptance, assistance, and hope. When you send the postcard to Frank, he is on the other end to receive it. The same person who has offered us an opportunity to share has taken an interest in us and is there for us, unconditionally.[51]

Now, despite all of Warren's good work, it is hard to believe that he loves *all* of the secret-tellers, and even harder to believe he loves them *unconditionally*. Even so, Fisher's comment about a benevolent, nonanxious presence receiving and holding the deepest secrets of our lives is a crucial one. Of course, it is exactly here, at this very point, that as good and as powerfully poignant as PostSecret and psychology are, they are not yet "good enough" in light of the testimony of Scripture and the divine epithet. And so, it is exactly here, at this very point, that we may return to the Bible and its God, "from whom no secrets are hid." According to Scripture, the psychological insights that are true and good—the inescapable need for and importance of honest disclosure (among many other things)—are nevertheless insufficient without the God Who Listens, Sees, and Knows. The stand-ins found in Warren's trustworthy reception of PostSecrets, or in a good therapist in a counseling session, are good as far as they go. Sometimes, we must be quick to add, "as far as they go" is *very far* indeed, and thus *very good*: the stand-in, in the best-case scenario may be seen as nothing less than God's representative, helping facilitate God's healing. But the best-case scenario is just that, and so we must also acknowledge that sometimes the stand-in does not go nearly far enough, because, even at its best, the stand-in only *re*-presents God. Holy Scripture, on the other hand—as we will see more closely in the chapters that follow—realizes and manifests, which is to say *discloses*, a place where all our secrets are "posted," thereby unifying, encouraging, changing, and healing us. But the candor of the canon does *yet still more*, since it does all that *coram Deo*, before the living God. Israel's honesty in the Old Testament, that is, does not simply have *an aura* of the sacred about it, nor is it merely *a kind* of prayer. Israel's honesty is laid out in the very presence of the Sacred Itself, quite frequently in the very pattern of prayer (as in the Psalms). So it is that Scripture realizes, manifests, and discloses not only *the place* where no secrets are hidden but equally also *the God* from whom they cannot be hid.

If we are honest, that, too, is a best-case scenario. Not all readers of Scripture experience the biblical texts that way, perhaps in part because not all preachers of Scripture preach the biblical texts that way. Whatever the case, this vision of the best-case scenario surpasses all rivals, since it includes the God Who Listens, Sees, and Knows. In this way, despite the similarities among PostSecret, psychology, and the kind of honesty found in Scripture, or the insights we can glean from PostSecret and psychology about the benefits of Israel's practices of disclosure, we also see that secret telling à la PostSecret or psychotherapy isn't quite enough—not, at least, according to the divine epithet or to the Scripture that gave rise to it. There is *something more* than just expressing our secrets so that we are no longer sick *with* them or sick *of* them. There is *Someone* more—there is this Other, this One Who Knows All Secrets.

The fact that it is *God* who knows our secrets makes telling them that much more important but also that much more fraught, more risky, more dangerous. In contrast to Warren or a good therapist, the divine presence revealed in Scripture is not always nonanxious, benevolent, and nonjudgmental—quite the opposite at times![52] Revealing our secrets to *that kind* of Presence is difficult. How far can we go? How much is permitted? Israel's testimony in Scripture suggests that we can go *the whole way*, that *all is permitted*: honesty about sin, yes, but also honesty about suffering and violence (and yet still more). That means that shame and disappointment, grief and sorrow, rage and curse are also among the secrets that cannot be hidden, that simply must be revealed and come to light. Scripture discloses all of these—among others—and, in Scripture's reperformance, whether in sermon, song, reading, or prayer, that honesty is made available, realized, and reused now. Israel's honesty is, again and in sum, a site and a script of and for full disclosure before God.

It is a sad fact, however, that Israel's honesty has often not been well received or curated in Christian preaching. Instead, Israel's honesty has often been misappropriated and misused, serving not as a model to be emulated but as grist for a simple-minded supersessionism if not full-blown anti-Semitism.[53] "That's what the Jews do," the mother said to her child in the pew that Sunday in New Jersey. "They had their chance," is what the pastor said in Southern California. It seems likely that both of those sentiments were spawned by old sermonic saws about "Foolish Israel" that can't stop sinning or rebelling or failing, *as if* the Christians gathered for worship, and perhaps also the preacher in the pulpit that day, were not similarly guilty of whatever "problem" (or, rather, "truth") Israel was gracious enough to share in the text at hand.[54] For the sake of emphasis, therefore, the claims of the present volume bear repeating: Israel's gracious honesty should inform our homiletic, serving as a model of truth-telling disclosure; furthermore, real benefits accrue when that example is emulated and serious detriments obtain when it is misunderstood and mishandled. When rightly understood and rightly handled—particularly in the pulpit—Israel's honesty becomes nothing less than our very own and sets us aright.[55] But when it comes to biblical interpretation, nothing is ever easy—with the same holding true for Christian preaching, a signal instance of biblical interpretation. Writing in the late nineteenth century, Frederic Farrer urged that expositors be people of "perfect candour" and that translators evidence "invincible honesty" lest things go seriously awry.[56] Again, easier said than done! But seen in the proper light, the candor of the Old Testament means that it is not simply a book *to be interpreted and preached* but also a book showing us *how to interpret and how to preach*.[57] Put differently, the best kind of preaching—the kind that is honest to God—is based on the honest testimony of Israel, manifested by the honest homilist.[58]

To return to an earlier point, the full range of biblical disclosure, which becomes also *our* disclosure, may be possible because (somewhat ironically) the divine epithet says nothing about our actions at all. It speaks only of God, asserting that no secret is hidden from the Lord. Whatever the secret—that is, whether truly profound or completely trivial—is of no matter: it is *known*. Whether the secret is told, disclosed by us in speech or writing or prayer, also seems to be of lesser import: according to the divine epithet and the Scripture that inspired it, secrets are disclosed *invariably and as a matter of course* simply because no secrets can be hidden from this God. In the Sermon on the Mount, Jesus speaks repeatedly of "your Father who sees what you do in secret" (Matt 6:4, 6, 18). Later in Matthew, Jesus asserts that "nothing is hidden that won't be revealed, and nothing secret that won't be brought out into the open" (Matt 10:26). And so again, the secrets are known or will be soon enough—whether we utter them or not.

And yet, the fact that our precious, dearly held (to our detriment) secrets are already or imminently "out there" makes their telling somehow thinkable and possible, not to mention *even more* significant and *even more* therapeutic. Secrets, we now know, are always on their way to going public, always in the process of coming to light. Indeed, when it comes to God, there is no "process" at all: the secrets are already revealed! A vast number of our problems seem to stem directly from trying to stop a process that is as inevitable as it is existential and theological. Our dear and dreadful secrets are *anything but* secret in the light of God. Why, then, do we hide them? And at what cost do we try?[59]

"We are only as sick as our secrets," says the psychological insight from Alcoholics Anonymous. The word *only* is not to be missed in this formulation. It suggests that we are not sick constantly, inevitably, irredeemably, but *only insofar as* we hide things that must come (and are coming) to light. That means, in turn, that we are only as healthy as our honest disclosure. It would seem, therefore, that we are caught *in between*: on the one hand, our secrets are always on their way to being revealed, even against our wills and our best efforts; on the other hand, the secrets are so deep, so painful and traumatic or vile, that we continue to fight against their revelation, doing our best to hide them ever deeper lest they be seen by others or by God. Of course, we should know better, from Scripture and psychology: the act of disclosure is good for our souls and good for our *psyches*. And we should also know, especially from Scripture, that God is trustworthy when it comes to our secrets—not that they will not come to light, which they most certainly will (see Ps 90:8; Matt 10:26; Mark 4:22; Luke 8:17; 12:2; Rom 2:16), but rather that in their coming to light, God may be trusted with them and with our healing. Indeed, our healing is predicated precisely on these secrets' full, honest coming-to-light.

In his penultimate PostSecret book, Warren testifies to the raw power of secret telling:

> I've seen secrets bring to life a hidden world that can inspire and comfort.

> I've seen how the very act of sharing a secret can make
> it true.
> I've seen how thousands of secrets, like different verses
> to the same song, sing of the search for that
> one special person we can tell all our secrets to.
> I have seen how a collection of earnest secrets can
> challenge each of us to liberate our own.[60]

The chapters that follow show how Israel's honesty in the Old Testament—nothing if not "a collection of earnest secrets" that "challenge each of us to liberate our own"—does all of the above for us now . . . and yet does still more because of "that one special person we can tell all our secrets to" but who knows them already long before that. The chapters that follow also show how Israel's honesty makes a way for preachers and their listeners to be fully honest to, with, and before God—naked, as it were, and yet free of shame (Gen 2:25), walking in the all-revealing light of the One who knows all secrets and hears all confessions.

2

Honest about Sin

The two troubling memories shared in the first chapter traded heavily in one way or another on Israel's failures and sins as recounted in the Old Testament. Both comments fell short, massively and miserably, by failing to recognize the first major point of the present book: *we only know of Israel's failures (and sins) because Israel was honest enough to share them with us in the first place.* Both comments therefore also missed the second major, and correlate, point: *Israel's honesty is something to imitate,* not misuse and abuse, because honesty *provides a way forward,* perhaps even the *only* way forward, *to reconciliation, health, and recovery.* The current chapter addresses Israel's honesty about sin and its connections to reconciliation.

What the New Jersey mother and the California pastor took as a record of inevitable and unavoidable failure on Israel's part is, upon closer inspection, nothing of the sort. It is, instead, Israel's *testimony* or *confession*—or, perhaps better, it is Israel's testimony *to* confession. Confession is, of course, widely regarded as the necessary prelude to forgiveness. Where there is no confession, there is in some ways nothing to forgive—not because wrongdoing hasn't taken place but because the wrongdoing hasn't been acknowledged; the aggrieved cannot forgive because the offending party, whether from ignorance or arrogance, is unfazed by their offense. The offended person feels otherwise! And so, without confession, there can be no true reconciliation between estranged people, no moving forward. That, at least, is how it feels and how it seems.

The failure to adequately reckon with Israel's honesty by the mother and the pastor is thus doubly troublesome. Yes, their remarks were anti-Semitic and supersessionist, but their remarks also reflect a profoundly *un*biblical understanding of forgiveness. Instead of celebrating Israel's honesty about failure, which yields to forgiveness, the New Jersey mother and California pastor berated those making confession, thereby not only mocking Israel but also locking Israel into a history of failure that was, in both of their deficient perspectives, ultimately beyond reconciliation, impossible to overcome. We could call that the equivalent of blaming not the victim but the penitent. Such a practice *prohibits*, not facilitates, forgiveness. Thankfully, Israel knows better:

> He [God] doesn't deal with us according to our sin
>   or repay us according to our wrongdoing,
> because as high as heaven is above the earth,
>   that's how large God's faithful love is for those who
>   honor him.
> As far as east is from west—
>   that's how far God has removed our sin from us.
>   (Ps 103:10–12)

An echo of sorts is present in the first epistle of Saint John:

> If we claim, "We don't have any sin," we deceive ourselves and the truth is not in us. But if we confess our sins, he is faithful and just to forgive us our sins and cleanse us from everything we've done wrong. (1 John 1:8–9)

And so, as noted in chapter 1, we might wonder if at root the problem that afflicted the mother and the minister was nothing less than a case of good old-fashioned projection: attributing problems that exist within our own selves to someone else.[1] "*I'm* not guilty or bad—definitely not like Israel! *They're* the sinful ones!" If that was the malady that afflicted the mother and the minister, the next verse in 1 John 1 hits very close to home indeed:

> If we claim, "We have never sinned," we make him a liar and his word is not in us. (v. 10)

It isn't only the New Testament that knows these truths about sin(s), sinning, and the importance of being honest about all of that. As is clear already in Psalm 103, the Old Testament knows it too, even if it doesn't put things quite as "doctrinally" as 1 John. Be that as it may, the Old Testament knows about all of this because Israel knows about these truths and models them for us again and again in the pages of Holy Scripture. Several texts that are remarkably candid about sin repay our careful attention if we care about the log in our own eye (see Matt 7:3–5) and if we also care about reconciliation with God and one another.

Israel's Honesty about Sin: Thoroughgoing and toward Transformation

Before proceeding further, we should be honest about Israel's honesty about sin. It is, in a word, *thoroughgoing*: striking in terms of its sheer extent. The reason Israel's history in the Old Testament can so easily be mischaracterized and caricaturized as a history of failure is because Israel itself frequently recounts—mercilessly, it seems—its past as falling definitively short of the glory of God, of God's desires and God's wishes. The false characterization one finds in both the pulpit (e.g., the California pastor) and the pew (e.g., the New Jersey mother) depends, therefore—at least to some degree—on how Israel presents itself, though we must quickly add that the caricature fails for the reasons already expressed. In Israel's case, all of this honesty about sin is not to blame itself forever but is instead *a matter of confession on the way to forgiveness and reconciliation*. The point, regardless, is simply that the Old Testament is stunningly candid about sin and shortcoming, wrongdoing and misdeed. In fact, some biblical voices go so far as to make a rhetorical trope of the idea that "our past history is almost entirely one of failure." Consider, for example, the words of that gifted preacher Moses in Deuteronomy:

> Once the Lord your God has driven them [the nations] out before you, don't think to yourself, It's because I'm righteous that the Lord brought me in to possess this land. . . . You aren't entering and taking possession of their land because you are righteous or because your heart is especially virtuous. . . . The Lord your God isn't giving

> you this excellent land for you to possess on account of your righteousness—because you are a stubborn people! Remember—don't ever forget!—how you made the Lord your God furious in the wilderness. From the very first day you stepped out of Egypt until you arrived at this place, you have been rebels against the Lord. Even at Horeb you angered the Lord! He was so enraged by you that he threatened to wipe you out. . . . Also at Taberah, again at Massah, and then again at Kibroth-hattaavah, you have been the kind of people who make the Lord angry. . . . You've been rebellious toward the Lord from the day I met you. (Deut 9:4–24)

As if that isn't a harsh enough message on its own (who could accept it? see John 6:60), it is possible that the last verse is to be read differently: "You've been rebellious toward the Lord from the day *he* met you," which would make Israel's pockmarked history very long indeed—as long, or so it would seem, as Israel has had life.[2]

It must be remembered that Moses here is in *preaching* mode and, further, is preaching directly *to Israel*. No doubt he is a gifted rhetor and has put his own homiletical spin on things, but it is clear that, despite this, he is preaching not, ultimately, to condemn Israel but instead *to transform* it. And so it is that the culmination of his oratory in this section of Deuteronomy is as follows:

> Now in light of all that, Israel, what does the Lord your God ask of you? Only this: to revere the Lord your God by walking in all his ways, by loving him, by serving the Lord your God with all your heart and being, and by

> keeping the Lord's commandments and his regulations that I'm commanding you right now. It's for your own good! (Deut 10:12–13)
>
> So love the Lord your God and follow his instruction, his regulations, his case laws, and his commandments always. (Deut 11:1)
>
> So keep every part of the commandment that I am giving you today so that you stay strong to enter and take possession of the land that you are crossing over to possess, and so that you might prolong your life on the fertile land that the Lord swore to your ancestors to give to them and their descendants—a land full of milk and honey. (Deut 11:8–9)

Moses's seemingly harsh judgments do not, therefore, condemn Israel to repeat a history of failure forever. His troping of Israel's past history as one of failure is in service, finally, not to condemnation but to transformation. The shortcomings he recounts are mere prelude to something *more*, something that transcends a troubled past: a future of full and effective obedience.[3]

Before Israel can get to that future, however, and before Moses's preaching can provoke the necessary change, certain sins simply had to be acknowledged. While Moses's sermon in Deuteronomy touches on a number of unfortunate episodes, the *coup de grâce* by far is what happened at Mount Sinai, which Deuteronomy calls "Mount Horeb." Moses strategically leaves this part of the story out of his earlier summary of the stages in Israel's journey from Egypt. Moses saves it, like the proverbial ace up one's sleeve, to make the point—emphatically and exactly when most effective—that it is not Israel's own innate righteousness that has led them to the land.⁴ Quite to the contrary, it is, instead,

> because of these nations' wickedness that the Lord is removing them before you.... It is because these nations are wicked—that's why the Lord your God is removing them before you, and because he wishes to establish the promise he made to your ancestors: to Abraham, Isaac, and Jacob. (Deut 9:4–5)

Here again Moses is *preaching* and *preaching to Israel*. He doesn't make much more, in this specific passage at any rate, of the other nations' wickedness, though God's promises to and love for the ancestors are consistent themes throughout Deuteronomy.⁵ The sermonic point, in any event, is clear: Moses's rhetorical move is ultimately to address and acknowledge *Israel's own wrongdoing*, not that of the nations. And in this particular sermon, no wrongdoing is more obvious than what took place at Mount Horeb. "Even at Horeb you angered the Lord!" Moses begins (9:8). Well, what happened at Horeb?

(Religious) Adultery on One's Wedding Night

The golden calf, of course, is what happened at Horeb. Walter Moberly has memorably described this particular debacle as "rather like committing adultery on one's wedding night."⁶ While Moses is atop the mountain, receiving the covenant commandments from God, the Israelites ask Aaron to "make us gods who can lead us" because they "don't have a clue" of what happened to Moses (Exod 32:1). And Aaron does it. After receiving gold items from the people, he makes a metal image of a bull calf, and the people declare, "These are your gods, Israel, who brought you up out of the land of Egypt!" (32:4).

This intriguing narrative fascinates in a whole host of ways. It's not entirely clear, for example, what Aaron—or the people, for that matter—is up to, at least at first. The language that both parties use, "gods," is *ĕlōhîm* in Hebrew, which is technically a plural form (morphologically). Despite that fact, *ĕlōhîm* is often used with reference to the one God—capital-*E* *Ĕlōhîm*, if you will—as in Genesis: "In the beginning, God [*Ĕlōhîm*] created the heavens and the earth" (Gen 1:1 NASB).

It is the presence of other grammatical complements that reveals if any given instance of *ĕlōhîm* is singular or plural: if an accompanying adjective or verb is plural, then so is *ĕlōhîm*; if singular, then singular. The verb in Genesis 1:1, for example, is singular: *bārā'* ("created"), indicating the one God's creative activity. In Exodus 32, the grammatical forms are plural and so

> Make us *gods* [plural *ĕlōhîm*] who can lead [*yēlĕkû*, a plural verb] us. (Exod 32:1)

and

> These are your gods [plural *ĕlōhîm*] who brought you up [*he'ĕlûkā*, a plural verb]. (Exod 32:4)[7]

The presence of plural *ĕlōhîm* in Exodus 32 is quite damning, of course, because only a few chapters earlier in Exodus, in the very first commandment of the Decalogue—itself the very first law Israel receives as part of its covenantal relationship with God—plural *ĕlōhîm* are expressly forbidden:

> You must have no other gods [plural *ĕlōhîm*] before me. (Exod 20:3).[8]

This injunction is followed hard and fast by another:

> Do not make an idol for yourself—no form whatsoever—of anything in the sky above or on the earth below or in the waters under the earth. Do not bow down to them or worship them. (Exod 20:4–5a)

The golden calf fails on both counts. It is not simply "another god"—some other divine entity than the Lord, which would have been bad enough and obviously out of line. No, the *singular* calf has somehow, someway become in Israel's acclamation a plural entity. The singular calf is now a plural *ĕlōhîm*, "gods," in what could not be a clearer violation of the first commandment. The problem is made worse still by how this singular calf turned plural gods is/are immediately credited with bringing Israel up out of Egypt, something that is otherwise the action of the one true *Ĕlōhîm* alone, as per the Decalogue's all-important prologue:

> I am the Lord your God [*Ĕlōhêkā*]—I brought you out [*hôṣē'tîkā*] of the Land of Egypt [*mē'ereṣ miṣrayim*], out of the house of bondage. (Exod 20:2; my translation)

But now, with the calf, everything is misunderstood, misconstrued, upside down, and wrong side out:

> These are your gods [*ĕlōhêkā*], Israel, who brought you up [*he'ĕlûkā*] out of the land of Egypt [*mē'ereṣ miṣrayim*]! (Exod 32:4b)

The golden calf fails the Decalogue test in a second way. The image that is made by Aaron is clearly in the form of something found here "on the earth below" (Exod 20:4b). Still further, Israel is explicitly said to have "bowed down" to the calf (32:8).

Both are clear violations, this time of the second commandment (20:4b–5a).

Adultery on one's wedding night, indeed! Right after solemnly swearing "I do"—both before and after the Decalogue (see 19:8; 24:7)—Israel breaks its vows, specifically the very first (and close second) of them, arguably the most important of its vows, in the most heinous of ways.

And then Israel writes it all down, telling us all about it, in detail, for posterity, forever.

More (Real) Adultery—This Time, Belated

Moberly's memorable connection between the golden calf and adultery isn't simply an apt analogy of his own devising: it's equally also a biblical metaphor. Idolatry was often construed and presented in marital terms as infidelity.[9] This trope is common in Prophets, for example, but it is also found elsewhere in the ancient Near East, where "the great sin" stood not only for adultery but also (and relatedly) for political disloyalty.[10] It is perhaps no surprise, in this light, that a prohibition against adultery is found in the Decalogue, which is the preeminent articulation of Israel's political-religious (i.e., *covenantal*) relationship with God.

The use of adultery in metaphorical constructions shouldn't be taken as evidence that adultery *only* had religious or political meaning, however. The seventh commandment is not glossed in any religious way and appears amid the latter part of the Decalogue, which deals especially with social, neighborly relationships.[11] *Real* adultery mattered, that is, and was a problem, "a great sin," whether it took place early on (say, on one's wedding night) or much later (say, "in the spring, when kings go off to war"; 2 Sam 11:1), which brings us, of course, to David and Bathsheba.

Here is another narrative that continues to fascinate readers and interpreters. I cannot do justice to it here. It must suffice for present purposes to once again note the extreme honesty of this story. At a time when monarchs are typically off doing the sorts of things monarchs typically do (not all of which are good!), David hangs back, preferring to send Joab and company off to do all the killing for him (2 Sam 11:1a). This, too, of course, is what monarchs tend to do: delegate death-dealing. And so, the opening verse recounts, "But David remained in Jerusalem" (11:1b).

Next, David proceeds to do something else that monarchs tend to do: abuse their power. Already back in 1 Samuel 8, when Israel first demanded a king "like all the other nations" (v. 5), the Lord instructed Samuel to "give them a clear warning, telling them how the king will rule over them" (v. 9). "This is how the king will rule over you," Samuel said:

> He will take your sons, and will use them for his chariots and his cavalry and as runners for his chariot. He will use them as his commanders of troops of one thousand and troops of fifty, or to do his plowing and his harvesting, or to make his weapons or parts for his chariots. He will take your daughters to be perfumers, cooks, or bakers. He will take your best fields, vineyards, and olive groves and give them to his servants. He will give one-tenth of your grain and your vineyards to his officials and servants. He will take your male and female servants, along with the best of your cattle and donkeys,

and make them do his work. He will take one-tenth of your flocks, and then you yourselves will become his slaves! (1 Sam 8:11–17)

The key term in this passage is, unmistakably, the verb "to take" (*lāqaḥ*), which repeatedly pounds on Israel's skull in this all-too-honest premonarchy assessment of monarchy. Four times in Hebrew (five in the above translation), the verb "to take" describes what verse 11a calls "the justice of the king" (*mišpāṭ melek*; my translation; CEB: "how the king will rule"). Royal justice is, from the start, presented as anything but: it is perverse, dominated repeatedly—almost exclusively—by acquisition, acquisition, and yet more acquisition. That is *royal* justice: the king takes. The objects of this royal taking are numerous, running from family (children, both sons and daughters) to property, livelihood, and possessions. And this does not yet mention the twice-used verb that means "to confiscate one-tenth" (*'āśar*) nor how the monarch's reallocation of funds and goods goes toward his own mostly militaristic purposes, with the final result being Israel's self-enslavement—back to Egypt, only this time with a native-born Israelite pharaoh! No wonder the solemn finale of this most grave warning is

> when that day comes, you will cry out [*zĕ'āqtem*] because of the king you chose for yourselves, but on that day the Lord won't answer you. (1 Sam 8:18)[12]

Alas, this warning had absolutely zero effect in Samuel's day:

> But the people refused to listen to Samuel and said, "No! There must be a king over us so we can be like all the other nations. Our king will judge us and lead us and fight our battles." (1 Sam 8:19–20)

HONEST ABOUT SIN

Except, of course, when the king does nothing of the sort and sends other people, people like Joab, to do his dirty work. When that happens, it should come as no surprise, since 1 Samuel 8 gave plenty of advance warning about monarchs and their conscripted troops and military hardware designed and destined to fight their battles for them.

Now, the royal outsourcing of violence doesn't mean kings can't still do a great deal of damage themselves, even when not on the battlefield. And that is exactly what David does, back in Jerusalem, in the lovely springtime:

> One evening, David got up from his couch and was pacing back and forth on the roof of the palace. From the roof he saw a woman bathing; the woman was very beautiful. David sent someone and inquired about the woman. The report came back: "Isn't this Eliam's daughter Bathsheba, the wife of Uriah the Hittite?" So David sent messengers to take her. When she came to him, he had sex with her. (2 Sam 11:2–4a)

The connections to 1 Samuel 8's warning about "royal justice" and "how kings rule" are even clearer in Hebrew: "David sent messengers and he took [*lāqaḥ*] her." Not only does the king *take*; the narrative is explicit that it was David who did it. *David* took her, the text says, even though he sent messengers to do it. They went to Bathsheba, but they did not perform the deed of taking, because David is the king, and kings are those who take. Samuel was a prophet in more ways than one.

In this case, what David takes is not something but some*one*— a person, the wife of another, Bathsheba, who is Eliam's daughter and Uriah's wife. But in the description of David's act, Bathsheba is not described in any of these ways but gets only a nondescript pronoun that figures her as nothing more than the object of David's verbal action: he took *her*. It doesn't matter who Bathsheba is, that she is a person or a daughter or the wife of another, because David is a king and king's take. She is his object—of taking and of desire. And so, "he had sex with her," the Hebrew text reports in two brief words, *wayyiškab 'immāh* (v. 4b), which belong to a series of two-word reports that propel all that follows:

He had sex with her [*wayyiškab 'immāh*]. (2 Sam 11:4b)

I'm pregnant [*hārāh 'ānōkî*]. (2 Sam 11:5b)

You are that man! [*'attāh hā 'îš*]. (2 Sam 12:7a)

I've sinned against the Lord! [*ḥāṭā'tî la-Yhwh*]. (2 Sam 12:13a)

The first two statements are obviously closely, even intimately, related. David's *taking* and Bathsheba's subsequent conception lead to a chain of events culminating in Uriah's death, which was planned, with malice aforethought, to cover up David's sin.

But some things cannot be covered up.

Not from God, from whom no secrets are hid! Even secret sins are eventually aired out, then set in the light of God (see Ps 90:8)—as David will learn momentarily, painfully, and from God's own mouth (2 Sam 12:12). So it is that, once Uriah is dead, with the last loose ends apparently tied up and Bathsheba relocated to David's house as his wife and mother to his son, the narrative asserts quite laconically but oh-so-ominously,

But what David had done was evil in the Lord's eyes. (2 Sam 11:27b)

This comment transitions immediately to Nathan's divine mission to David, armed with nothing more than a sermon illustration about a rich man with tons of stuff and a poor man who had nothing but one small lamb that ate from his table and "was like a daughter to him" (2 Sam 12:3b).

Nathan's parable is a familiar one and needn't be rehearsed in full here. It is enough to note how the parable underscores the severity and atrocity of David's sin.[13] According to the dynamics of the story, when the rich man takes (v. 4: *lāqaḥ* again!) the poor man's ewe for a dinner engagement, it isn't a simple case of picking up lamb chops from the store for a nice evening at home. This is the poor man's *daughter*, taken (as kings are wont to do) by force and power, killed, then cooked, then offered up as a dish for some random traveler's culinary pleasure. It is *a daughter* that is treated this way! Still further, this is the poor man's *only* daughter—of this kind, at any rate (v. 3b). He had nothing else to his name (v. 3a) and certainly nothing to replace this particular, well-beloved child.

David takes the bait; he is incensed at the injustice of this account. He calls for judgment, maybe even the death penalty, on this rich man because he "had no compassion" (*lō'-ḥāmal*, v. 6). Then comes the next two-word utterance: *'attāh hā 'îš*, "*You are that man!*" (v. 7a).

David is the guilty party, who deserves the worst of punishments. *David* is the one who has taken something, *someone*, much beloved by another—though we readers already knew as much (2 Sam 11:4a). David, per the mapping of Nathan's story, is the one who has failed to show compassion, a phrasing that casts his act of adultery, murder, and cover-up in a much larger light. By means of the verb *ḥāmal* ("to feel compassion, take pity on" [12:6, also in v. 4]; CEB: "wasn't willing"), David's actions are portrayed as decidedly *un*compassionate, *un*merciful—as lacking or denying care and consideration. That judgment is indisputable in the case of Uriah's death. But what of the adulterous affair? Many modern people, or so it seems, are foolish enough to think that adultery is limited to two consenting adults. But nothing could be further from the truth![14] The use of *ḥāmal* suggests that adultery, too, lacks compassion, mercy, and consideration. "But for whom?" we might ask. The most obvious response is the spouse who has been cheated on, but perhaps the other spouse—the one involved in the adultery—is another, close second. That, in fact, must be the case in 2 Samuel 11–12, where we are told nothing of Bathsheba's feelings about any of what transpires, nor of any level of complicity in the affair with David. In point of fact, the burden of the entire account—the parable and the story that precedes it—is that she is anything *but* complicit: she has been "taken" by the rich man, David, from the bosom of a caring husband who proves, in the narrative, to be an outsider (a Hittite) more pious than David himself (11:11). In the end, then, Uriah, too, is also something of a lamb: one led to the slaughter (11:24).

After identifying "the man" in question, Nathan connects all the dots for David. First, the murder:

> You have struck down Uriah the Hittite with the sword. (2 Sam 12:9)

Next, the taking—twice:

> You have . . . taken [*lāqaḥ*] his wife as your own. (2 Sam 12:9)

> You . . . took [*lāqaḥ*] the wife of Uriah the Hittite as your own. (2 Sam 12:10)

In brief, in 2 Samuel 11–12, Israel gets—in the person of David—exactly what it asked for in 1 Samuel 8: a merciless *taker* without regard and with zero compassion.

With the crimes identified and the defendant pronounced guilty, Nathan proceeds to judgment: the sword will never leave David's house (2 Sam 12:10), trouble will come from within his own family (v. 11a), and that which was intimate and private will be profaned and exposed (v. 11b). "You did what you did secretly," God says through Nathan, "but I will do what I am doing before all Israel in the light of day" (v. 12). One could easily imagine additional clauses here:

> You did what you did secretly,
> *and your secrets have made you sick,*
> but I will do what I am doing before all Israel in the
> light of day
> *because from me no secrets are hid.*

In this second text concerning adultery in the Old Testament,[15] the honest disclosure of sin is the result of divine initiative, which uncovers a devastating secret. There is, as here, such a thing as *the divine exposure of sin*. There is no getting around that, for better or for worse, because it falls within God's power and purview: "You have set our iniquities before you, our secret sins in the light of your countenance" (Ps 90:8 NRSV). But despite God's revelation of what we might call David's "PostSecret"—against David's own will—it should be underscored that this nadir in David's story, no less than its zenith (see 2 Sam 7), is preserved and recorded in Scripture. As if ripped from the latest headlines, 2 Samuel 11–12 recounts the worst of scandals about Israel's most renowned king, involving illicit sex, conspiracy, and murder. Once again, Israel is brutally honest in its assessment, looking unblinkingly at David and his (mis)deeds.

> And then Israel writes it all down, telling us all about it, in detail, for posterity, forever.

Confession toward Forgiveness, Part 1: David in Story and Psalm

Israel tells us more about David than just his sin, of course. Indeed, in this way, Israel's honesty about David's sin provides a model for thinking about Israel's honesty about other accounts of its sin, as, for instance, in the case of the golden calf. Before returning to "Calfgate," however, or more general learnings about Israel's honesty with reference to sin, David's own honesty about his sin should be considered. David's response to Nathan's parable is quick and immediate, almost staccato. There is absolutely no dissembling, no beating around the bush, no excuse—just the next installment in the two-word drama of "Uriah and Bathsheba-gate":

> I've sinned against the Lord! (*ḥāṭā'tî la-Yhwh*; 2 Sam 12:13a)

Perhaps the only thing that can rival the rapidity of David's confession is how swiftly it is met with absolution. Without skipping a beat, without even starting a new verse (as it were), Nathan absolves his adulterous and murderous monarch:

HONEST ABOUT SIN

Now the Lord has put away your sin; you shall not die.[16] (12:13b NRSV)

There is a dread consequence, however, for David's sin, despite his confession: David will live, but his son will not (12:14).

Several things are worth observing at this point. First, Israel remembers its greatest king's worst sins and broadcasts them for all to hear. Honesty like this—about politics, no less, and in the highest office of the land—is surely in rare supply in our own, more recent, days. In fact, that kind of honesty seems downright unimaginable now. It would be impolitic, terrible for approval ratings, and devastating for reelection (or so it seems). Second, Israel remembers that its greatest king, when exposed and confronted by his worst sins, confessed that he was, in fact, 100 percent *guilty as charged*. Such a move is even rarer these days, virtually inconceivable, especially among today's politicos. Contemporary politicians get exposed all the time, of course, and with regularity, thanks to an insatiable public demand for salacious news on our social media outlets. But such exposure is rarely, if ever, accompanied by admission, humility, and speedy resignation. Now, it is denial, cover-up, pleading the Fifth! The third observation is perhaps the most unthinkable of all, especially for us, here and now. It is simply that honesty about sin—true confession of profound wrongdoing—leads to transformation and forgiveness, even if some consequences unavoidably linger.[17] It is surely a sign of shame and impoverishment that it is so hard for us, now, to imagine the possibility of forgiveness following confession, even and perhaps especially in the public square.[18]

Surely there is a debilitating, unhelpful and unhealthy cycle at work in our world with regard to honesty about sin. It seems probable that our inability to be honest about wrongdoing—our own sin and sinfulness—means that we cannot move to forgiveness. Or perhaps the equation should be reversed. Maybe it is the (seeming) impossibility of forgiveness that leads us to be as duplicitous as possible about our sin. Better to keep up appearances, hoping that we are not found out. Of course, when we do that, not only are we not found out, we are also not forgiven.

Scripture knows better. Again, 1 John:

> If we claim "We don't have any sin," we deceive ourselves and the truth is not in us. But if we confess our sins, he is faithful and just to forgive us our sins and cleanse us from everything we've done wrong. (1 John 1:8–9)

God knows better too—this is the God from whom no secrets are hid, after all. But this is also the God who is, at one and the same time, "rich in mercy" (Eph 2:4).

We are only as sick as our secrets, Alcoholics Anonymous says famously. David, thanks to Nathan's confrontation and his own honest confession, is no longer sick on his secrets of infidelity and murder, though he is soon bereaved of an infant child and at odds with another, much older, son. The profundity and pathos of what plays out in David's house after 2 Samuel 12 shows that the absolution offered by Nathan, while speedy, is hardly a panacea. Perhaps that is the narrative's way to assuage any reader who finds David's prompt, two-word confession a bit hasty and worries if it might be *too* quick if not a tad bit . . . well, disingenuous.

Perhaps similar concerns gave rise to the interesting connections that have been drawn, already within Scripture itself, between 2 Samuel 12 and Psalm 51. If David's "I've sinned" strikes us as too brief, and therefore not quite sufficient, Psalm 51 swoops in. If we are honest, we'd like to hear David be more contrite, say a bit more than just a two-word utterance, especially given the severity of what he's done. We'd like to hear him talk about how he is constantly aware of his wrongdoings and how his sin is always smack-dab in front of his face, inescapable. We'd like to hear him say that he knows God is correct in judging him. We'd like to hear him beg for mercy and forgiveness. All of that and more is exactly what Psalm 51 delivers, and in great poetic detail. In the superscription it is explicitly identified as "a psalm of David, when the prophet Nathan came to him just after he had been with Bathsheba."

Psalm 51 is a famous text, not least because it is one of the seven "penitential psalms"—along with Psalms 6, 32, 38, 102, 130, and 143 (see also the Prayer of Manasseh)—so called because of these poems' expression of regret over wrongdoing. In these compositions the psalmists are more than ready "to concede guilt."[19] The opening lines of Psalm 51 are particularly well known:

> Have mercy on me, God, according to your faithful
>   love!
>   Wipe away my wrongdoings according to your
>   great compassion!
> Wash me completely clean of my guilt;
>   purify me from my sin!
> Because I know my wrongdoings,
>   my sin is always right in front of me.
> I've sinned against you—you alone.
>   I've committed evil in your sight.
> That's why you are justified when you render your
>   verdict,
>   completely correct when you issue your judgment.
>   (Ps 51:1–4)

These four verses alone (not to mention the rest of the psalm) are somehow more satisfying than the two words "I've sinned." Readers of 2 Samuel would like to see David more penitent, and the penitential Psalm 51 is happy to provide such a script. But the script we find in Psalm 51 is itself not entirely satisfying vis-à-vis 2 Samuel: "I've sinned against you—you alone," Psalm 51:4 says, and that doesn't strike us as quite right. What about Uriah? What about Bathsheba? At the very least, 2 Samuel 12 seems clear that David was guilty of not showing compassion (*ḥāmal*) to them. That David *sinned* against them, too (in the process), seems obvious.

The questions about sinning against Bathsheba and Uriah are real and not to be shirked, but the poet of Psalm 51 is caught up in prayer to God with everything now riding on the psalmist's relationship with the Lord. In this sense, Psalm 51 is actually not too different from 2 Samuel 12:13's brief two-word utterance *ḥāṭā'tî la-Yhwh*: "I've sinned against the Lord!" In 2 Samuel 12:13, that is, Uriah and Bathsheba also go unnamed, perhaps because they've already been present in Nathan's parable in verses 1–4 and in his point-by-point explication in verses 7–10. It was, after all, "what David had done"—the entirety of it, *en masse* and *en bloc*—that was so evil in the Lord's eyes (2 Sam 11:27). And so, David confesses his sin *against God* in both the story and in the psalm.

The divine recipient of confession makes good sense, further, if only because "sin" is a rather heavy, theological term. We don't use it much these days, even in church. It's been dying a slow death since the 1970s, if not long before that, when Karl Menninger wrote his best-selling book *Whatever Became of Sin?*[20] Instead of *sin*, we prefer to speak today of *problems*, *addictions*, *sickness*, or perhaps *a criminal record*. None of these alternative terms are necessarily bad, especially when they are true, but the word *sin* says something more. Saying *sin* ups the ante; it's a word that envisions God in the room in the case of this particular wrongdoing. And once God is in the room, all other things don't seem quite as important. Probably because they aren't! The other things *are* still important, to be sure, but only relatively so in comparison with the God who is now present, invoked by this theological term, *sin*. The specific matter at hand is no longer merely an "offense" or a "wrongdoing" of some general variety. No, to speak of *sin* means that the situation is truly grievous if for no other reason than the fact that God is now *in the mix* and *part of the discussion*. Sin language is God language. To speak of *sin* means something has gone wrong—very wrong indeed, with serious repercussions—while at the same time indicating that that "something" that has gone wrong somehow involves God.

So, yes, of course, David has sinned against Uriah and Bathsheba. His killing and taking, taking and killing, are egregious abuses of power whether he was a king or not. And yet these acts are *still more*. They are *sin*. Sin *against God*. That is what David is honest about—and unstintingly so—according to the narrative of 2 Samuel and in the poetry of Psalm 51. And Israel remembers all this and memorializes it. Yes, David is the best of kings who made the worst of mistakes. And yes, David, the best-and-worst king, was also forgiven, even if his confession was überbrief, as it was in 2 Samuel 12, and even if it strikes us as somehow incomplete and unsatisfying even in the much longer Psalm 51.

Confession toward Forgiveness, Part 2: Israel after Adultery

Israel's honesty about David's sin and David's own honesty about his sin are worth wondering about with reference to the golden calf story. In this story, too, there is almost unbearable candor about the community of faith's *faithlessness* at a moment when it seems like it should have been remarkably easy to keep faith. There they are at God's holy mountain after all, amid impressive pyrotechnics! Surely that would be a time to be faithful with ease. But no. And so, "within the history of Israel," writes Nathan MacDonald, "the story of the Golden Calf functions as an *epic fail*."[21] The making and worshipping of an idol, acclaimed as plural *gods*, right when Moses is atop God's mountain, receiving the God-inscribed tablets of the covenant (Exod 31:18), brings to mind another "mountain-top experience" where others, too, found it difficult to believe:

> Now the eleven disciples went to Galilee, to the mountain where Jesus told them to go. When they saw him, they worshipped him, but some doubted. (Matt 28:16–17)

The question, clearly, is not whether profound moments of faithlessness occur. Mount Horeb and the mountain in Matthew 28 offer irrefutable evidence that they happen all the time, even at the most inexplicable of times. The question, rather, is what to do in the face of such shortcomings that are so real, so *ill*-timed, that they cannot be ducked but simply have to be acknowledged.

The answer, of course, is simply to acknowledge them. That is what David does when confronted by Nathan so that his secret sins are no longer held inside, pathologically.[22] Great

King David, popularly understood rightly or wrongly (more the latter, in my judgment) to be "a man after [God's] own heart" (1 Sam 13:14 KJV) is nothing more or less than *an adulterous, murderous sinner*. Nathan's judgment makes clear that these latter qualities are not "after God's own heart." And yet, even so, there David is, an adulterous, murderous sinner *confessing* immediately, quickly, without excuse in front of God, Nathan, and any and all within earshot (and then also to everyone else who ends up reading Holy Scripture). And that is also exactly what Israel does when it recounts, in full disclosure, the golden calf debacle, its own equivalent to marital infidelity on the very first night of its covenantal marriage to God. The recounting of what took place at Horeb/Sinai, that is, *is* confession: it is Israel coming clean about its worst sin. And this honest confession about sin leads to absolution—for David, yes, thanks to Nathan, but also for Israel, thanks to Moses's shrewd intercession (Exod 32:11–14).

Israel's honesty about sin—corporately with the calf, and representatively with David—is thus in service to transformation and reconciliation with God. In the case of corporate Israel, the book of Exodus has more to contribute to that discussion than just Moses's savvy prayer skills, as important as those are. For immediately after Moses's extended interchange with God that ultimately convinces the Lord to continue the trek to Canaan (33:12–34:9) comes a new iteration of the covenant, with a new, but similar (see 34:1), version of the Decalogue (34:10–28). Israel is restored—taken back, as it were, to that first wedding night and given a second chance. This time, things work out; the covenant takes. The rest of Exodus depicts Israel at full stretch, in full obedience as it executes—to a T—the instructions for the tabernacle, where God will take up residence in Israel's midst.

And that is, in fact, exactly what happens, and that is, in fact, precisely how Exodus ends:

> When Moses had finished all the work, the cloud covered the meeting tent and the Lord's glorious presence filled the dwelling. Moses couldn't enter the meeting tent because the cloud had settled on it, and the Lord's glorious presence filled the dwelling. Whenever the cloud rose from the dwelling, the Israelites would set out on their journeys. But if the cloud didn't rise, then they didn't set out until the day it rose. The Lord's cloud stayed over the dwelling during the day, with lightning in it at night, clearly visible to the whole household of Israel at every stage of their journey. (40:33b–38)

This ending would have been unthinkable, altogether impossible, without the honesty about sin that leads to reconciliation. Israel confesses its sins, writes them all down honestly, and is transformed. That is the not-so-dirty and not-so-little secret about candidly confessing secrets.[23] And, as if that weren't enough good news about how confession facilitates reconciliation, after the book of Exodus comes the book of Leviticus, which begins with an extended "manual of sacrifice" containing detailed instructions on "the craft of forgiveness":[24] how Israel may be restored whenever they do wrong and acknowledge the same—when they are, in brief and in sum, *honest about sin*.[25] In fact, in one sense, the entirety of the sacrificial system may be seen as an elaborate acknowledgment of sin: a way to be honest to God about wrongdoing.

In this way, corporate Israel knows, with David its royal representative, God's truth about confession—honesty about sin—and so can revoice and reperform it in prayer:

> You [God] want truth in the most hidden places;
> you teach me wisdom in the most secret space.
> (Ps 51:6)
>
> The sacrifice acceptable to God is a broken spirit;
> a broken and contrite heart, O God, you will not
> despise. (Ps 51:17 NRSV)[26]

Paul echoes the point, much later, in a different idiom: "If we judged ourselves, we would not be judged" (1 Cor 11:31 NRSV)—evidently because the wrongdoing would be set aright and early on. But even when we are "judged by the Lord, we are disciplined so that we may not be condemned," Paul adds (1 Cor 11:32 NRSV). The Old Testament agrees, as Israel's new-smelling tabernacle and sweet-smelling sacrifices attest, as does David's ongoing life with God despite and in spite of the results that followed God's judgment of his sin. Let this sink in: even Israel's adultery on its wedding night can be rectified; even sexual scandal that ends in murder can be forgiven. Honesty about sin facilitates reconciliation. And if that is true for "great sins," like those at Mount Horeb/Sinai and at Jerusalem in springtime, how much more true is that for other sins, including our countless, lesser "peccadilloes"?[27] Let that sink in too.

(Dis)Honesty about Sin, Now and in the Pulpit

Israel's candor about sin is clear, and it resonates, in various ways, in the New Testament's own honest disclosure—say, with Peter's denial at a key moment in Christ's passion, or with Saul-turned-Paul's persecuting past. Some betrayals are so profound, some histories so sordid, that no amount of spin could ever make them go away. In our own days, however, honest confession about sin seems to be in very short supply. Unlike Israel, we seem prone to evasion and self-justification, denial and cover-up. In their book *Mistakes Were Made (but Not by Me)*, the social psychologists Carol Tavris and Elliot Aronson state that such

> self-justification has costs and benefits. By itself, it's not necessarily a bad thing. It lets us sleep at night. Without it we would prolong the awful pangs of embarrassment. We would torture ourselves with regret. . . . We would agonize in the aftermath of almost every decision. . . . Yet mindless self-justification, like quicksand, can draw us deeper into disaster. It blocks our ability to even see our errors, let alone correct them. It distorts reality, keeping us from getting all the information we need and assessing issues clearly. It prolongs and widens rifts between lovers, friends, and nations. It keeps us from letting go of unhealthy habits. It permits the guilty to avoid taking responsibility for their deeds. . . . None of us can live without making blunders. . . . To err is human, but humans then have a choice between covering up or fessing up. . . . We are forever being told that we should learn from our mistakes, but how can we learn unless we first admit that we made any?[28]

Uttering the impersonal, passively constructed sentence "Mistakes were made"—with the implication that they were not made by the speaker—is very different, in Tavris and Aronson's perspective, than saying "*I* made a mistake." A whole host of problems emerge from the first option, as Tavris and Aronson go on to demonstrate, whereas a whole host of benefits can follow from the second.[29] Of course, Scripture already knew this millennia before Tavris and Aronson wrote their book.[30]

But again, things are different now. In Tavris and Aronson's opinion, "America is a mistake-phobic culture."[31] One wonders what they might say about the Christian church, riddled with scandal after scandal, with clergy and other church leaders often more interested in cover-up than confession, and with religious bureaucrats more eager to pass offending ministers on to the next unsuspecting parish than to defrock them and offer restitution to the victims. What Israel gives us in the Old Testament is a more excellent way. "The mind wants to protect itself from the pain of dissonance with the balm of self-justification; but the soul wants to confess," Tavris and Aronson assert.[32] In Scripture, Israel concurs and then does more: Israel *models* such confession, extensively and unblinkingly, explicitly and implicitly, in story and in song.

Once more and not for the last time,

Israel writes it all down, telling us all about it, in detail, for posterity, forever.

God will not despise a broken and contrite heart, says the psalmist, but Christians, including preachers (whether from Southern California or elsewhere) and no doubt well-meaning parents in pews (in New Jersey and beyond), often *have* despised such hearts. And the hearts they have despised belong to none other than those who prove to be expert practitioners in confession and forgiveness—hearts that also belong to the Lord, "the God of those who repent" (Pr Man 1:13 NRSV) with whom there is "great power to redeem" (Ps 130:7 NRSV). Rather than apprentice ourselves to their craft—to our great benefit and to our reconciliation with God and one another!—it has far too often been the case that we have misunderstood their honesty, turned their skills in candid confession against them, belittling them in the process, all the while projecting our own sin and shortcomings elsewhere, to our detriment, since that has prevented our own honest and desperately needed confession. It is high time for preaching to stop despising Israel's broken and contrite heart. It is high time to learn from Israel's model of honest confession of sin.[33] It is high time to practice such honesty in the pulpit, for the transformation of all who hear.

We already know this—or we *should*. We know it (or should) not only from Scripture but also from the work of people like Tavris and Aronson and from people like Desmond Tutu and the Truth and Reconciliation Commission (TRC) in South Africa, which offered total amnesty for those who committed atrocities during apartheid but only after their complete honesty.[34] Only full honesty yielded full amnesty. There is no future without forgiveness, the great archbishop has taught us, but reconciliation depends first and foremost on extensive and explicit confession. It depends extensively, maybe exclusively, on truth telling about wrongdoing. Honesty about sin can make—and has made—all the difference in the world. Preaching that follows Israel's lead, that is equally honest about sin, can make the very same difference.

> Create a clean heart for me, God;
>   put a new, faithful spirit deep inside me!
> Please don't throw me out of your presence;
>   please don't take your holy spirit away from me.
> Return the joy of your salvation to me
>   and sustain me with a willing spirit.
> Then I will teach wrongdoers your ways,
>   and sinners will come back to you. (Ps 51:10–13)

3

Honest about Suffering

The last chapter asserted that Israel was unfailingly honest about sin and, in that process, offered us not weapons to use against Israel but an example to emulate, since honest confession proves to be the gateway to forgiveness and reconciliation. The texts discussed in the last chapter also hinted at the fact that sin often has a comrade in arms—suffering. Sin is frequently associated with suffering in Scripture and in more than one way. Sin can *lead to* subsequent suffering, for example, due to divine judgment. That is part, at least, of what David learns in the aftermath of his sins against Uriah and Bathsheba (and God). Even his honest confession cannot eliminate the dreadful consequences, which include, by God's own lips, the real and profound "trouble" that comes "against you from inside your own family" (2 Sam 12:11). David acknowledges the reality of post-sin suffering due to divine judgment in Psalm 51, "just after he had been with Bathsheba":

> I know my wrongdoings,
>   my sin is always right in front of me . . .

> You are justified when *you render your verdict,*
> completely correct *when you issue your judgment* . . .
> Let me hear joy and celebration again;
> let *the bones you crushed* rejoice once more.
> (Ps 51:3, 4b, 8; emphasis added)

And David knows it a bit later as he flees Jerusalem for his life and is cursed by Shimei, Gera's son, for being a despicable murderer, one who was finally getting paid back—by none other than the Lord—for all his bloodshed (2 Sam 16:7–8).[1] "Leave him alone," David says to his servants who want to end Shimei's life for insulting their debased king, "let him curse, because the Lord told him to. Perhaps the Lord will see my distress" (2 Sam 16:11b–12a).

And David knows about sin's relationship to suffering even more painfully, only slightly later, when he hears the news about the death of his usurping son:

> Oh, my son Absalom! Oh, my son!
> My son Absalom! If only I had died instead of you!
> Oh, Absalom, my son! My son! (2 Sam 18:33)

This first pairing of sin and suffering suggests that *judged sin produces deserved suffering* as punishment; and this is, in fact, a rather pervasive perspective in the Bible. The disobedience of the northern kingdom of Israel and the southern kingdom of Judah, both of which eventuate in destruction and exile, is easily the largest, most extensive sermon illustration of this point found in the Bible. First, the north:

> And the Israelites continued walking in all the sins that Jeroboam did. They didn't deviate from them, and the

HONEST ABOUT SUFFERING

Lord finally removed Israel from his presence. That was exactly what he had warned through all his servants the prophets. So Israel was exiled from its land [*wayyigal... mē'al 'admātô*] to Assyria. (2 Kgs 17:22–23; cf. Amos 7:11, 17)

Then, later, but ineluctably, the south experiences the same result with the very same formulation: "So Judah was exiled from its land [*wayyigal... mē'al 'admātô*]" (2 Kgs 25:21b; cf. Jer 52:27).

But there is a second pairing of sin and suffering that suggests a different relationship and a different ordering. In addition to the idea that sin produces deserved suffering, Scripture also knows that *undeserved suffering can often emerge directly from sin*. The sin in question in this second formulation is typically *external* to the sufferer. The suffering, in turn, is *caused*, which means it is typically caused *by others*. This second pairing will be the point of entry into the present chapter's focus on *Israel's honesty about suffering*, an honesty that *facilitates healing*.

Israel's Primal Suffering

Israel's honesty about suffering must begin with its most fundamental instantiation, the enslavement in Egypt as recounted in the book of Exodus. There are, without doubt, canonically prior articulations of suffering that are found in the book of Genesis. Sarai's harsh treatment (*'ānāh*, "to oppress, humiliate, do violence to")[2] of Hagar in Genesis 16, for example, comes to mind, which leads to Hagar's flight and distress (Gen 16:6; also 21:16).[3] The very first use of the verb *'ānāh* in the Old Testament, however, is earlier still. It is found in Genesis 15, in an anticipatory comment God makes to Abram as he sleeps through an important covenant ceremony: "Know well that your offspring shall be strangers in a land not theirs, and they shall be enslaved and oppressed [*'innû*, from *'ānāh*] four hundred years" (Gen 15:13 NJPSV).

Grief, sorrow, and distress are expressed in many ways in the Bible, certainly more than by means of the single verb *'ānāh*,[4] but Genesis 15:13 is nevertheless significant in foreshadowing Israel's corporate suffering in Egypt, even if that "house of bondage" goes unnamed, for whatever reason and for the time being.

Unsurprisingly—but also unfortunately for Israel—God's statement in Genesis 15 proves true just a few pages later, when, flourishing down in Egyptland (Exod 1:1–7), Israel finds itself under "a new king . . . who did not know Joseph" (1:8). That notice *sounds* ominous, and that impression is confirmed by the new pharaoh's subsequent policies. These begin with the need to "deal shrewdly" with the Israelites; otherwise, "if war breaks out, they will join our enemies, fight against us, and then escape from the land [*wĕ'ālāh min-hā 'āreṣ*]" (Exod 1:10). The last clause is rendered differently in the New Jewish Publication Society Version (NJPSV): the Israelites might "rise from the ground." Both translations, that of the Common English Bible (CEB) and that of the NJPSV, are acceptable and instructive in their own way. With regard to the CEB, the departure—the great escape—from Egypt is frequently described with the verb *'ālāh*, "to go up." What Pharaoh fears will happen does, in fact, happen, even though it happens on another king's watch. The successful departure of the people is thus foreshadowed here in Pharaoh's concerns over *'ālāh*: Israel *might* escape and, in fact, Israel *will* escape. The NJPSV's rendering is less a case of foreshadowing than it is of poignancy. The phrase "rise from the ground" shows where Israel currently is, or soon will be—namely, underfoot and under the thumb of a despotic pharaoh who slides, as despots so easily do, from simple "shrewdness" to tyranny in the verses that immediately follow:

> As a result, the Egyptians put foremen of forced work gangs over the Israelites to harass [*'annōtô*, from *'ānāh*] them with hard work. They had to build storage cities named Pithom and Rameses for pharaoh. But the more they were oppressed [*yĕ'annû*, from *'ānāh*], the more they grew and spread, so much so that the Egyptians started to look at the Israelites with disgust and dread. So the Egyptians enslaved [*ya'ăbidû*, from *'ābad*] the Israelites. They made their lives miserable with hard labor, making mortar and bricks, doing field work, and by forcing them to do all kinds of other cruel work. (Exod 1:11–14)

This short passage is overfull with phrasing that places Israel firmly on the underside of Egyptian society. The verbs "harass," "oppress," and "enslave" and the terms "hard work," "hard labor," and "cruel work" make up a veritable lexicon of suffering, drafted and enforced by Pharaoh.

And he is just getting warmed up. For some odd reason, Israel's calculus is "the more oppressed, the more growth" (1:12a), which, characteristically, is misunderstood in Egypt, where that kind of math equates only to "more Egyptian disgust and dread" (1:12b). So Pharaoh takes things to the next level. Why settle for enslavement when genocide will do? Pharaoh's repeated mandates to kill all Hebrew boys is just such an attempt (1:15–22), since the surviving girls would presumably intermarry with the

Egyptians and thus be assimilated into Egyptian culture. In Pharaoh's mind, that would be the end of Israel proper and thus the elimination of any (potential) internal foe.

This is all horrific on many levels and for many reasons. There can be no doubt, therefore, that the news of this pharaoh's death came as a moment of great joy and hope for suffering Israel: "A long time passed, and the Egyptian king died" (2:23a). Finally, and at last! This "long time" has been a case of *far too long*.

But the (potential) joy is cut short, the hope very short lived. Yes, there has been a regime change, but the policies remain firmly in place. No change there. The new king might, as was not uncommon in the ancient world, have chosen at his accession to power to lighten some loads, cancel some debts, free some prisoners.[5] But no, not this time. Not, at least, in the case of Israel. Though his predecessor's genocidal designs were thwarted by brave midwives who chose civil disobedience over complicity in mass murder, the new pharaoh continues the prior administration's practices of oppression and enslavement. And so, no surprise, Israel continues to suffer. Immediately after the death of the old pharaoh, within the very same verse, Exodus dolefully reports that Israel was "still groaning because of their hard work. They cried out, and their cry to be rescued from the hard work rose up to God" (2:23b).

This is an even shorter passage (just a half verse!), but it is again overfull with words connoting suffering. Three different verbs are used: "groaning," "cried out," and "cry to be rescued." As if that weren't enough, the next verse adds a fourth: "cry of grief" (2:24). The cause of such pain is also mentioned more than once, but in this case, the cause is the same—"the hard work" and, again, "the hard work" (*hā ʿăbōdāh*), the repetition like a drumbeat of pain on Israel's skull, or, better, on Israel's whip-scarred back.

Israel is honest about its suffering here. Honest enough to make us wince, perhaps, if we weren't so desensitized by the violence of our own world. Israel's candid texts about suffering, if appropriately received and carefully reflected in honest preaching, can actually work to *re*sensitize us, which would help in reading Scripture and also in reading the world.[6] Be that as it may, Israel's suffering couldn't be clearer in Exodus, and it all stems from Pharaoh's despotic nationalism and racism—in a word, from his *sin*. Pharaoh's sin leads to Israel's suffering. The text is crystal clear about these matters because Israel is honest about them.

But there is more to say.

Israel recounts its suffering here in numerous ways—as an enslaved group, as forced workers, as subjected to mass extermination efforts (more than once), and through various verbs and terms. But then something altogether unexpected happens. Their cries of pain on account of all their great suffering rose up to God, Exodus reports (2:23b). Then comes an astonishing turn: "God heard their cry of grief, and God remembered his covenant with Abraham, Isaac, and Jacob. God looked at the Israelites, and God understood" (Exod 2:24–25). At first, the cry is said to have risen up (*'ālāh* again), eventually making its way to God, though it isn't explicitly said that Israel's cry was originally directed there. Those who suffer pain like Israel's don't usually have the luxury to be polite about where, exactly, to address their complaints. They are in pain and the prayer to stop such pain is urgent, sometimes as brief as one blurted-out word, "Violence!"[7] Pharaoh *could* have heard Israel's cry. No doubt he *did* hear Israel's cry, but he wouldn't heed it. No matter. Israel's suffering groan keeps moving, looking for any ears that will listen until they finally reach the very ears of God.

And that is the end—or, at least, the beginning of the end. The end of Pharaoh. The end of Egypt. The end of enslaved Israel.

> God heard... God remembered... God looked... God understood.

Four verbs, as if to match Israel's prior four verbs of suffering. Four different verbs, all with Israel as the sole locus of divine attention and concern. Pharaoh should be afraid. The kingdom of heaven is about to draw near.

The importance of this moment cannot be overstated. Israel is in profound suffering and is candid about that. All seems lost. And then, suddenly, all *isn't* lost because suffering gives way to deliverance. Israel's groans have awoken God. The divine sense perceptions are all now fully open, open to one thing and one thing only: Israel in pain. No wonder there will be hell to pay back in Egyptland.[8] And no wonder the next chapter begins with God's calling a deliverer—Moses, a wanted fugitive and convicted felon—to head the rescue mission.

It is important to highlight two things about Israel's primal suffering, which is reported so honestly in the Old Testament. *First*, as Walter Brueggemann has seen so well, *everything begins in grief*.[9] In many ways, Israel's history, especially as a corporate body, and as a corporate body in covenantal relationship with the Lord, begins here, in suffering, in Egypt, frequently called "the house of slavery" (*bêt 'ăbādîm*)[10] and that Deuteronomy and Jeremiah memorably speak of as nothing less than an "iron furnace" (Deut 4:20; Jer 11:4). Israel is honest about all this suffering because it is, of course, true but also because it is the beginning of change. Perhaps, with God's (and Moses's) help, suffering may come to an end—and it does! But what ends in this case is nothing less than true, real, profound suffering. There is no covering over, prettying up, or denying what actually happened down in Egyptland. Perhaps it is for this reason that the exodus is spoken of so often in the Old Testament, with the New Testament following suit.[11] It is simply *that* important—important enough that it must never be forgotten. It is worth observing, in this regard, that the prologue to the Decalogue identifies the God who commands as "the Lord your God who brought you out of Egypt, out of the house of slavery" (Exod 20:2). Judaism is the only religion attentive to the Ten Commandments that numbers this as the first of the ten.[12] The first commandment is *to remember*. To remember *suffering*. Because everything begins in suffering. And because Israel's God delivers from suffering. These things, *both of these things*, must never be forgotten. They must always be remembered, treasured, even obeyed—as the very first commandment!

The *second* thing to highlight is that while suffering does change, yielding to healing, this happens slowly. The chronology specified in Genesis 15 tallies in advance Israel's suffering in Egypt at four hundred years, the biblical equivalent of ten full generations. Surely the extent and severity of ten generations of suffering left an indelible mark that can only be healed with great lengths of time and equally great amounts of care.

This explains a good bit of what follows in the book of Exodus, after God's sense perceptions are opened to Israel's pain and God selects a deliverer (and his sidekick) to do the work. There is, at the start, the joyous reception of the good news announced by Moses and Aaron upon their return to Egypt and their convening of the elders:

> Aaron told them everything that the Lord had told to Moses, and he performed the signs in front of the people. The people believed. When they heard that the Lord had paid attention to the Israelites and had seen their oppression [*ănî*, from *ānāh*], they bowed down and worshipped. (Exod 4:30–31)

But things turn sour quickly after that. The initial parley with Pharaoh goes south, resulting in *more*, not less, oppression for Israel, which leads to anger and division among the Israelites. When Israel's leaders fail to win any remediation from Pharaoh directly (no surprise there), their pain boils over into rage against their new would-be revolutionaries, Moses and Aaron: "Let the Lord see and judge what you've done! You've made us stink in the opinion of Pharaoh and his servants. You've given them a reason to kill us" (Exod 5:21). Moses, understandably, is upset by all these developments and takes it to the Lord in prayer:

> My Lord, why have you abused [*hărē'ōtāh*, from *rā'ā*] this people? Why did you send me for this? Ever since I first came to Pharaoh to speak in your name, he has abused [*hēra'*, from *rā'ā*] this people. And you've done absolutely nothing to rescue your people. (Exod 5:22–23)

Once again, Israel's honesty in this account is both remarkable and revealing. Suffering can and often does turn to rage when it is not brought to an end, when things are not set right. And such rage gets passed up the chain, to different subjects—who become, rightly or wrongly, targets—including, ultimately, God. Suffering is a complicated thing. Suffering is a theological thing. Thus avers Israel, in all honesty, with great sincerity and in great detail, without much concern over who ends up looking bad: Pharaoh and Egypt, Israel itself, the great Moses and Aaron, even God. As with sin, so also with suffering:

> And then Israel writes it all down, telling us all about it, in detail, for posterity, forever.

Not to be missed amid all this pain and anger is Israel's deep sorrow. The arrival of Moses and Aaron was great news of great joy, but it had no staying power. It didn't last. The long experience of suffering in Egypt had repeatedly demonstrated that things were usually otherwise, that Israel typically got no relief, no break, not even on the Sabbath (see Deut 5:15). No wonder Exodus goes on to report, in the very next chapter, that the Israelites "would not listen to Moses, *because of their broken spirit and their cruel slavery*" (Exod 6:9 NRSV; emphasis added).[13]

This, too, is a full display of honesty. Despite the testimony of Psalm 30:5, weeping sometimes lasts more than just the nighttime, and joy doesn't always come in the morning. Deep and profound suffering is not overturned, changed into joy in an evening. Not after four hundred years of enslavement! Israel's suffering yields slowly—ever so slowly—to healing. God must prove repeatedly good and faithful to Israel for its broken spirit to begin to mend.[14] Surely this explains in part why there are so many "I am" and "I will be" statements in Exodus because they assert the divine presence, in various capacities and with different capabilities and in ways that Israel most needs, from early to late in the book:[15]

> I am the God of your father, Abraham's God, Isaac's God, and Jacob's God. (Exod 3:6)
>
> I will be with you. (Exod 3:12 NRSV)

I Am Who I Am. (Exod 3:14)

I am the Lord. I'll bring you out from Egyptian forced labor. I'll rescue you from your slavery to them. I'll set you free with great power and with momentous events of justice. (Exod 6:6)

I am the Lord who heals you. (Exod 15:26)

I am the Lord your God who brought you out of Egypt, out of the house of slavery. (Exod 20:2)

I am loyal and gracious to the thousandth generation of those who love me and keep my commandments. (Exod 20:6)

If your fellow Israelite cries out to me, I will listen, because I am compassionate. (Exod 22:27; my translation)

These statements also extend well beyond Exodus:

I am holy. (Lev 10:3; 11:44–45; 19:2)

I am the Lord, who brought you up from the land of Egypt to be your God. (Lev 11:45; 22:33)

I am the Lord, who makes you holy. (Lev 20:8; 21:8; 22:32)[16]

I am the Lord your God, who brought you out of the land of Egypt to give you Canaan's land and to be your God. (Lev 25:38)

I am the Lord your God, who brought you out of Egypt's land—who brought you out from being Egypt's slaves. I broke your bonds and made you stand up straight. (Lev 26:13)

I am your share and your inheritance. (Num 18:20)

Now, look here: I myself, I'm the one; there are no other gods with me. (Deut 32:39)

Perhaps, given the anticipation of the Egyptian sojourn and slavery in Genesis 15, God's statement to Abram in that chapter is also pertinent: "I am your protector. Your reward will be very great" (Gen 15:1).

Much later, the New Testament, too, picks up this pattern (e.g., Matt 28:20; John 6:35, 41, 48, 51; 8:12; 9:5; 10:7, 9, 11, 14; 11:25; 14:6; 15:1, 5).

It is not surprising that there is a good deal of overlap between many of these statements, especially in the Pentateuch: they are variations on a theme, with the dominant tune the deliverance from Egyptland and God's direct involvement in the exodus. That primary melody is necessary to counter the earlier incessant drumbeat of Pharaoh's "the hard work, the hard work." God must prove good—repeatedly—for Israel's "broken spirit" (*miqqōṣer rûaḥ*) to heal and for Israel to catch its breath again, especially if that breath is to be exhaled again, someday, in praise.

Surely the need to prove good to Israel also explains why the Lord repeatedly hardens Pharaoh's heart in the account of the plagues. Even when Pharaoh is done hardening his own heart, when Pharaoh has clearly had enough (after Plague 7), the Lord God of Israel is just getting warmed up, with the worst strike yet to come (Exod 12:29–32). No doubt this contest results in the Lord's winning honor or glory at Pharaoh's expense (see Exod

14:4, 17, 18). But it is also "that they may know" who this Lord really is (see Exod 7:5, 17; 10:2; 14:4, 18). The "they" who learn this lesson includes Pharaoh and his army, his officials and all of Egypt, to be sure, but it also includes Israel, which now has stories to flesh out and accompany God's potentially abstract "I am" statements or God's as-yet-futuristic "I will be" promises. These prove not to be abstract in the least but rather proof of God's accompanying, healing presence, responding to Israel's suffering. And they come to pass in the not-too-far-off future as God passes through Egypt at midnight (11:4; 12:12, 23) and as Israel passes through the sea as if on dry land (14:19; 15:16).

Lastly, Israel's slow healing helps explain its own ongoing struggles with faithlessness. Simply put, it's hard to change after four hundred years. It's hard to trust. It's hard to believe, fully, that rather than Pharaoh's *slave* (*'ebed*), one is now God's treasured "most precious possession" (*sĕgŭllāh*; 19:5).[17] Said differently, Israel's honesty about its own suffering—its extent, its severity, its duration—is interwoven with its honesty about other topics, including its own sin (see chapter 2). The shift from serving Pharaoh to serving the Lord is a slow and hard one, all the more so because of suffering. Israel is honest—painfully honest—about all that pain. Preachers can follow Israel's example, not by parading the preacher's own suffering and sin before the congregation, but by preaching these honest texts in the way the texts themselves preach: through remarkable, even gut-wrenching candor. These honest texts provide preachers and congregants with scripts to recite about suffering as well as sites where that suffering can be transformed.[18] No longer slave, now *sĕgŭllāh*!

Israel's Poetic Suffering

Much in the poetic tradition of the Old Testament resonates with Israel's honesty about its primordial suffering in Egypt, where it was born, and in enslavement, where it was shaped. First and most obviously, there are many references to Egypt and the exodus in the Prophets and in the Psalms.[19] There is thus plenty of evidence of the second of the two sin-suffering dynamics described above—namely, that others' sins not infrequently cause Israel to suffer. Among many examples is the following rather famous lyric, which will be taken up more fully in chapter 4:

> Alongside Babylon's streams, there we sat down,
>   crying because we remembered Zion.
> We hung our lyres up in the trees there
>   because that's where our captors asked us to sing;
>   our tormentors requested songs of joy:
>   "Sing us a song about Zion!" they said.
> But how could we possibly sing the Lord's song on
>   foreign soil? (Ps 137:1–4)

The captors and tormentors in this text are the Babylonians, with the psalm coming from Judean exiles deported from their homeland, bereaved of kin and country, traumatized and brutalized, and as a final insult, psychologically taunted to sing about all that they've lost at Babylon's hand.

While powerful and poignant, the specifics of Psalm 137 might strike one as somewhat odd because the historical books of the Old Testament depict the exile as the inevitable and apparently fully justified deserts of Israel's own disobedience, its own sin. From this perspective, it is not *others' wrongdoing* that has produced Israel's suffering; it is *Israel's own wrongdoing*, which makes the entire complex running from Joshua through Kings yet another, quite massive instance of Israel's confessing *its own sin*. Is it right, then, to speak of Babylon's destruction of Jerusalem in 587 BCE as sin *against* Judah? Probably not, in the perspective of Joshua through Kings, but maybe so, according to the prophet Zechariah:

> Thus said the Lord of Hosts: I am very jealous for Jerusalem—for Zion—and I am very angry with those nations that are at ease; for I was only angry a little, but they overdid the punishment. Assuredly, thus said the Lord: I graciously return to Jerusalem. My House shall be built in her—declares the Lord of Hosts—the measuring line is being applied to Jerusalem. Proclaim further: Thus said the Lord of Hosts: My towns shall yet overflow with bounty. For the Lord will again comfort Zion; He will choose Jerusalem again. (Zech 1:14–17 NJPSV)[20]

With Zechariah, Psalm 137 would likely fall in the *maybe so* camp (Jerusalem's destruction is the result of *Babylon's* sin), if only because it is an exilic psalm, and as observed in chapter 2, the Psalter as a whole is not particularly enamored with sin as a primary explanation of the psalmists' plights. Penitential psalms like Psalm 51, as a result, are something of a "second opinion" with regard to what typically ails the psalmists.[21] "Sinful" is simply *not* a dominant definition of who Israel is in the Psalms—the penitential psalms aside—perhaps because Israel is so honest about its sin elsewhere in Scripture (witness the golden calf or Joshua–Kings, etc.).[22] And so, in Psalm 137, with a little help from other texts like Zechariah 1 or Obadiah (among others), the role of enemy sin in producing Israel's suffering is amply attested.

This leads to two important observations about Israel's honest disclosure about suffering in its poetry.

First, among the Psalms are some poems that Gert Kwakkel and others have called "songs of innocence."[23] In these texts—in marked contrast to the penitential psalms—the psalmists assert their totally innocent and upright behavior. For example:

> Lord, my God, if I have done this—
>   if my hands have done anything wrong,
> if I have repaid a friend with evil
>   or oppressed a foe for no reason—
> then let my enemy not only chase but catch me,
>   trampling my life into the ground,
>   laying my reputation in the dirt. . . .
> The Lord will judge the peoples.
>   Establish justice for me, Lord,
>   according to my righteousness
>   and according to my integrity. (Ps 7:3–5, 8)

> You have examined my heart, testing me at night.
>   You've looked me over closely, but haven't found
>   anything wrong.
>   My mouth doesn't sin. . . .
> My steps are set firmly on your paths;
>   my feet haven't slipped. (Ps 17:3, 5)

> Establish justice for me, Lord,
>   because I have walked with integrity.

> I've trusted the Lord without wavering. . . .
> Because your faithful love is right in front of me—
> > I walk in your truth!
> I don't spend time with people up to no good;
> > I don't keep company with liars.
> I detest the company of evildoers,
> > and I don't sit with wicked people.
> I wash my hands—they are innocent! . . .
> But me? I walk with integrity.
> > Save me! Have mercy on me! (Ps 26:1, 3–6b, 11)[24]

Such language suggests that at least sometimes when Israel suffers, it does so *completely undeservedly*. Such a position on suffering may explain the sentiment in a poem like Psalm 137, especially vis-à-vis Joshua through Kings.[25] Undeserved suffering, too, is part of what Israel candidly confesses about its trials and tribulations. And, add these psalms of innocence, that perspective is not only honest; it is *true*. Preachers, who are kind of the first responders to grief, know more than their fair share about undeserved suffering. Indeed, according to Craig Barnes, a preacher's own calling might qualify as an example thereof.[26] Whatever the case, however undeserved suffering is known, emulating Israel's honesty in the pulpit—not to mention pastoral care—should not be difficult for the honest to God preacher. Sometimes there is no good answer to suffering because there is no answer at all.

Second, in the aggregate, Israel's honesty about suffering is quite multifaceted when it comes to causation. If the dominant narrative of Joshua through Kings reflects Israel confessing its exilic ends as entirely deserved due to its own disobedience, then other texts—like Psalms 137 or 7, 17, 26, and the like—see things otherwise. In this stalemate, another text deserves attention. It is the book of Lamentations, which is arguably Israel's most poignant and plaintive reflection on the destruction of Jerusalem in 587 BCE.

What Lamentations offers is nothing less than a complex and complicated engagement with suffering and its several causes. Israel's suffering, personified and given voice as destroyed Zion, is recounted in stomach-turning detail (see, e.g., 2:11–12, 19–20; 4:2–4, 10). The opening verse—even the very first word—signals how much is at stake, how much has been lost:

> Oh, no [*'êkāh*]!
> She sits alone, the city that was once full of people.
> Once great among nations, she has become like a
>   widow.
> Once a queen over provinces, she has become a slave.
>   (Lam 1:1)

Verse 3 clarifies the poetic personification and identifies the situation:

> Judah was exiled after suffering [*'ănî*, from *'ānāh*] and
>   hard service [*'ăbōdāh*].
> She lives among the nations; she finds no rest.
> All who were chasing her caught her—right in the
>   middle of her distress.[27] (Lam 1:3)

Jerusalem's suffering is laid out in great detail in what follows, but the mention of pursuers in 1:3 already suggests that quite a lot is going on in Lamentations; simply put, Israel's great suffering cannot be reduced to a single cause.[28] Verse 2 already says as much:

> She weeps bitterly in the night, her tears on her cheek.
> None of her lovers comfort her.
> All her friends lied to her; they have become her
>   enemies. (Lam 1:2)

Israel has been betrayed by former allies become foes, but personified Jerusalem has also "sinned greatly" (1:8). She confesses this because she is expert in confession:

> —the Lord is right, because I disobeyed his word. (Lam 1:18a)

> —my heart is wrung within me, because I have been very rebellious. (Lam 1:20b NRSV)[29]

But again, the matter is complex. Not everything is Israel's fault. Sometimes, instead, what has happened is because of enemies (1:2, 10, 16), sometimes because of the Lord (1:15), sometimes a combination of the two (1:14), with Israel's own guilt also peppered liberally throughout the poetry and the pain. The end result is, once more, a complicated portrait of suffering, one that includes moments of profound hope (3:21, 24, 56–58) and also of deepest despair (3:41–51)—not to mention violent imprecation (1:21b–22; 3:64–66; 4:21–22; cf. Pr Azar 1:21; see further chapter 4 below). This complexity, too, is part of being honest about suffering, which so often resists any monocausal explanation, especially one offered by us who see so little and not very far.

The complexity of suffering and its causes is clear in Lamentations, even if it is hard to sort out. What is more difficult to understand is if and how Israel's honest account of its suffering in this book facilitates its healing. The evidence seems, at first, quite meager. Yet perhaps the very articulation of pain, in one's own voice, is a sign of hope, proof of life at the very least, and thus a harbinger of something to come—something *beyond* suffering.[30] There is also, of course, the well-known section in the middle of Lamentations 3 that has been often seized upon by interpreters as an oasis of hope in the middle of a desert of suffering:

> I call all this to mind—therefore, I will wait [NRSV: I have hope].
> Certainly the faithful love of the Lord hasn't ended;
>   certainly God's compassion isn't through!
> They are renewed every morning. Great is your
>   faithfulness.
> I think: The Lord is my portion! Therefore, I'll wait for
>   him.
> The Lord is good to those who hope in him, to the
>   person who seeks him.
> It's good to wait in silence for the Lord's deliverance.
> It's good for a man to carry a yoke in his youth.
> He should sit alone and be silent when God lays it on
>   him.
> He should put his mouth in the dirt—perhaps there is
>   hope.
> He should offer his cheek for a blow; he should be
>   filled with shame.
> My Lord definitely won't reject forever.
> Although he has caused grief,
>   he will show compassion in measure with his
>   covenant loyalty.
> He definitely doesn't enjoy affliction, making humans
>   suffer. (Lam 3:21–33)

Close inspection reveals that this passage, too, is far from a simple or straightforward antidote of hope—a point confirmed by what follows later in Lamentations 3 (see vv. 42–45), not to mention Lamentations 4–5, all of which return to the bleak wasteland of suffering. It is thus difficult to know what, exactly—let alone *how much*—to make of Lamentations 3. In some ways, this hopeful passage demands special attention due to its more positive content and central positioning in the book. In other ways, though, this passage seems, at best, the briefest of respites in a book that returns quickly and dreadfully to heartbreaking articulations of grief, sorrow, and pain. Indeed, the very last verse of the book, while admittedly open to more than one interpretation, seems to be among Israel's most sober assessments of its suffering with God:

> For truly, You have rejected us,
> Bitterly raged against us. (Lam 5:22 NJPSV)

The severity, if not utter hopelessness, of this line has led the Jewish tradition to repeat the prior verse, verse 21, a second time after verse 22 in liturgical readings, so as to end on a more positive and hopeful note. The result is as follows:

> Take us back, O Lord, to Yourself,
> And let us come back;
> Renew our days as of old!
> For truly, You have rejected us,
> Bitterly raged against us.
>> Take us back, O Lord, to Yourself,
>> And let us come back;
>> Renew our days as of old! (Lam 5:21–22, 21 NJPSV)

This practice of repeating verse 21 could, of course, be seen as little more than a liturgical "fix," a smoothing over of what cannot, in the final analysis, be smoothed over. But why shouldn't the liturgy be allowed to facilitate a move to healing, especially when the suffering is so thoroughgoing and overwhelming? In desperate times, help must be sought wherever it may be found, and liturgy is precisely such a source. Elsewhere in Scripture, Israel well knows—in many and profound ways—that God has not, in fact, rejected it, and certainly not utterly. Repeating verse 21 after verse 22 is a small movement, but one that draws on deep resources, which helps move Israel ever so slowly toward healing after its shocking honesty across five chapters of Lamentations.

There is something more to say about Israel's honesty about suffering in Lamentations and its facilitation of healing; it has to do with the poetic form of the book. The most obvious aspect of that form is that Lamentations is composed as an alphabetic acrostic. In alphabetic acrostic poetry, each poetic line begins with a successive letter of the alphabet. Since the Hebrew alphabet has 22 letters, each chapter of Lamentations has 22 verses—one verse per letter—with the exception of chapter 3, which is a triple acrostic: three verses, each beginning with one letter, followed by three verses with the next letter, and so on, to total 66 verses.[31]

Alphabetic acrostics are known elsewhere in the Bible, and so the form in Lamentations is not unique;[32] neither does the acrostic form strike one as the most difficult or impressive within the poetic arsenal. In point of fact, acrostic poetry seems simplistic compared to something like a sonnet in iambic pentameter let alone a more complex poetic form like a villanelle or *terza rima*. The use of the alphabetic acrostic form in Lamentations is noteworthy, however, because its use in this particular case may be *anything but* simplistic. In the case of Lamentations, the acrostic form itself may be a herald of hope, despite and in spite of the pathos-ridden content of the book. Preachers who care about biblical forms and preach in their own styles will want to pay close attention to the acrostic form of Lamentations and what can be learned from it.

Among other things, what can be learned from the acrostic form is that it is an effective way to encompass a great deal of content—even chaotic, grief-filled content—capture it in form, and thus somehow manage it and control it. On the one hand, the acrostic form suggests *a totality*: Lamentations is a veritable "A to Z" of grief, as it were. Everything is included in this poetry; nothing is left out, not even one letter of the alphabet. Thus says the acrostic. On the other hand, the acrostic form suggests *a limitation*: the grief lasts only for the duration of the alphabet. The grief comes to an end—poetically, at least—with the last letter. Upon reaching the final letter of the alphabet, the poet can set her pen down for the day. That is enough. The suffering has been catalogued, in its entirety, from A to Z, and at the same time, it has been contained. The end of the alphabet has been reached. It is finished. For now, at least. Until the next day or the next poem. This, too, is what the acrostic as a form communicates.

Although not properly an acrostic, it is worth comparing at this point the poem by former US poet laureate Billy Collins entitled "The Names." Collins wrote this poem as a memorial for the tragic events of September 11, 2001.[33] In the poem he moves, alphabetically, through representative surnames of the victims, from "A" (Ackerman) until "the final jolt of Z" (Ziminsky). The poem concludes by acknowledging that there are "So many names, there is barely room on the walls of the heart."[34] While that is no doubt true, it is equally true that the alphabetic form has provided a way for Collins to somehow include all of these names within the limited compass of a single poem and to manage their overwhelming, heartbreaking scope.

So also, and similarly, in Lamentations, where we find evidence of what Walter Brueggemann memorably calls "the formfulness of grief."[35] By this term Brueggemann means to signal the intriguing correspondence between the set literary pattern of the lament psalms and other patterns of grief, such as that identified by Elisabeth Kübler-Ross in her study of death and dying.[36] Form, Brueggemann avers, brings some sort of order to what is otherwise a chaotic, orderless experience like the experiences of suffering recounted in the Psalter and the book of Lamentations. An additional, instructive poetic comparison, beyond Collins's "The Names," might be the "terrible sonnets" of Gerard Manley Hopkins (1844–89), so called because they were written during a particularly difficult time in the poet's life. In these sonnets Hopkins's already complex poetic style seems to be taken to an entirely different level. The first stanza from one of these sonnets, "Carrion Comfort," illustrates the point:

> Not, I'll not, carrion comfort, Despair, not feast on
>   thee;
> Not untwist—slack they may be—these last strands
>   of man
> In me or, most weary, cry I can no more. I can;
> Can something, hope, wish day come, not choose not
>   to be.[37]

The complexity of these four lines requires careful rereading to even begin to untangle. The syntax is convoluted, with the *a-b-b-a* rhyme scheme complicated by numerous instances of internal rhyme and dense repetition. This kind of complex poetry is how Hopkins reflected, and reflected upon, his suffering at this time in his life. Form, alphabetic or otherwise, is one way to contain grief and so perhaps move it toward healing, even if at first that movement is barely perceptible, evident only in poetic devices.[38]

In Lamentations, of course, the form chosen to manage suffering is the alphabetic acrostic. But given the horror of Jerusalem's destruction, even this capacious form falters. As it happens, only Lamentations 1 is a true alphabetic acrostic in proper alphabetical order. Already in Lamentations 2 the acrostic form begins to break down by having two letters (and thus two verses) out of proper order (2:16–17). The same holds true—and for the very same letters of the alphabet—in chapter 3 (vv. 46–51) and chapter 4 (vv. 16–17), which suggests that this pattern is not a failure on the part of the poet but present by design. It is a way of signaling that even the alphabetic acrostic form cannot fully or finally contain Israel's suffering in Lamentations. A to Z turns out to be insufficient. The *coup de grâce* is found in Lamentations 5, where the alphabetic acrostic form is abandoned altogether, leaving, at best, only a trace behind. Chapter 5, too, has twenty-two verses echoing the twenty-two letters of the Hebrew alphabet that were deployed throughout chapters 1–4, but no acrostic is actually present, no A to Z of grief. In Lamentations 5, the form—even the alphabet—has failed.

Or is it perhaps instead that the form is opening up—that the alphabetic A to Z of suffering is no longer needed, that it is being transcended somehow and is now on the way to something else, something new? We shouldn't be too hasty here: Lamentations 5 contains poetry that is every bit as gut-wrenching as what has come before. But at the end of the day, maybe the abandoning of the acrostic form isn't finally a failure of form or poet, but a portent of something else—something yet to come. The last stanza of the book is plaintive, to be sure, but not too far off from what is found in many of the psalms within the Psalter:

> But you, Lord, will rule forever;
>   your throne lasts from one generation to the next.
> Why do you forget us continually;
>   why do you abandon us for such a long time?
> Return us, Lord, to yourself. Please let us return!
>   Give us new days, like those long ago—
> unless [*kî 'im*] you have completely rejected us,
>   or have become too angry with us. (Lam 5:19–22)

As noted earlier, the final verse—in some interpretations and translations—is understood to be hopeless enough that it can only be mitigated by repeating verse 21. But such an understanding of verse 22 is neither inevitable nor necessary. The CEB's rendering, among others, holds the door open with "unless": perhaps the Lord *hasn't* rejected Israel despite its great suffering and Jerusalem's brutal destruction. The presence of this "unless" means that the end of the book may end, not with a period and full stop, but with an ellipsis that extends outward, unresolved:

> Return us to yourself, O Lord—and we will return!
>   Make our days new again, like they were of old,
> unless you have utterly rejected us,
>   your wrath against us too much . . . (my translation)[39]

If so, the resulting question, of course, is, What might lie on the other side of this elliptical "unless"? As noted earlier, it is the special burden of several other texts in the Old Testament to demonstrate that God has *not*, in fact, finally and ultimately rejected Israel despite exile, wrath, and judgment. There *is*, in fact, life with God on the far side of the ellipsis. Israel's suffering will eventually be deemed complete; it will come to an end (see, e.g., Isa 40:1–2; Jer 31:8–14). These other texts make this point explicitly and extensively, but a future on the others side of "unless" is already hinted at, even if only barely, at the end of Lamentations. The last chapter and the book as a whole therefore reflect Israel's painful honesty about suffering *and also* by various strategies, including poetic form and raw honesty, begin to move that suffering toward healing.[40]

Lamentations is not alone. As already observed, the lament psalms, too, traffic in a literary form that simultaneously captures suffering and somehow constrains it toward healing. The conventional literary form of the lament psalm is nicely displayed in Psalm 13:

> [1]How long will you forget me, Lord? Forever? *complaint*
> How long will you hide your face from me?
> [2]How long will I be left to my own wits,
> agony filling my heart? Daily?
> How long will my enemy keep defeating me?
> [3]Look at me! Answer me, Lord my God! *petition*
> Restore sight to my eyes! Otherwise, I'll sleep
> the sleep of death,
> [4]and my enemy will say, "I won!"
> My foes will rejoice over my downfall.
> [5]But I have trusted in your faithful love. *confession of trust*
> My heart will rejoice in your salvation.
> [6]Yes, I will sing to the Lord because he has been
> good to me. *vow to praise*

Though no two lament psalms are exactly the same, there is widespread consensus that they generally follow this pattern.[41] The pattern includes the elements of *complaint*, wherein the psalmist recounts the several problems she faces (including the suffering she has experienced), and *petition*, wherein the psalmist articulates her requests to God, as well as a *confession of trust* and a *vow to praise* that, following the complaint and petition, can sometimes seem like non sequiturs. How, in Psalm 13, can the psalmist move so suddenly, even abruptly, from the complaints and pleas of verses 1–4 to the confident words found in verses 5–6? In Psalm 22, the most famous of lament psalms for Christians, given Christ's citation of it from the cross, the shift happens in the middle of a verse, between two halves of a single line of Hebrew poetry (Ps 22:21): "Save me from the mouth of the lion"—the psalmist requests. Then, suddenly, inexplicably, "From the horns of the wild oxen you have answered me!" the psalmist exclaims.

In the first half of this verse, the mood is imperative: *Save me, God!* In the second half, the salvation is achieved, done, complete; the mood is now indicative: *You have answered me!*

This "rapid change of mood" in the lament psalms has been the subject of numerous studies.[42] Various theories have been proposed to account for it, with perhaps the most popular being that a priest heard these prayers and, at the appropriate time, after the petition had been made, responded to the supplicant with some words of assurance. An example is found in 1 Samuel, in the exchange between Hannah and the priest Eli at Shiloh. After Hannah explains to Eli that she has been "praying out of [her] great worry and trouble" (1 Sam 1:16), Eli responds, "Then go in peace. And may the God of Israel give you what you've asked from him" (1:17).

One can easily imagine that such a statement, if said by a priest to a supplicant who had just uttered Psalm 13:4, could easily enough have produced verses 5–6—"I have trusted! I will sing!"

The problem, of course, is that there is precious little (if any) evidence that such words of assurance were a regular part of the recitation of the psalms. There is no exchange quite like 1 Samuel 1 anywhere in the Psalter. This explanation of priestly assurance remains, therefore, speculative and, as a result, dissatisfying. While other options might be considered, my own judgment is that *the literary form of the lament itself* may be what makes this shift possible.[43] That is to say, in brief, that *Israel's honest lament is precisely what allows it to shift to new life, to healing, and ultimately to praise.* One can hardly imagine greater testimony to the power of honest disclosure with regard to suffering. And so, as a result, one cannot help but see how important, crucial, and indispensable honesty about suffering truly is. Honest disclosure about suffering is, in the Psalms, *the only way* to something *beyond* suffering, the only way to praise, wholeness, happiness. No new life comes through denial and cover-up. But new life can, and does, come through candor about suffering, whenever it comes and wherever it comes from.

New life *through*, never *around*, suffering is not easy—precisely because that path lies directly through the very midst of pain, the valley of the shadow of grief (and worse). It is thus not surprising to find one lament psalm, Psalm 88, that does not make this stereotypical shift to praise. Here, the standard literary form of the lament psalm is broken . . . in pieces! This poem rearranges the usual elements of the lament form as it goes from address (v. 1a), to petition (vv. 1b–2), and then to complaint (vv. 3–12).

Then comes verse 13, which sounds a great deal like a confession of trust, or at least the beginning of one:

> But I cry out to you, Lord!
> My prayer meets you first thing in the morning!

But then, all bets are off. What follows immediately after this verse is one of the deepest and darkest complaints found in the entire Psalter. Here is no prayer "out of the depths" (see Ps 130:1 NRSV) but a prayer that remains fully and resolutely *in the depths*:

> Why do you reject my very being, Lord?
> Why do you hide your face from me?
> Since I was young I've been afflicted, I've been dying.
> I've endured your terrors. I'm lifeless.
> Your fiery anger has overwhelmed me;
> your terrors have destroyed me.
> They surround me all day long like water;
> they engulf me completely.
> You've made my loved ones and companions distant.
> My only friend is darkness. (Ps 88:14–18)

And that is how Psalm 88 ends, with the poet's only companion, the ever-present darkness, surrounding her.[44] Verse 13 was, at best, a feint; the psalmist gestured toward confession of trust only to show that, in this case—no less than in the alphabetic acrostic in Lamentations—the form could only do so much and, in this particular case, not nearly enough.

Perhaps Psalm 88 is the exception that proves the rule, but perhaps it also shows that candor about suffering doesn't always yield to healing—not always, at any rate—and not always easily. Rarely easily! Even with a good literary form to help! But if this is the case with Psalm 88, it finally is not much different from the book of Lamentations, even if it is much smaller in size. That is because in this psalm, no less than in Lamentations, the grief-stricken voice that speaks is proof of life, a sign that the psalmist is still alive and may, in the future, still have hope. Further, Psalm 88 is not the last in the Psalter. Many more psalms are lined up in the queue. So it is that one who reads the psalms seriatim encounters what appears to be the nadir of nadirs in Psalm 88 but then, ever so slowly (as is so often the case with healing), begins to emerge from its pit (see 88:4)—first in Psalm 89, which also ends somberly before its concluding doxology (v. 52); then in Psalm 90, which is a sober-eyed reflection on the limited span of human life (v. 12); and then into the last half of the Psalter, where the majority of the hymns of praise cluster and where everything, all of life, indeed everything that has breath, culminates in unbounded, comprehensive doxology: "Praise the Lord!" (150:6).

Psalm 88 is not alone, therefore. The psalmist turns out to have other friends besides darkness only. This psalm (and psalmist) takes its (and her) place within a larger cycle of honesty about suffering that leads sooner or later to healing as that is expressed not only in the other lament psalms that end in confidence and praise but also in the shape of the Psalter as a whole. Psalm 88 may be the most troubling of the Psalter's candid articulations of sorrow, but it is not alone—not left alone—and it is not the final word. Israel knows that there is no replacement for honest testimony about suffering, even suffering that seems hopeless but turns out, in the end, not to be without hope. Israel knows that it is honesty that enables a new life with its Lord. Israel knows this from its primordial experience in Egypt and from its equally primal poetry.

And then Israel writes it all down, telling us all about it, in detail, for posterity, forever.

(Dis)Honesty about Suffering, Now and in the Pulpit

That Israel *writes* all of this down is no small matter in light of research conducted by James W. Pennebaker and others who have demonstrated the significant health benefits that accrue from honest disclosure, especially in written form.[45] Pennebaker's work shows that holding things in—*not* disclosing, *not* being honest—takes a major toll on the body, including immune function. In his own words,

> The main discoveries . . . indicate that actively holding back or inhibiting our thoughts and feelings can be hard work. Over time, the work of inhibition gradually undermines the body's defenses. Like other stressors, inhibition can affect immune function, the action of the heart and vascular systems and even the biochemical workings of the brain and nervous systems. In short, excessive holding back of thoughts, feelings, and behaviors can place people at risk for both major and minor diseases.[46]

Things can be and are different, however, if one opens up, as revealed in the following passage from Pennebaker, which was partially cited in chapter 1:

> Whereas inhibition is potentially harmful, confronting our deepest thoughts and feelings can have remarkable short- and long-term health benefits. Confession,

whether by writing or talking, can neutralize many of the problems of inhibition. Furthermore, writing or talking about upsetting things can influence our basic values, our daily thinking patterns, and feelings about ourselves. In short, there appears to be something akin to an urge to confess. Not disclosing our thoughts and feelings can be unhealthy. Divulging them can be healthy.[47]

The helpful aspects of disclosure also obtain in cases of wrongdoing such that Pennebaker's work could easily have been considered in the previous chapter about sin. As he notes, "Even when the costs are high, the confession of actions that violate our personal values can reduce anxiety and physiological stress. . . . Revealing pent-up thoughts and feelings can be liberating. *Even if they send you to prison.*"[48] "Or," Israel would quickly add, "into exile."

Whatever the precise content of the disclosure, Pennebaker's research has demonstrated that inhibition or nonverbalization (failure to disclose)

* is physical work—it requires physical exertion;
* affects short-term biological changes (as, for instance, indicated by lie detectors) and long-term health (in terms of the cumulative toll it takes on the whole body); and
* influences thinking abilities by preventing us from "understanding and assimilating" the event in question.[49]

Pennebaker calls the "opposite pole of active inhibition" *confrontation*, which "refers to individuals' actively thinking and/or talking about significant experiences as well as acknowledging their emotions."[50] Confrontation counters the many problems inherent in nonverbalization. It

* reduces the effects of inhibition, immediately reducing its "physiological work"; and
* forces a rethinking of events, helping people to "understand and ultimately, assimilate the event."[51]

Pennebaker's research involves very real, very physical outcomes. This is not a simple matter of "It's nice to tell the truth, Sally" or "Be honest, Billy!" It is far more serious than that. Pennebaker has been able to show, for example, that not disclosing a childhood trauma can make people more likely to be diagnosed "with virtually every major and minor health problem ... cancer, high blood pressure, ulcers, flu, headaches, even earaches."[52] "Oddly," Pennebaker goes on to say, "it made no difference what the particular trauma had been. The only distinguishing feature was that the trauma had not been talked about to others. A sexual trauma that was not confided was no worse than a death in the family that was not discussed."[53] Pennebaker reached similar conclusions when he moved from traumas experienced early in life to those later in life, such as, for example, the death of a spouse: "The more that people talked to others about the death of their spouse, the fewer health problems they reported having. Not talking with others about their spouses' death was clearly a health risk."[54]

According to Pennebaker's research, the people who did not open up about their spouse's death and were, as a result, prone to illness tended to follow two inhibitory strategies: the first was "to move forward and try not to think about the spouse or the death"; the second was to live in denial, pretending the traumatic experience had never happened.[55] Neither approach proved effective.

Those who did not disclose tended to become obsessed with their traumas and ruminated on them—something that was correlated with poor physical health in the year immediately following the spouse's death.[56] In contrast, those who talked about their suffering ended up thinking about their loss less frequently than those who did not.

From early on, but especially in more recent publications, Pennebaker has placed special emphasis on *expressive writing*—on how the disclosure of emotions through writing is a special means to health and the easing of emotional pain.[57] In other words, "we don't need to talk to others to tell our untold stories";[58] people who simply write about "their deepest thoughts and feelings about traumas" experience "improved moods, more positive outlook, and greater physical health."[59] This is not, according to Pennebaker, a simple matter of catharsis or venting, if only because his experiments revealed that writing about traumatic experiences was often quite painful for those who did it. But the payoff was significant—truly beneficial—and was frequently described by the writers themselves in terms of *insight*: "Rather than explaining that it felt good to get negative emotions off their chests, respondents noted how they understood themselves better."[60] Pennebaker's conclusion is "that our thought processes can heal"—and that that healing happens precisely through honest disclosure about suffering put into language and committed to writing. Frank Warren's PostSecret project operates with the same insight (see chapter 1). So does the Old Testament:

> And then Israel writes it all down, telling us all about it, in detail, for posterity, forever.

The Old Testament anticipates Pennebaker's findings (and Warren's project) by millennia; or put differently, the Old

HONEST ABOUT SUFFERING

Testament offers additional evidence that honesty about suffering—even and perhaps especially in writing, by "posting secrets"—is directly related to healing. Beneficial results also obtain, of course, for honesty about sin, discussed in the previous chapter,[61] as well as honesty about violence, to be discussed in the next. Whatever the case, what Israel offers us in all its candor is a model that can be emulated—a model that *should* be emulated because it provides a way to healing and wholeness. Honesty about suffering facilitates healing. Israel knew that. The Old Testament reflects that. Pennebaker, in more recent times, has confirmed it empirically. Preaching also provides its own kind of confirmation. Honest preaching about the hard topics, like suffering, can be exactly what is needed to make an intractable issue somehow suddenly tractable. And preachers know firsthand how writing an honest sermon on a candid text can transport their souls far beyond what seemed possible before that point. Honest preaching about honest texts can make a real difference, moving all who hear toward healing—and not just of the spiritual variety.

Pennebaker discovered something else during his research on people who had lost their spouses: it specifically concerned *prayer*. "The more people prayed about their deceased spouses, the healthier they were," he writes. "Prayer, in fact, worked the same way as talking to friends about the death. It is easy to see why this is true: Prayer is a form of disclosure or confiding."[62] As demonstrated in the present chapter and the others in this book, much of Israel's honesty is precisely couched in prayer, as in the Psalms. Indeed, even in its narrative honesty, what Israel repeatedly offers through its practices of candid disclosure is nothing less than a confiding in others, including, especially, its Lord. These confessions, addressed to and/or heard by the Secret-Knowing God, are, therefore, nothing less than prayers.

It goes without saying that the honest disclosure Israel offers, in both story and psalm, is something we can read, belatedly, today. When we do that, God isn't the only one who hears and sees secrets that have now come to light. We hear and see them as well, which means that Israel is *confiding in us*. And that makes these written expressions of honesty very precious indeed. What will we do with this confidence that Israel has entrusted to us? These not-so-secret secrets are not simply things to be read, that is, but also treasured. Still further, and once again, these treasures can (and *should*) be received as models to imitate in homiletical practice no less than in personal devotion. The main takeaways for preachers, therefore, include at least the following:

1. Honest disclosure about suffering isn't optional but required if we are to move toward healing. There is no new life via denial or cover-up; healing and newness come instead (if not only) through honest disclosure about suffering. In brief: if Christian preaching wants to be about healing, it must sound the difficult notes and not drown them out incessantly with triumphal chords, no matter how beautiful they may be. The Blues, too, are beautiful—and healing.[63]
2. The suffering that must be expressed in honest preaching may be self-inflicted, the result of our own wrongdoing, or may instead be caused by others. Both aspects of suffering must be recognized and acknowledged, including in the pulpit. The fact that suffering can be inflicted on one person by another person means that disclosure about suffering may frequently need to include honest confession about our own sin and wrongdoing (see

chapter 2). It may also mean that we will need to be honest about our own rage about the sin and wrongdoing that has been done to us (see chapter 4).
3. Certain literary elements and forms are helpful in facilitating the move from suffering to healing. Generally speaking, giving voice to suffering and to those who suffer helps, as do, more specifically, certain kinds of literary patterns—in Israel's case, the latter included things like the alphabetic acrostic or the structure of an individual lament psalm. Preachers who give voice to the text and their people and do so at the point of their intersection every Sunday, if not Monday through Saturday, and who preach using the (endlessly pliable) literary form of the sermon should have little difficulty finding points of connection here between biblical and sermonic forms of honest disclosure.

More will be said about Israel's honesty and our homiletic in chapter 5. I end the present chapter with one more instance—whether echo or anticipation—of Pennebaker's honesty-to-health dynamic in Israel's prayers, this one from Psalm 32. Though it speaks explicitly of sin, it also (not surprisingly) contains traces of suffering, since these are so often connected. In either case, the psalmist is once again nothing if not honest.

> When I kept quiet, my bones wore out;
>   I was groaning all day long—every day, every
>   night!—
> because your hand was heavy upon me.
>   My energy was sapped as if in a summer drought.

So I admitted my sin to you;
   I didn't conceal my guilt.
"I'll confess my sins to the Lord," is what I said.
   Then you removed the guilt of my sin.
That's why all the faithful should pray to you during
      troubled times,
   so that a great flood of water won't reach them.
You are my secret hideout!
   You protect me from trouble.
   You surround me with songs of rescue! (Ps 32:3–7)

4

Honest about Violence

As we turn to the third and last topic of honesty to be considered in this book, honesty about violence, we find ourselves on familiar ground. The previous two chapters have had occasion to note a good bit of overlap between sin, suffering, and violence—so much so that much of what has been said in those earlier chapters applies, mutatis mutandis, in the present one. An example of the interconnections may be found in the Bible's very first mention of sin (*ḥaṭṭāʾt*), in the story of Cain and Abel, where sin is associated with the first violent act of human history, the fratricide that occurs between the first two brothers, the first children of the first human couple (Gen 4:7). After the very first murder, we read immediately of the very first prayer, as Abel's blood gurgles into the ground:

> The Lord said, "What did you do? The voice of your brother's blood is crying [*ṣōʿăqîm*] to me from the ground" (Gen 4:10)

The word here for "crying [out] to" comes from the root *ṣā'aq*, which is one of the key verbs used to describe Israel's primal suffering in Egypt, discussed in the previous chapter:

> A long time passed, and the Egyptian king died. The Israelites were still groaning because of their hard work. They cried out [*yiz'āqû*]¹ and their cry to be rescued from the hard work rose up to God. God heard their cry of grief, and God remembered his covenant with Abraham, Isaac, and Jacob. God looked at the Israelites, and God understood. (Exod 2:23–25)

Abel's blood is, in a word, *praying*—calling out from its distress, from its great suffering that has been caused by Cain's sin of violence. And in the case of this particular murder, Abel's blood knows exactly where it should pray, *to whom* it should pray: God. At the very least, we would have to say that, according to Genesis 4, God has an ear for precisely these kinds of prayers. Israel's cries in Exodus 2 don't seem to be originally oriented to the Lord, after all, but the Lord hears them nevertheless.[2] As I said in chapter 3, people who are experiencing pain—especially from violent acts—don't have much time for niceties. Sometimes just one word ("Violence!") or an inarticulate groan will do.[3] And that holds true for Abel's blood just as it does for enslaved Israel.

Sin-suffering-violence is clearly a matrix of sorts. These three things are neither exactly coterminous nor entirely discrete sets. There is significant overlap and interrelationship between and among these three subjects, about which Israel is so honest. We, too, know much about this matrix, even if we aren't always honest about it in the pulpit. We are painfully aware that this "unholy trinity" of sin, suffering, and violence has operated far too often within the church itself, with the sins of Christians individually or as a corporate body often leading to and/or emerging from cycles of suffering and violence. Church scandal after church scandal are proof of the point—with the vast majority of those not making it to the newsfeed.

Another example of this matrix in action is seen in David's life. As noted in the previous chapter, Shimei is portrayed as cursing David as he flees Jerusalem after Absalom's coup:

> Get out of here! Get out of here! You are a murderer! You are despicable! The Lord has paid you back for all the blood of Saul's family, in whose place you rule, and the Lord has handed the kingdom over to your son Absalom. You are in this trouble because you are a murderer! (2 Sam 16:7–8)

Strong words! Especially the twice-made accusation that David is nothing less than a "murderer," in Hebrew "a man of blood/bloodshed" (*'îš haddāmîm . . . 'îš dāmîm*).[4]

Shimei's cursing is one thing, certainly bad enough. Even worse, however, is when it is God who comes to the same conclusion about David, which is what happens in Chronicles, where David's proclivity for bloodshed is the reason given for why Solomon, not David himself, will construct the temple. David relays the divine judgment to his son:

> The Lord's word came to me: You've shed a great amount of blood [*dām*] and fought massive battles. You will not build a temple for my name because you've spilled too much blood [*dāmîm*] on the ground before me. (1 Chr 22:8; my translation)

The Hebrew word for "blood" here is the same, used twice and in two different forms—singular and plural—probably to be clear and comprehensive.[5] And should there be any lingering doubt, each time the term is modified: we are talking about *a great deal of blood, too much* blood (*rōb, rabbîm*), and it has been *poured out, spilled, shed* (*šāpak*). That is *not* what blood was designed to do; when blood does that—or rather, when someone does that to blood—it means something has gone wrong, a violent act has transpired.[6]

The relationship between Samuel–Kings and Chronicles is a complicated one and cannot be resolved here. Even so, in any correlation of their differing accounts of David's career, the story in 1 Chronicles 22 comes long after David's misdeeds with Uriah and Bathsheba.[7] The consequences of David's sin(s)—especially his violence—linger, that is, for a very long time indeed, just as Nathan predicted, despite David's immediate confession in 2 Samuel 12 and the more effusive penance recounted in Psalm 51.[8] Indeed, upon closer inspection, Psalm 51, too, refers to David's blood-soaked violence:

> Deliver me from violence [*dāmîm*], God, God of my salvation,
>   so that my tongue can sing of your righteousness.
>   (Ps 51:14)

It is easy enough to relate this line to other prayers in the Psalter that request deliverance *from violent enemies* (e.g., Pss 7:1–2; 17:8–12; 35:4; etc.), and perhaps that is the case here in Psalm 51. But within the larger scope of Israel's many stories about David—the many stories about his own blood shedding—it is also not hard to imagine that the flawed king seeks relief here from *his own violence*. Within the echo chamber of Scripture, only David's appeal to God, twice, in confession of sin, can

HONEST ABOUT VIOLENCE

apparently counter Shimei's commands, twice, to leave Jerusalem because David is, twice, a killer:

Shimei:
Get out of here [ṣēʾ]! Get out of here [ṣēʾ]!
You are a violent man [ʾîš haddāmîm] . . . you are a
violent man [ʾîš dāmîm]! (2 Sam 16:7-8)

David:
Deliver me from violence [dāmîm], God [ʾĕlōhîm],
God of my salvation [ʾĕlōhê tĕšûʿātî] . . . ! (Ps 51:14)

Unlike Cain, who feigns ignorance regarding his dead brother's whereabouts, David is honest about his sin, including, in this understanding of Psalm 51, his own violence, which runs far beyond the hit he took out on Uriah. Once more we see clearly that sin often leads to suffering of various kinds, that sin not infrequently includes or leads to violence, and that sins of violence are not infrequently the cause of suffering par excellence.

Over the course of the present book, we have come to see that while there is a *sin-suffering-violence* matrix, there is also a corresponding nexus on the other side of honest disclosure, *reconciliation-healing-recovery*. These better angels of truthful confession also evidence significant overlap even though they, too, are not identical. Reconciliation, after all, is a kind of healing of relationships, whether human-human or human-divine, and healing and recovery are often closely related, especially in certain therapeutic situations.[9] It is the burden of the present chapter to discuss the last item in each triad and the role honesty plays in connecting them: namely, how *honesty about violence facilitates recovery*.

Before proceeding, it is important to recognize that both of the items under consideration, *violence* and *recovery*, are massive and fraught, especially in our day, with great concerns often expressed over violence in the Bible, on the one hand, and, on the other, massive human effort expended toward recovery (and healing) even as societal violence runs perilously close to out of control.[10] Any brief treatment of these important matters therefore threatens to be beyond trite. At precisely this point, however, the matrix of *sin-suffering-violence* and the nexus of *reconciliation-healing-recovery* may be helpful by reminding us that the various issues are many, deep, and intertwined. Help from one may help with the others in making progress and moving forward.

In what follows, I speak first of honest disclosure about *violence done to Israel* before turning to Israel's honesty *about its own violence*. These types of violence are quite different, of course, if only due to the fact that the subjects and objects change with regard to who is doing the violence and who is experiencing it. This difference also means that the nature of the recovery on the other side of honesty about violence is also distinct. What is constant, in either case, is Israel's exemplary candor, which can be learned from and imitated in the pulpit and beyond it.

"God Damn It" and Other Things People Say (or, Better, *Pray*)

The imprecatory or cursing psalms are among the most infamous in the Psalter if not the entire Bible.[11] In these texts, the psalmists curse their enemies in great and at times gory detail. The following, from Psalm 58, is an especially vicious passage:

HONEST ABOUT VIOLENCE

> God, break their teeth out of their mouths!
>   Tear out the lions' jawbones, Lord!
> Let them dissolve like water flowing away.
>   When they bend the bow,
>   let their arrows be like headless shafts.
> Like the snail that dissolves into slime,
>   like a woman's stillborn child,
>   let them never see the sun. (Ps 58:6–8)

It seems more than a bit ironic that the superscription to this psalm includes the phrase "Do not destroy" (*'al-tašḥēt*)[12] because it seems that this psalmist would like nothing more than the destruction of her enemies![13]

A good number of psalms, not just the half dozen usually categorized as imprecatory, contain elements of cursing. One example is the beloved Psalm 139, which, after its long discussion of God's constant (if not also comforting) presence, ends in an unexpected turn:

> If only, God, you would kill the wicked!
>   If only murderers would get away from me—
> the people who talk about you,
>   but only for wicked schemes;
> the people who are your enemies,
>   who use your name as if it were of no significance.
> Don't I hate everyone who hates you?
>   Don't I despise those who attack you?
> Yes, I hate them—through and through!
>   They've become my enemies too.
> Examine me, God! Look at my heart!
>   Put me to the test! Know my anxious thoughts!

> Look to see if there is any idolatrous way in me,
>   then lead me on the eternal path! (Ps 139:19–24)

Nowadays, most people would likely consider verses 19–22, if not an "idolatrous way," then at least something that deserves divine examination, testing, and correction so as to lead the psalmist on an "eternal path" (vv. 23–24). That is patently *not* how Israel understood matters according to the witness of Psalm 139, and that fact deserves further reflection and careful consideration. How does the psalmist's "perfect hatred" mentioned in verse 22 (NRSV; CEB: "through and through") pass under the divine radar?

Psalm 139 is proof that cursing elements are found mixed in with many psalms (as also in Lamentations; see 1:21–22; 3:64–66; 4:21–22)—so much so that, as C. S. Lewis remarked, "the bad parts will not 'come away clean'; they may . . . be intertwined with the most exquisite things."[14] If that is an accurate assessment (and I myself think it is), it suggests that the problem of cursing one's enemies is a larger issue to address than just a handful of unusual, "gone-off-the-rails" psalms. Indeed, in the contemporary context, the problem posed by *the cursing psalms* as well as by *cursing in the Psalms* might be something of a stand-in for major problems that contemporary readers struggle over in Scripture: things having to do with biblical ethics writ large, not just the specific issue of ethics toward enemies in the Psalter. Put differently, are these cursing psalms nothing but one more example of what may be described as the barbaric, premodern, and pre-Christian nature of the Old Testament? These types of questions are complicated ones that cannot be resolved easily or quickly.[15] That said, the imprecatory psalms deserve further discussion because they continue to loom large as a special case of "problematic text" for many modern readers. They also deserve further attention because these psalms bear directly on the issue of violence and honesty about violence.

Even casual Bible readers seem to know about the big problems of violence, revenge, and the like that lurk in the cursing psalms. The president of the "problematic text club" is likely Psalm 137, if only because the first two-thirds of the psalm (vv. 1–6) have been popularized and often set to music as, for example, in "By the Willows" from the musical *Godspell*. The last third of the psalm has been every bit as *in*famous, however. After a moving, heart-stirring beginning and middle, the last part of the psalm seems—to cite Lewis again—to contain a "spirit of hatred which strikes us in the face . . . like the heat from a furnace mouth."[16] Many people find the heat too much to bear and get out of this particular (psalmic) kitchen.

Psalm 137 is worth citing in full and discussing in some detail because, whatever else we might want to say about it, it is another installment in Israel's record of honest dealings. In the case of Psalm 137, the honesty is first and foremost about violence done to Israel. But the psalm is also quite frank about how the violence done to Israel leads it to say some other things about violence in (re)turn.

Psalm 137

¹Alongside Babylon's streams, there we sat down,
    crying because we remembered Zion.
²We hung our lyres up in the trees there
³because that's where our captors asked us to sing;
    our tormentors requested songs of joy:
        "Sing us a song about Zion!" they said.

⁴But how could we possibly sing
  the Lord's song on foreign soil?
⁵Jerusalem! If I forget you,
  let my strong hand wither!
⁶Let my tongue stick to the roof of my mouth
  if I don't remember you,
  if I don't make Jerusalem my greatest joy.
⁷Lord, remember what the Edomites did on Jerusalem's
    dark day:
  "Rip it down, rip it down! All the way to its
    foundations!" they yelled.
⁸Daughter Babylon, you destroyer,
  a blessing on the one who pays you back
    the very deed you did to us!
⁹A blessing on the one who seizes your children
  and smashes them against the rock!

There is much to say about this psalm, a good bit of which would relate to the discussion of suffering in chapter 3. Not unlike Lamentations, we have in Psalm 137 a poem that recounts Israel's great suffering due to the destruction of Jerusalem. Israel is forthright about the violence that has been done to it, which is captured in this particular psalm by the citation of Edom's exultation over Jerusalem's fall (v. 7) and by the prayer for precise payback for Babylon's cruel deeds (v. 8a).[17] After this comes the most brutal strike of all: the children, the seizing and smashing, the rock (v. 9).

Several observations about this grief-wracked, violence-filled poem must be made. First, it will come as no surprise to anyone who has read much at all of the Old Testament that Israel is forthcoming about its suffering and that its suffering in this particular psalm (as in many other passages) is the result of enemy violence. What may be surprising, however—and quite important—is *exactly how* forthcoming Israel is about the horrors of 587 BCE. To be sure, this is not without parallel: the book of Lamentations is every bit as candid, and disturbing, as Psalm 137 and has the further, rather dubious merit of being considerably longer, which draws out the grief and violence even further. Be that as it may, Psalm 137 joins Lamentations as something of a sister text. It, too, mourns the same thing, the same trauma: "Jerusalem's dark day" (v. 7).

Second, it is important to note, at a very basic level, how the poet in this psalm *verbalizes* the trauma of 587 BCE. Such verbalization is noteworthy because, according to psychiatrist Judith Lewis Herman, "the ordinary response to atrocities is to banish them from consciousness. Certain violations of the social compact are too terrible to utter aloud: this is the meaning of the word *unspeakable*."[18]

As Herman goes on to demonstrate, the silence following trauma is not simply—if ever—a matter of decorum, having to do with what is or is not polite to talk about at the dinner table. Instead, in many cases, it is *physiological*: "Preliminary results of brain scanning studies of patients with PTSD, using the sophisticated technique of positron emission tomography, suggest that during flashbacks, specific areas of the brain involved with language and communication may indeed be inactivated."[19]

Whatever the reason for silence after trauma, that silence is, at best, temporary because "atrocities . . . refuse to be buried," according to Herman.[20] And so, she continues, "equally as powerful as the desire to deny atrocities is the conviction that denial does not work. . . . *Remembering and telling the truth about terrible events are prerequisites both for the restoration of the social order and the healing of individual victims.*"[21] Herman calls the conflict between denying (or keeping silent about) traumatic experiences and the urge to talk about them "the central dialectic of psychological trauma."[22]

It would be, of course, a gross oversimplification to say that a short poem like Psalm 137 resolves or somehow transcends this profound dialectic. And yet there can be no doubt that in this psalm and others like it, Israel does not banish its suffering from consciousness, deny it, and/or refuse to utter it. Rather, Israel evidently also believed that "denial does not work."[23] Unspeakable things *can* be told. And they *must be* told because, per Herman, "remembering and telling the truth about terrible events" are the sine qua nons "for the restoration of the social order and the healing of individual victims."[24] Israel knew this well. As a result, the Old Testament knows it too. And so does Psalm 137:

* In Psalm 137, Israel *remembers*: Israel remembers *Zion* (v. 1). Israel remembers *destroyed Zion*, ripped down all the way to its foundations (v. 7). The psalmist weeps over this memory (v. 1) and worries that she will forget Jerusalem (pre- or postdestruction?), uttering a curse on herself should she ever do so (vv. 5–6).
* In Psalm 137, Israel also *tells the truth about terrible events*—the truth about destroyed Jerusalem, obviously, but also the truth about forced migration to Babylon, about captivity, and about cruel mockery on the part of Israel's tormenters.

Remembering and telling are prerequisites for restoration and healing, or, to use a different term from Herman's book, for *recovery* from trauma. So it is that *honesty about violence*—in the case of Psalm 137, violence done against Israel—*facilitates recovery*.

HONEST ABOUT VIOLENCE

A third important observation about Psalm 137 occurs at the confluence of this point about *required honesty toward recovery* in the face of what is *unspeakable trauma*. It seems highly significant that the emphatic request in verse 8 for precise payback to Babylon moves directly, in verse 9, to the comment about seizing and smashing the Babylonian children. Perhaps the two verses are more closely related than is typically thought. Rather than verse 9 being some sort of unthinkable outburst—a case of emotions running amok or worse—it may, instead, be understood as a calculated strike, a carefully considered request for perfect payback as, in fact, verse 8 imagines (and prays!). If so, that would mean that the outcome hoped for in the future according to verse 9 corresponds to a prior, already achieved outcome from the past: the poet's own child (children?) bashed against a rock.[25] If so, the sentiment found in verse 9 may become somehow less off-putting than it appeared initially. Or perhaps the sentiment *remains* off-putting but becomes, suddenly, more understandable—something that readers can more easily empathize with than they could have before. Rather than an undisciplined fit of berserker rage, verse 9 may be nothing more but also nothing less than the words of a grief-stricken, bereaved mother who can't get that rock out of her head, the rock against which that Babylonian tormentor bashed her child to death. If so, the trauma of the psalmist is vast and deep, truly unspeakable in its horror. And perhaps that is why, when that trauma is spoken of in the psalm, verse 9 does so rather obliquely. "Tell all the Truth," Emily Dickinson wrote, "but tell it slant"—especially, perhaps, when the truth in question is truly traumatic.[26] Telling that kind of truth is hard, traumatic in its own right.

Psalm 137 is an astonishing piece of honesty about violence—violence done against Israel. It stuns and shocks. But the psalm's stunning candor also proves to be an instance of the kind of honesty about trauma that leads to recovery when seen through the lens of Herman's work, which identifies three stages to recovery, with honest disclosure being the central, and in many ways key, transforming stage:

- The first stage is about "the establishment of safety."[27]
- In the second stage, "the survivor tells the story of the trauma . . . completely, in depth, and in detail."[28]
- The work of the third stage is "creating a future": the survivor "has mourned the old self that the trauma destroyed; now she must develop a new self."[29]

The (re)telling that is the work of the second stage is what Israel accomplishes in its own candid reportage in both story *and* song. It bears repeating that Israel does not tell us everything just once. Quite to the contrary, Israel's honest disclosure about suffering generally and its suffering after traumatic violence specifically is found in many different places in the Old Testament, *across* the Old Testament, even if one narrows the trauma in question to the particular (but world-shattering) event of Jerusalem's fall. Beyond Psalm 137 and Lamentations, for example, that signal moment in Israel's history is discussed, extensively or otherwise, in Obadiah, Jeremiah, Ezekiel, 2 Kings, and so forth. Perhaps these multiple retellings are proof of Herman's axiom "Trauma is contagious."[30] Whatever the case, *repeated retelling* is therapeutic because, as Herman has shown, it helps to lessen the intense feeling of trauma:

> After many repetitions, the moment comes when the telling of the trauma story no longer arouses quite such intense feeling. It has become a part of the survivor's

experience, but only one part of it. The story is a memory like other memories, and it begins to fade as other memories do. Her grief, too, begins to lose its vividness. It occurs to the survivor that perhaps the trauma is not the most important, or even the most interesting, part of her story.... When the "action of telling a story" has come to its conclusion, the traumatic experience truly belongs to the past.[31]

But, Herman adds, the traumatized "need not worry" because "she will never forget" what has happened to her.[32] Surely this *retelling unto recovery* but also this *retelling that will never forget* is accomplished not only by Israel's "multiple takes" on its suffering in the wake of violent trauma but also by the canonization of these various "takes" that subsequently help all who read to remember, retell, and recover too. Israel's honesty is, again, exemplary at this point, setting a model for all to see and put into practice. The numerous versions and interpretations of the year 587 BCE found in the Old Testament are not, therefore, some sort of repository of historical factoids recounting a long-ago and long-gone instantiation of pain. They are instead the very (and varied) means by which we, too, can disclose traumatic suffering—*now, here, among us*—and in so doing, move toward recovery.

None of Herman's three stages of recovery are easy, nor is any easily achieved. In fact, she writes that "the most common cause of stagnation in the second stage of recovery" is "resistance to mourning."[33] Such resistance is easily correlated with what Pennebaker calls "inhibition" (see chapter 3). Either way, the honesty that facilitates movement toward healing and recovery is stifled. In the Old Testament, however, Israel's repeated instances of overwhelming candor would seem to function as a direct counter to denial and inhibition, stagnation and resistance. But even here things aren't always so easy. Herman proceeds to note that "resistance to mourning can take on numerous disguises. Most frequently it appears as a fantasy of magical resolution through revenge, forgiveness, or compensation."[34] In this list, the revenge fantasy, in particular, seems to warrant careful consideration in the case of the imprecatory psalms.

According to Herman, a "revenge fantasy is often a mirror image of the traumatic memory, in which the roles of perpetrator and victim are reversed."[35] On the face of things, that sounds exactly like what we find in Psalm 137 as described above. The psalmist begins indirectly, with Edom, addressing the Lord for the first and, notably, only time in the poem, asking God to "remember to the Edomites" (*zĕkōr . . . libnê 'ĕdôm*). The Hebrew construction with the verb "remember" (*zākar*) and the preposition "to" (*lĕ-*) is not, by itself, an inherently negative or adversarial kind of remembering; in fact, *zākar* + *lĕ-* can be used to denote positive instances of divine recall.[36] NRSV's translation of verse 7 as "Remember, O Lord, *against* the Edomites" is thus doing some interpretive work for us, but not without good reason given the larger context of the psalm. That larger context, as described earlier, moves directly from Edom to the hoped-for payback of Babylon in verse 8. Exactly here Herman's work seems applicable, since "hoped-for payback" sounds like nothing less than "revenge fantasy." That suspicion seems confirmed in verse 9, especially via the interpretation offered earlier, in which, per Herman, "the roles of perpetrator and victim are reversed": smashed baby for smashed baby.

But before we find ourselves adopting a self-righteous posture toward the psalmist or this particular psalm, several things might be noted. First and most importantly, "feelings of rage and murderous revenge fantasies are *normal responses to abuse treatment*."[37] In other words, while a revenge fantasy *can* be a sign of resistance to mourning, it needn't be. It can just as well be part of the retelling process that slowly but surely lessens the impact of a terrible trauma, facilitating the traumatized victim's recovery. At one point in her book, Herman recounts the spontaneous sharing of a revenge fantasy among a women's support group, describing the initial articulation of the fantasy by the survivor, who was immediately encouraged and supported by the other women in the group. The fantasy grew in intensity as it was shared, with several in the group laughing with delight at the victimizer finally getting what he had coming. "Even the quietest and most inhibited members" weren't frightened and were "able to join in the laughter," Herman writes.[38] Then slowly the laughter faded and things got serious again. In Herman's judgment, this kind of sharing process causes these fantasies to "lose much of their intensity" such that victims "are able to recognize how little they actually need revenge."[39]

Second, in the case of Psalm 137, the psalmist is most certainly not concocting a strategy to resist mourning, since the poet leads off, from the very start, with the admission that she is aggrieved.[40] She sits down, weeping as she remembers her beloved Zion and the Lord's songs that celebrated Jerusalem.

This leads to a third, very important observation—namely, that in the ancient world, the notion of precise payback was not primarily a vehicle for revenge fantasy but, instead, a means for the proper execution of justice—no more, no less.[41] In this light, Psalm 137:8–9, when read together and understood as integrally related, are not a vindictive lashing-out—a "mere" revenge fantasy—but a deep hope that justice be served precisely, exactly, no more but also no less.⁴² If so, verses 8–9 ought not be seen as somehow barbaric or backward, as if they were premodern, pre-civilized, or pre-Christian. Quite to the contrary, if only because the Bible is full of testimony to the sublime nature of justice and to justice as one of the most sublime qualities of God.⁴³ No wonder the psalmist prays to the "God of paybacks" (*'ēl něqāmôt*; Ps 94:1), variously rendered in different translations:

> O Lord, you God of vengeance, you God of vengeance, shine forth! (NRSV)
>
> God of retribution, Lord, God of retribution, appear! (NJPSV)
>
> Lord, avenging God—avenging God, show yourself! (CEB)

Erich Zenger has conclusively demonstrated that the imprecatory psalms are predicated on God's justice and God's justice alone—they do not lean on the psalmist's own understanding.⁴⁴ And the call, prayer, and hope for divine justice would seem to have no ending here on earth. Amazingly, according to Revelation, even in heaven the martyrs continue to beg for it:

> They cried out with a loud voice, "Holy and true Master, how long will you wait before you pass judgment? How long before you require justice for our blood, which was shed by those who live on earth?" (Rev 6:10).

In sum: yes, Psalm 137 *is* brutal—brutally honest about violence. In this psalm (and other texts like it), Israel is honest about the violence that has been done to it, which has led to unimaginable suffering. But this honesty turns out to be nothing less than a retelling strategy that, in the end, proves to be critical for any possible recovery. Even the imprecatory psalms, that is, so full of rage and wrath, *precisely because of their expression of that rage and wrath*, offer evidence that the poets who wrote them and those who read them *are on the way* to a new and different future—a new self, in Herman's words—even if we don't fully "get there" within the framework of any one specific poem. And yet, even if we haven't yet completely arrived, we are nevertheless on the move toward newness and recovery. This dynamic of honesty facilitating profound healing is precisely what was observed in the lament psalms in chapter 3.[45] That is no surprise, since the imprecatory psalms are a subtype of the lament form.

The final verses of Psalm 137 shift from Israel's honesty about the *violence done to it* to honesty about the *violence Israel would like to see done*, though, in my judgment, the end of this psalm is too often mistaken as mere vindictiveness. On the contrary, what we have seen is that the retelling of trauma, which often includes the desire for revenge, is a way to unburden the self, to mourn what needs to be mourned, and so move to newness.[46] Surely we censor such psalms to our own peril, cutting off a way toward recovery—a way modeled by Israel in its candor and made available to us now through canon. In the canon, that is, we have not only the record of Israel's retelling unto recovery but an example of how we might do the same. Every time someone reads (or prays) these texts, they function to realize the same type of disclosure in the reader (or supplicant) *at the same time* precisely *by means of this process*.[47] Seen in this way, even the most intransigent of imprecatory psalm not only models full honesty, it becomes a means by which we ourselves become honest—*finally and at long last!*—disclosing everything, including our experiences of and feelings about violence and trauma, whether that trauma be *our own* or *someone else's* or *someone-else's-as-our-own*.

Said differently, the psalms—even and perhaps especially the cursing psalms—offer a script for those of us not yet comfortable with being honest about our own traumas.[48] If that is the case, there is no cause for concern because this script offers us specific words to adopt as our own, even if the scenarios aren't perfectly matched, and thus a "trying out" of another person's disclosure on the way to our own. That can be useful for those who have suffered unspeakable violence, because they now have words to speak. But it can also be useful for those who haven't experienced such horrors—or haven't in the same way or to a similar degree—because at this point the psalms offer us windows onto another world, onto *another's world*. In this way, Ellen Davis says, the psalms are not only therapeutic but educative because they help "keep compassion alive"—if, that is, we allow these sacred poems to "instruct our compassion."[49]

There can be no doubt that Israel is honest about violence in the Psalter, writing it all down and praying it all out loud. Whenever the psalms are read or prayed now, they manifest the same honesty, and we who read or pray them suddenly find ourselves caught up in the same, even when the candor runs beyond what we would perhaps otherwise say, especially in polite company, or when a psalm puts things more righteously (in terms of divine justice) than we ourselves might in our more petty vindictive modes. Whatever the specific case, when this transference of honesty happens—from Israel to us—we are put on the road to recovery, miraculously and mercifully, precisely because honest disclosure is the only way to get there. We now know, thanks to the work of Herman and others but also thanks to the Psalter long before that, that honesty about violence is the primary facilitator of recovery.[50]

HONEST ABOUT VIOLENCE

One of the PostSecrets from California, cited in chapter 1, deserves recollection here as capturing the endgame of this honesty:

> On Thursday, I enjoyed dropping my postcard into the post office box and watching it disappear. My secret does not own me anymore. *I don't need revenge.*[51]

The psalms concur—even the psalms of divine vengeance! That is because they know the truth captured in Deuteronomy, cited belatedly by Paul (Rom 12:19) and the author of Hebrews (10:30):

> Vengeance is mine, and recompense,
>   for the time when their foot shall slip;
> because the day of their calamity is at hand,
>   their doom comes swiftly.
> Indeed the Lord will vindicate his people,
>   have compassion on his servants,
> when he sees that their power is gone. (Deut 32:35–36a NRSV)

God's seeing to payback means, ultimately, that we don't have to.

It should be repeated that the dynamics of honesty about violence must not be simplistically understood; the path to recovery—any final endgame—will be long and hard. Perhaps that is why there are 150 psalms in the Psalter. Perhaps that is why Israel retells its honesties again and again—inside and outside the Psalter—with Scripture itself canonizing all these many retellings. And perhaps that is why there is still more to say about Israel's honesty about violence, since that honesty concerns not only the violence done to it, or the violence it would like to see done, but the violence it did itself. It is thus time to turn, finally, to honesty about this last aspect of violence. I start with a story.

Israel's Own Violence, or The Cursing Psalms, the Conquest of Canaan, and the Things We Watch for Fun

The student (let's call him Joe) came up to me after class, somewhat exercised but also oddly peaceful, almost Zen-like. The class was entitled "Preaching Torah," and I had just done my best song and dance about violence in the Pentateuch, especially in Deuteronomy, where it is something of a harbinger of things to come in Joshua and beyond. Joe clearly didn't like that violence, nor was he particularly impressed by my song and dance. That explains why he was exercised. The oddly peaceful part is how Joe told me that he wasn't especially bothered by violence in the Old Testament because it had all been fixed, taken away, transcended (insert your favorite verb here) because of—drum roll, please—"the nonviolence of Jesus."

"Uh huh," I said. "But, um, what about various things Jesus says in the New Testament that don't seem particularly nonviolent?"

"I guess I'm, like, talking about the cross," Joe replied.

"Right," I said. "OK. But, like, isn't the cross—the crucifixion—kind of violent?" I asked.

Joe replied, "I guess I'm just thinking of the big thing, you know, the big Jesus event as canceling the violent stuff."

"Yeah, well, um, I'm not sure that's going to work," I said.

I don't remember what happened next. We were clearly at an impasse, and it was time for the next class to begin, so we had to leave the room. At the moment, I thought that perhaps I

HONEST ABOUT VIOLENCE

had made a point with Joe, but years later I ran into him randomly in another town in another state while out to breakfast with my family. He had long since graduated but hadn't forgotten my song and dance about violence in Deuteronomy. He was still not impressed by it and, in truth, seemed far less Zen-like about the matter in round two!

I can't speak for Joe or his disapproval of me, but I can say something about why I didn't like Joe's own particular "fix" to violence. I have exegetical reasons, like the content of specific biblical passages (in the Old Testament and New), and also have big theological problems (like the relationship of the Testaments) for disagreeing with Joe.[52] But insofar as the big theological questions depend (or *should*) on the exegetical work, and insofar as the exegetical work depends (or *should*) on fine details that are somehow *there*—in the text and in the tradition—I think now, in retrospect, that what bothered me most about Joe's take is that it *just wasn't honest*. It wasn't honest about the fine details of the text; it wasn't, therefore, an honest exegesis, and so you couldn't build a larger theological account on it. Because, let's face it: The Bible—*both* Testaments—has its fair share of violence. That means that violence is not limited to Israel alone, or to the Old Testament, or to that altogether wrongheaded and heretical construction known as "The Old Testament God" (in contrast to some friendly neighborhood New Testament variety). And that means the New Testament—even Jesus, I'm afraid—has its fair share of violence.[53] We need to be honest about that. Any reckoning with Israel's honesty about violence must reckon with violence in *all* of Scripture, with the same holding true for preaching as itself a kind of reckoning.

There are other things that preaching must be honest about when it comes to the violence in Scripture. Sure, the Bible has its fair share of violence but probably *not more than its fair share*—how would such a metric even be assessed? What is a "fair share" of violence in the first place? The very phrasing itself is disturbing. Violence is a very large, very far-flung human problem. It lives no special, extralarge life in religion or Scripture as opposed to, say, in politics or science or our entertainment media. That point entered, it is nevertheless true that the particular problem of enacted violence in Scripture has become a major locus of interpretive concern. A cottage industry of books has emerged dealing with this issue, especially in the Old Testament, and especially when the violence in question is predicated of God.[54]

These books are not uniform. Some come from atheists inimical to all forms of faith; at other times, the criticism is internal to the Christian communion. At still other times, the books are attempts to account for (*apologize*, in the classical sense of the term) biblical violence, justifying it or explaining it away in some way—whether successfully or not is another question. Whatever the case, the literature is now vast and deep and cannot be recounted here. Once again, violence and recovery are enormous topics, precluding any definitive treatment, even across many books. If nothing else, that explains the present spate of publications! In what follows, therefore, I will restrict myself to two important points that emerge from Israel's honesty about its own participation in violence: the first is how that violence is *contained and constrained*—how Scripture itself, that is, offers an innerbiblical critique of violence;[55] the second is how Israel's honesty about its own violence says something about our own proclivities toward violence.[56]

The first task is to ponder how Israel's honesty about its own violence often contains within it various strategies by which that selfsame violence is limited and critiqued. For example, David's violence and its critique by Shimei, on the one hand, and the Chronicler, on the other, have already been noted and are cases in point. Unfortunately, David's life story does not end with his acceptance of Shimei's curse. Instead, at the very end of his life, David proves adept at "outsourcing personal revenge."[57] On his deathbed, David charges Solomon to keep the faith (1 Kgs 2:1–4) but then asks him to deal with Joab (2:5–6) and Shimei, who "cursed me viciously" (2:8). David defers to Solomon's wisdom in both cases (vv. 6, 9)[58] but offers specific suggestions for how Solomon might treat his old enemies:

* For Joab: "Do not let his gray head go down to Sheol in peace" (1 Kgs 2:6 NRSV)
* For Shimei: "You must bring his gray head down with blood to Sheol" (1 Kgs 2:9 NRSV)

While the constructions are similar, the second scenario concerning Shimei is the worst of the two, given the addition of "with blood" (*bĕ-dām*; cf. CEB: "Give him a violent death"). Matthew Lynch has argued that David does not actually ask Solomon to shed Shimei's blood, because that "would be unconscionable to express in terms so direct."[59] Instead, David draws on legal language, asking Solomon to not acquit Shimei (CEB: "don't excuse him"). To bring Shimei down to Sheol with blood would thus "mean that David returns Shimei's own bloodshed (in the form of curse) back upon him."[60] As the story unfolds, we see that Solomon effectively puts Shimei on parole (2:36–37), which Shimei agrees to (2:38) but which he subsequently violates at the expense of his own life (2:39–46). While this dénouement exculpates Solomon and David from direct responsibility—Shimei is to be blamed for his own untimely demise—it is still striking that at the very end of his life—indeed, in his very last words—David is still a man of *dām*, of blood and bloodshed, just like Shimei said he was. David's has a long history of violence that is contained, finally, only by his death.[61] That, too, is part of the honest report Israel offers about its "greatest" king and his history of violence. Violence is an old habit for some. It leaves a long legacy, but it will, eventually, come to an end, even if only with the death of those who are so prone to enact it.

The imprecatory psalms, too, offer constraints on violence, limiting it mostly by uttering their violent sentiments *within the bounds of prayer*.[62] Indeed, as Patrick Miller has eloquently written, "Rather than asking if we could ever justifiably pray such a prayer as this [Psalm 137], assuming that the issue is simply a matter of choice, of rational decision, we might better ask whether such *thoughts* as expressed here have any other permissible context than *conversation with God*, from whom no secrets are hid, from whom no rage or anger can be concealed."[63]

Put differently, Miller is suggesting that there is *no* acceptable place to utter brutal sentiments about our enemies, such as those found in the cursing psalms, *except* within prayer to the Lord. Miller goes on to observe how the context of prayer allows troubling sentiments about enemies to be *released* and to be *restrained* at one and the same time:

> The unrestrained, justifiable but not justifiable, thoughts are let loose—but within a particular framework. In this sense, the rage and brutality are not allowed to go public. They are real in this psalm, and there are terrible moments when they are real in human life. To pray such rage is at one and the same time to let it go and to hold

HONEST ABOUT VIOLENCE

it back. It is not now a part of our dealing with our neighbor-enemy. It is a part of our life with God.[64]

Such prayer, first, *releases* this violence because it *must* be released. It is noteworthy that Miller invokes the divine epithet discussed in chapter 1: prayer is made to the God from whom no secrets are hid, and since we are only as sick as our secrets, our violent thoughts, too, must be uttered in all candor. To do otherwise would be to repress, to become more and more sickly—sick on our own secret wishes, griefs, and sorrows. Perhaps, in light of Pennebaker's research, we might even become physically ill as a result of our nonverbalization. We would, certainly and at the very least, be unhealthy before God, hiding something that cannot, in the end, be covered up, denied, or hidden. The cursing psalms let our violence go . . . but *safely*—in prayer to the God who listens and who already knows, who sees and somehow understands and remembers (cf. Exod 2:24–25; Ps 137:7).

Second, and simultaneously, this type of prayer *restrains* our violence. The violence has been uttered before the Lord, *to* the Lord, who can receive this violence in a way our enemies simply cannot, accepting it, as it were, in a way our enemies simply will not. So to pray in this way is to be utterly honest before God and at the same time to keep oneself from expressing anger in an upraised fist or a cocked and loaded gun. Instead, the anger is raised to God in prayer, leveled at the Lord. In Miller's words, "The ferocity of the psalm gives voice to and channels the ferocity of the soul, turning the fallen countenance that has retaliation and murder in its eyes [see Gen 4:7]—or calls for execution—into a raging prayer that finally leaves the matter where Moses (Deut 32:35) and Paul (Rom 12:18–21) both tell us it belongs—in the hands of God."[65]

Here again, one thinks of the dynamics of one of the Post-Secrets: "My secret does not own me anymore. *I don't need revenge.*"⁶⁶ Still further, who knows what God, sole proprietor of payback, might do with our prayers, or our enemies, once we have prayed this kind of prayer and placed our enemies in God's hands? As Ellen Davis memorably puts it, the fact that payback is God's prerogative and not ours is "*a severely limiting condition. For God's action is free, directed not only to our healing but to the healing of the whole moral order. Through these psalms we demand that our enemies be driven into God's hands. But who can say what will happen to them there? For God is manifest in judgment of our enemies but also, alas, in mercy toward them. Thus these vengeful psalms have a relationship with other forms of prayer for our enemies.*"⁶⁷

God may just have mercy on our dreaded enemies—the very ones whose horrific acts of violence have caused us great suffering and that have called forth violent thoughts (and prayers!) of our own in response. That is a hard pill to swallow when it comes to enemies who have done us great wrong, but one doesn't have to think very hard of biblical examples of how divine mercy is shown to the most undeserving of persons in the most extreme of moments:

> When they arrived at the place called The Skull, they crucified him, along with the criminals, one on his right and the other on his left. Jesus said, "Father, forgive them, for they don't know what they're doing." (Luke 23:33–34a)

Lest such mercy be deemed impossible for us mere mortals, unlike the incarnate Christ, we need only read a bit further to find another, perhaps more attainable, example:

> As they battered him with stones, Stephen prayed, "Lord Jesus, accept my life!" Falling to his knees, he shouted, "Lord, don't hold this sin against them!" Then he died. (Acts 7:59–60)

If we are being honest, another, equally unattractive outcome of prayed violence is that God might have a word of judgment, not for our opponents, but for us. Perhaps our enemies are not God's enemies after all. Perhaps God feels differently about them than we do and would like us to follow suit. Whatever the case—God's forgiveness of our enemies or the Lord's judgment of us—the kind of prayer captured in the cursing psalms limits the violence in our hearts because the situation is no longer one between us and our enemies alone: it is now, per Miller, "part of our life with God." God is now in the room, and that means that we are smack-dab in the middle of the sin-suffering-violence matrix, with its overlaps and interconnections, with honesty our primary way forward to the nexus of forgiveness, healing, and recovery.

Taken together, the previous considerations demonstrate that *praying these violent prayers is, in the end, a very real, very concrete way to contain and limit their violence,* maybe even bring it to an end—an ending, not in death, as was the case with David, but in prayer to the Lord who hears and sees, who judges the thoughts and inclinations of the heart (cf. Heb 4:12). And so, again, with Davis, we can see that to pray such psalms and to pray in this way, is "severely limiting" because it leaves things to God, not to us. In the imprecatory psalms, judgment is ultimately *God's* work, *not* Israel's work, and that greatly restricts any notion that judgment is something that human beings could or should implement on their own.[68] In brief, it makes divine judgment something impossible for humans to imitate; there is no place for *imitatio Dei* here, only *non*imitation.[69] Payback is God's business, not ours.

    This is an appropriate point to turn and consider what strikes many contemporary readers as the most worrisome instance of violence in the Bible—namely, the conquest of Canaan discussed in Deuteronomy, Joshua, and Judges. Yet here again one encounters the same sort of severely limiting condition to be at work insofar as the taking of the land is at God's command; it does not stem from something like Israel's desire for property or safety. There is not space in this chapter to fully engage the problem of the conquest, which is a deeply vexed issue. It must suffice to say that there are a number of ways that the violence of the conquest account(s) is carefully contained and constrained, limited to a one-time event back then and back there, not to be replicated in the future.[70] Perhaps the closest thing we get to a representation of some of Israel's "sacral war" strategies is found at the end of the book of Esther, where the situation is presented as a defensive action on the part of the Jews living in the Persian Empire.[71] That is very different from Joshua and the battle at Jericho, however.[72] And so it comes as no surprise, much later, when one reads about gearing up for battle, to hear that "our struggle is not against flesh and blood" (Eph 6:12 NIV). That's because so much flesh-and-blood struggle has been limited and confined to way back when, back there, once upon a time.

    There are also ways that the taking of the land of Canaan is carefully, even legally, justified by taking the matter of ownership (title) all the way back to Genesis (e.g., 15:7, 12–16; 17:8) and to God's sole proprietorship of any and all land, including this specific piece of property (Lev 25:23).[73] Then, too, there are numerous exceptions to "anti-Canaanitism"—or, more generally, xenophobia—both at the time of the conquest (see Josh 6:25; 9:1–27; 13:13; 15:63; 16:10; 17:12) and thereafter, including the extraordinary stories preserved in Ruth, Jonah, and Matthew 15:22–28. So, again, the God-sanctioned nature of the conquest is ultimately "a severely limiting condition"—not least because of the constraints and controls placed upon it by none other than the Lord, including various exceptions to the rules. Israel's violence in the conquest of Canaan is, in sum, severely limited, and in this way (among others), the canon of Scripture contains the violence that was part of that action. If Israel is honest about (1) participating in violence at the time of the conquest, which it is, that honesty also includes (2) these (and other) ways that that violence was restricted and brought to an end.

Both of these types of honesty are important when it comes to the violence that Israel itself conducted. The latter—the honesty about limitations to violence—is especially important, but it doesn't fix everything by any stretch of the imagination. The narratives about the conquest still exist in the pages of Holy Scripture, because Israel was honest enough to include them, and they remain difficult. "This is the hard part," writes Stephen Chapman, about these candid accounts—namely, that "God was not able, given the violence of the world, to preserve Israel purely nonviolently," and so God's purposes in history have occasionally intersected with violence.[74] Israel is honest about this "hard part," including the fact that this part is, in fact, *hard*. That is why Israel is at pains—and in more than one way and in more than one violent scenario—to limit and contain its violence. That, too, is part of Israel's remarkable honesty about its own violence. "Yes," Israel admits, "we have been violent." "And yes," Israel adds, "we are working hard at trying not to be violent anymore." That sounds like nothing if not *recovery*—like being *on the way* to recovery, at the very least.[75]

I do not believe that the preceding discussion will convince every reader. Many may, with my former student Joe, be singularly unimpressed with this particular song and dance about violence in Scripture. The issues at hand are, again, complex and deeply vexed. But my larger point is simply that one must engage the matter closely with as much candor as Israel itself manifests. Our assessment of Israel's honest account of violence must attend to the fine details present in that testimony. To do otherwise is to be cavalier about and play loose with the good-faith confession Israel has bequeathed to all who read Scripture. The devil is in the details, we often say. Israel, I imagine, would put things otherwise: the Deity is in the details, and if we care not for careful engagement with those details, the fault lies not with Israel, who has confessed all these things in great detail and in writing, but with us, who care not for honest testimony—perhaps because we are frightened by that kind of honesty in some way. Let preachers beware! But let preachers also take inspiration and encouragement to do hard interpretive work within their sermons. Where else will it be done? We can no longer assume people devote extensive attention to Scripture outside of church, whether on their own or with others. Even if they did, such readers often lack the preparation and training that professional clergy enjoy (but sadly often squander). Let the sermon function, then, as a locus for honest interpretation that does full justice to Israel's honest testimony.

(Dis)Honesty about Violence, Now and in the Pulpit

The idea that Israel's honesty might frighten us in some way leads, at last, to the second point that emerges from Israel's honesty about its own participation in violence—namely, how that might cast light on us and our own violent proclivities. To cut to the quick: I think it is worth wondering if some modern concerns over Israel's violence in Scripture are, in the end, little more than cases of psychological projection.[76] Projection is a common defense mechanism "in which intolerable feelings, impulses, or thoughts are falsely attributed to other people."[77] It is sometimes called "externalization," because by means of projection, people unconsciously attribute "inner impulses to the external world."[78] So to cite just one example, "a patient might deny feelings of anger but be very sensitive to and preoccupied with angry feelings in others around her."[79] It was Anna Freud who offered the first detailed study of projection, building on her famous father's initial ideas.[80]

Not every defense mechanism is pathological, though many can and frequently do function in unhealthy ways, especially when employed excessively. It is important to stress, however, that *everyone* uses defense mechanisms of one sort or another, at different times and in different ways, and sometimes quite harmlessly. Psychologist Nancy McWilliams writes that, in and of themselves, these processes "pose a problem only if we lack more mature psychological skills or if these defenses are used to the exclusion of possible others. . . . *It is the absence of mature defenses, not the presence of primitive ones, that characterizes borderline or psychotic structure.*"[81]

McWilliams states that defense mechanisms like projection are used by people who are trying (unconsciously) to accomplish one or both of the following goals:

> (1) the avoidance or management of some powerful, threatening feeling, usually anxiety but sometimes overwhelming grief, shame, envy, and other disorganizing emotional experiences; and (2) the maintenance of self-esteem.[82]

The first sounds like nothing so much as what Pennebaker calls inhibition/nonverbalization or what Herman describes as resistance to the mourning so crucial for recovery (see above). Projection, seen in this light, is nothing but a dead end; it offers no way forward to healing.

A mature, nonpathological example of projection might very well be empathy, whereby one can imagine what it is like to walk in someone else's shoes.[83] But in unhealthy forms, projection often leads to significant misunderstanding and profound "interpersonal damage."[84] McWilliams explains,

> When the projected attitudes seriously distort the object on whom they are projected, or when what is projected consists of disowned and highly negative parts of the self, all kinds of difficulties can ensue. Others resent being misperceived and may retaliate when treated, for example, as judgmental, envious, or persecutory (attitudes that are among the most common of those that tend to be ignored in the self and ascribed to others).[85]

Someone who depends overmuch on projection as the central way to understand the world or cope with life and who, as a result, exists in a state of denial (about themselves) with regard to what is projected (onto others) can be identified as someone with "a paranoid character."[86]

What does projection and paranoia have to do with violence in the Bible, specifically Israel's honesty about violence in the Old Testament? Much, in my judgment, and in every way. It is my deep suspicion that much contemporary concern about violence in the Bible is the result of or at least greatly impacted by projection. This scenario is not unthinkable. As André LaCocque has commented, "Psychologically speaking, the projection on others of the onus for evil and unhappiness is remarkably universal."[87] I suspect that many Christians would like to say that violence is only a problem *there* and *then*, in ancient Israel and in the Old Testament—not in the early church or the New Testament!—but that it is not a problem here, right now, with and in us. But nothing could be further from the truth. Woe is us, for we are violent individuals and live among a people of violence (cf. Isa 6:5). It is, in fact, apparently impossible to escape participating in violence these days. Societies predicated on "the rule of law" depend, in no small measure, on violence, or at least on the potential and threat of violence exercised by governments and their "peace-keeping" forces. Beyond the law, which in a best iteration wishes to maintain a good and just society, the United States has a deadly love affair with firearms, which has resulted in staggering statistics regarding gun violence and death. Mass shootings are now just another part of the American way. Life, liberty, and the right to carry. Not even the mass shooting at Sandy Hook Elementary School in Newtown, Connecticut, in 2012, where twenty children, six and seven years of age, were gunned down, proved enough to change gun policy in this country. Only the global COVID-19 pandemic finally brought a stoppage to the gun carnage from mass shootings on American soil . . . but only temporarily. Sadly, as I finish this book and health restrictions are lessening in various parts of the United States, so also have mass shootings reappeared in the news.

And then there is our entertainment: full to overflowing with violence—and sex, including sexual violence. The violence we see on a regular basis, not just in the news, but in our leisure time for our enjoyment (!), rivals if not surpasses any violence in the Bible in terms of its sheer amount and its graphic gruesomeness, all of which leads to profound desensitization. And so it is, as the poet Denise Levertov has put it, "the disasters numb within us" because we've "breathed grits" of violence "all our lives"; "our lungs are pocked with it, / the mucous membrane of our dreams / coated with it, the imagination / filmed over with the gray of it."[88] Levertov knows things could be different, better. Humanity, she writes, can be "delicate," can respond to caresses, can see the stars, laugh, and create.[89] Despite those virtues, we still turn "without surprise, with mere regret / to the scheduled" atrocities of violence.[90] Of late but for a long time now, what we turn to without surprise and mere regret is the latest mass shooting, right on schedule.

If this is true, or, rather *because* it is true, the matter(s) of violence is, in a very real sense, *internal* to us. It is not a matter of "violent Israel" in that "violent Old Testament." Instead, *we* are the ones who are violent and warlike, here and now—and at a far more profound and disturbing level than what Israel honestly recounts for us in Scripture. Indeed, we are *entertained* by violence, *choosing* to spend massive amounts of time, energy, and money on violence *for our leisure*. But if confronted with the many ways we comply with violence, we dissemble, deny, and deflect. "Not us," we say, adding, "Gun laws really wouldn't do much good, anyway."

HONEST ABOUT VIOLENCE

It isn't hard to imagine that, were we to confront Israel about the problem of violence, it would respond soberly, "Why, yes, I've suffered violence, and, yes, regrettably, I have to admit that I've also participated in it." "But," Israel might then ask with a querulous look, "who are you to call me violent? I'm at least honest about the matter. Can the same be said for you?" While we stammered around a bit trying to concoct a self-righteous reply, Israel might continue: "Not only am I honest about violence, I'm trying to shut it down, cut it off, end it. What about you?" "Well," we'd likely stammer, "gun legislation *really wouldn't work*, you know . . ."

It's not hard to imagine the very same scenario with any one of the "vindictive psalmists" of the imprecatory psalms. Are we any better? I seriously doubt it. We utter the same vitriol but are at a disadvantage because we rarely do so in the context of prayer. Instead, we do it on social media. As Walter Brueggemann has written, "The yearning for vengeance is *here*, among *us* and within *us* and with power. It is not only there in the Psalms but it is here in the human heart and the human community. . . . *Willy-nilly, we are vengeful creatures*."[91]

The same, of course, could be said of the psalmists—they, too, are "vengeful creatures." But that isn't anything they didn't frankly admit about themselves, already, first. And it isn't anything that they didn't candidly acknowledge, out in the open, before God and before others—or anyone within earshot to hear. But we, today, in pulpit and pew, prefer to stuff our violence down, repress it, deny it, and project it elsewhere. Then we go home and turn on the gory news or stream the latest gory show.

If we don't recognize the model of candor set by Israel about its own violence—violence done to it and done by it—and emulate Israel with similar forthrightness, we will end up no different than the mother from New Jersey discussed in chapter 1, quick to decry Israel's violence while having a great big log—make that a semiautomatic weapon—sticking out of our own eye (cf. Matt 7:4). It'd be far better, and a real step toward recovery, to admit candidly, with Richard B. Hays, that "on the question of violence, the church is deeply compromised and committed to nationalism, violence, and idolatry."[92] It is worth noting at this point that the New Testament recognizes and follows Israel's honesty, and not only in Revelation 6:10 with its heavenly saints begging for payback. In Romans 15:3, Paul cites a line from Psalm 69, an imprecatory psalm and, after applying it to Christ (!), adds in the very next verse:

> Whatever was written in the past was written for our instruction so that we could have hope through endurance and through the encouragement of the scriptures. (Rom 15:4)[93]

Imagine that: an imprecatory psalm *written for our instruction so that we could have hope*! Imagine that: an imprecatory psalm as *the encouragement of the Scriptures*! That, apparently, is what Paul, at least, imagined. And so there is apparently very good reason that some of the cursing psalms include "do not destroy" in their superscriptions. These texts are too precious to get rid of—do not destroy them! Or censor them. Still further, despite their virulent sentiments, at the end of the day, these psalms actually function to *prevent* us from destroying anyone or anything. They say—or rather pray—a way to not destroy. And so these psalms are good for our souls, therapeutic in fact; they are a means by which we can "hold our anger in good faith."[94]

More could always be said. Despite the length of this chapter, I haven't discussed in any detail how God, not just Israel, is implicated in the violence found in both Testaments of the Christian Bible. Nor have I spoken as fully as I might on how preachers might follow Israel's lead in honesty toward recovery when it comes to violence. I turn to both of these matters, along with others, in the final chapter. But before doing so, I end, as in the previous two chapters, with a text from the Psalter, this one from Psalm 76. The psalm sounds familiar notes: God's powerful victory against enemies is celebrated—a victory that came about because God announced judgment (v. 8) and established justice (v. 9a), rising up "to save all of the earth's poor" (v. 9b). Then comes a remarkable verse, which is difficult in Hebrew but seems to capture in miniature the dynamics of imprecation discussed in this chapter:

> Even human rage will turn to your praise
>   when you dress yourself with whatever remains of
>   your wrath. (Ps 76:10)

Even human rage turns to God's praise! Perhaps that is because God is acquainted with wrath. This is, after all, a God who is "a righteous judge, a God who is angry [zōʿēm] at evil every single day" (Ps 7:11). Though the psalm discusses human rage (singular ḥēmāh), the talk is ultimately of *God's* wraths (plural ḥēmōt) and what remains of that (šěʾērît). God will evidently decide what to wear from the wardrobe of divine wraths on any given day. Whatever God dons will be sufficient for those who pray, whose own rage will turn to praise because God is the Lord of Payback and because that is how things work in these poems that allow us to express *and* limit all our many angers before the throne of mercy *and* judgment. And so, though Psalm 76:10 might remain enigmatic, there is no doubt about how this psalm ends.[95] In light of the God who dresses up in wrath and acts against the powerful few who would flaunt divine justice and mistreat the earth's poor, the psalmist can only blurt out in joy and command:

> Make promises to the Lord your God and keep them!
> Let all around him bring gifts to the awesome one.
> He breaks the spirit of princes.
> He is terrifying to all the kings of the earth.
> (Ps 76:11–12)

Now who, *honestly*, doesn't think that is something to rejoice about?

5

The Importance of Being Earnest—or, Rather, of Preaching Honestly

Oscar Wilde penned his farcical play *The Importance of Being Earnest* in the 1890s. True to its name and its form, the comedy has much to do with the name Ernest and, in the final line, contains a wordplay involving that name and the adjective "earnest." One of the characters, Jack, who, according to the play, should've been named Ernest, turns to his aunt, Lady Bracknell, and says, "I've now realized for the first time in my life the vital Importance of Being Earnest."[1] The importance of being *Ernest*, yes, given what transpires in the comedy, but *earnest*? Maybe not, as the point of the farce seems quite to the contrary. Aurally, of course, audiences cannot be entirely certain which earnest/Ernest it is so important for Jack to be. The title of the play, in its written form, clarifies matters at least somewhat.

The present book is neither a play nor intended as a comedy, but the title of Wilde's work seems somehow appropriate for this final chapter. In light of what has been said in prior chapters about Israel's honesty with reference to sin, suffering, and violence, is it—at the end of the day—simply a matter of *being earnest* about these topics?

Yes and no.

First, the negations. The primary concern of this volume—not least due to the series in which it appears—is less about *being* honest than it is about *preaching* honest(ly). Now one might reasonably assume that these two things go together, or should at any rate, and that wouldn't be all wrong. But as I'll discuss more fully below, the two can also be teased apart, and for good reason. To anticipate what follows: honest to God *preaching* isn't a matter of the preacher herself simply *being* honest by disclosing anything and everything of her own sin, suffering, and violence. Not in the least! Honest to God preaching should take a very different form than a kind of weekly "truth dump" from the pulpit.[2] Still further, the focus of the present book is not about being *earnest*—a term meaning "serious, not frivolous; showing sincere and intense feeling or conviction; lacking playfulness"[3]—but rather about *honesty*, which means that *truth*, not just personal sincerity, is in play. So to summarize the negative replies to the question, one must strike both "being" and "earnest" when it comes to Wilde's title. The talk here is of *preaching*, not being, and *honesty*, not earnestness.

But second, there is something positive that can be said in reply to the question raised above. Honest to God preaching that speaks of sin, suffering, and violence will, in my judgment, take seriously—*earnestly* even—Israel's modeling of the same. As the previous chapters have tried to show, Israel is not only honest in its truth telling; it is also *serious*, maybe even *intense* when it comes to telling the truth. This means that, in some sense, Israel is quite earnest after all, and so maybe Wilde's title isn't all bad or all wrong when it comes to honest to God preaching.

In this last chapter, I will revisit the work of the previous chapters, drawing out further implications of what it might mean to earnestly follow Israel's model and preach "honest(ly) to God" about sin, suffering, and violence. I will do so by looking at this "honest to God" phrase from two different angles: honest discourse *before* God and discourse that is honest *about* God. I will then introduce an odd if not off-putting interlocutor into the conversation—the nothing-if-not-honest biblical sage known as Qoheleth. *Qoheleth* is the Hebrew title for the book of Ecclesiastes, so called after its primary speaker, whose own name was understood by none other than Martin Luther to mean "the Preacher" (*der Prediger*) in his translation of the Bible. If Luther was right, Qoheleth the Preacher has some very intriguing things to teach us about preaching honestly.

Honest to God Preaching, Part 1: Honest Discourse *before* God

Let's begin with honest to God preaching understood as honest discourse *before* God on matters like sin, suffering, and violence. Though I've already said it, I want to be clear that honest to God preaching should *not* be confused with preachers being transparent about anything and everything in their lives. It is not hard to imagine how that kind of transparency could quickly become highly embarrassing or seriously inappropriate—or both—especially when the topics demanding honest discussion are those covered in this book. Serious care must be taken, therefore, that honest preaching is *not* misconstrued as saying way too much in a public context. That kind of "oversharing" is a judgment that has sometimes been made of "confessional poets" like Robert Lowell, John Berryman, and Anne Sexton. In their poetry, confessional poets often revealed personal confidences, admitted mental illnesses and extramarital affairs, or discussed any number of (at the time of writing) taboo subjects.[4] Taboos have the habit of changing over the course of the years, and so the confessional poets don't sound quite as shocking now as they did to their first readers. Even more importantly, stigmas surrounding things like mental illness, to cite just one example, should surely be done away with through more education and less closeting. In such cases, honesty is, proverbially, "the best policy." Prior chapters have repeatedly shown that denial and cover-up are unhelpful and unhealthy. That said, with some topics, at least in some contexts—particularly public ones—discretion does remain the better part of personal disclosure.[5] And so it is that confessional poetry has occasionally struck readers and critics as saying *a bit too much*, as when Lowell incorporated private correspondence with his wife into his book *The Dolphin*.[6]

We must proceed very carefully here, navigating between the proverbial Scylla of telling too much and Charybdis of telling too little. If we must avoid embarrassing, inappropriate transparency, we must also avoid a kind of preaching wherein the preacher is always a squeaky clean example of morality and righteousness for all to see—and to be impressed with! If the first problem is one of *oversharing*, the second is one of *overselling*. Jesus's words about those who like to give to the poor, pray, and fast just so as to be seen by others come to mind (Matt 6:2–6, 16–18), as does the word *hypocrite*—which is the term Jesus himself prefers to describe such individuals (6:2, 5, 16).[7] Also leaping to mind are the countless examples of clergy wrongdoing and impropriety:

scandal after scandal after scandal. In the worst-case scenario, therefore, preaching as if the preacher is always right and good is nothing less than one more case of denial and cover-up, if not worse: a keeping of secrets that will only make the preacher sick. Those types of secrets will, one way or another, sooner or later, be exposed. Happily, there is a difference between the preacher being fully aware of her own sins and blabbering on and on about them—in detail—from the pulpit. Honest disclosure can include discretion, and the truth can be told "slant" (Dickinson), as is evident even in the otherwise shocking candor of a text like Psalm 137. To be sure, part of Aristotelian persuasion depends on an audience believing in the *ethos* of the speaker—with honesty an important part of that—but here again we find ourselves in a narrow channel of water with dangers on both sides.[8] Tell too little, not be honest enough, and the speaker seems unapproachable, her ethics unattainable. Why even try? Tell too much, overshare, and the speaker is altogether unremarkable, her ethics uninspiring. Why even listen?

Thankfully, preaching honestly isn't ultimately about the preacher's own self anyway. The preacher can be an honest preacher, emulating Israel's own honesty, not by being candid about her own sins, sufferings, and violence in the pulpit (though, perhaps, here and there, now and then, some intimations of some failures might usefully be shared—*discreetly*) but, instead, *by honestly replicating Israel's own honesty*. Scripture is already plenty honest about sin, suffering, and violence. More than enough for any preacher. There is no need to do Israel one better. *Scripture's* honesty, not *self*-honesty, is the order of the day. It will be, and *is*, enough to reflect Israel's honesty in the pulpit, honor that honesty, and then ponder how it might impinge upon and impact our homiletic and our lives.

At this point, we could return to where I began in chapter 1. The kind of honest preaching I am arguing for does not and will not misuse Scripture's honesty by deploying it as a weapon to denigrate, insult, or otherwise abuse biblical Israel (or any of its representatives). To do that would be to dishonor Israel's honesty. To do that would be to seriously misunderstand the honesty of Scripture and to effectively miss out on the benefits that come on the far side of Israel's honesty. Once more:

* It is *honesty about sin* that facilitates *reconciliation*.
* It is *honesty about suffering* that facilitates *healing*.
* It is *honesty about violence* that facilitates *recovery*.

If the *honest* part is taken out of these equations, the benefits quickly disappear. Honesty is what permits the transformation of the *sin-suffering-violence matrix* into the *nexus of reconciliation-healing-recovery*. To curtail such honesty, avoid it, fail to emulate it means we will be left to our own devices—and our own vices—devoid of hope for a different and better future, bereft of a more excellent way.

The stories I shared in the opening chapter about the New Jersey mother and the California pastor are once again instructive. Both individuals failed to recognize and receive Israel's honesty about sin as nothing less than sincere confession and a worthy example of truth telling. Instead, both of these people seriously mistook Israel's honesty, then weaponized it, using it against the Old Testament and biblical Israel as well as contemporary Jews and Judaism: locking all of the above into an inescapable history of faithlessness and hopelessness. Thankfully Israel, and Scripture as a whole, knows better—thanks to honest disclosure.

Preachers can do better than that mother and that minister, and with very little difficulty—truly minimal effort—by simply following Israel's lead. And preachers can do that, not by blabbing on and on about their own struggles in their sermons, but by carefully reading and then preaching Israel's own honesty. Honest to God preachers will place themselves and their congregations—with appropriate discretion, to be sure, and with all due tact and rhetorical savvy—alongside Israel and our candid canon of Scripture for the sake of forgiveness, healing, and recovery. Given those lofty and beneficent goals, those truly therapeutic results, why on earth would any preacher do otherwise?

There is, of course, more than one way to emulate Israel's honesty and do it effectively. Gifted preachers rarely need someone to tell them how to do their jobs—especially someone who isn't a full-time preacher. Even so, I would like to offer at least a few concrete suggestions about imitating Israel's honesty in our homiletic. The ideas run from more general to more specific, from things covered elsewhere in this book to further particulars:

* Preachers should *preach candid texts about sin, suffering, and violence* not as foils for some sort of Christian triumphalism or valorization of the New Testament (or the Christian church) over the Old Testament (and biblical Israel) but as *loci of faithful confession*—true confession on the part of faithful people that leads to reconciliation, healing, and recovery.
* Preachers should preach candid texts as loci of confession *intentionally and transparently*, explicitly identifying the honest nature of these texts and the benefits that honesty brings, pointing out how such benefits are in fact made possible primarily if not exclusively by honest disclosure.

* Preachers should *preach candid texts about sin as a locus of confession about wrongdoing* that *moves toward transformation and forgiveness*. The worst of sins must be confessed—for example, the worst cases of betrayal, infidelity, unfaithfulness. These sins—*even these!*—can be forgiven in the end, despite their gravity, profundity, and accompanying shame. The work of the Truth and Reconciliation Commission (TRC) in postapartheid South Africa is a concrete example within living memory of what Israel models for us in Holy Scripture. Full honesty yields full amnesty.[9] Anything less than absolute candor will not do when it comes to sin. Yes, "mistakes were made," some of which were *exceedingly egregious* and of the *most unforgiveable* kind. In the course of honest confession, it turns out that the mistakes in question were made *by us*. This fact simply must be admitted. When it is, it turns out that these "mistakes" are quite *forgivable* after all: even murder and adultery, which our culture, including church culture, typically deems impossible to remediate. Scripture says otherwise about individuals like "great" King David and groups like Israel at Sinai, speaking frankly about sin *but also* about its transformation and forgiveness.
* Preachers should preach honest texts about sin toward these positive ends, *letting Israel's honest testimonies about sin function as sites wherein congregants can listen in and repeat back*—adopting and adapting, as need be—and in the process find themselves, their own sin, and their own reconciliation prefigured and made manifest in these selfsame texts. Is (y)our sin as bad as Israel's infidelity at Mount Sinai? Or as unconscionable as David's

abuse of power with Bathsheba and Uriah? Perhaps so, perhaps not. Either way, the sins recounted so candidly by Israel can stand in as something like a "worst-case scenario" into which we can substitute our own lesser (or not) wrongdoings and somehow find, on the backside of confession, God's compassionate and accompanying presence (Exod 32:14; 33:14, 17; 34:6–7) or hear "you are forgiven" (2 Sam 12:13). When that happens, our own lips can't help but respond with

> The sacrifice acceptable to God is a broken spirit;
>   a broken and contrite heart, O God, you
>   will not despise. (Ps 51:17 NRSV)

and

> You, O Lord, are the God of those who repent,
> and in me you will manifest your goodness;
> for, unworthy as I am, you will save me
>   according to your great mercy,
> and I will praise you continually all the days of
>   my life.
> For all the host of heaven sings your praise,
>   and yours is the glory forever. Amen. (Pr
>   Man 1:13–15 NRSV)

Preaching honestly about sin and reconciliation can prevent—with little difficulty and minimal effort—the profound theological errors so often present in the pulpit and evident in the minister from Southern California.

✳ Preachers should *preach candid texts about suffering, including its deep connections to sin.* We often suffer because of *our own* wrongdoing; there can be no doubt about that after reading Israel's accounts of Sinai and David. But we also suffer because of *others'* wrongdoing; there can be no doubt about that either after reading Exodus. Pharaoh's shadow looms large in the Old Testament. It cannot and must never be forgotten. The combination of our own and others' complicity in causing suffering means that we know, just as Israel did millennia ago, that the causes of suffering are multiple and complicated, often very hard if not impossible to tease apart. Preachers need to be honest about this fact too. Sermons that emphasize suffering due to our own misdeeds, therefore, must also recognize that the witness of Scripture and human life complicates all understandings that would be too simple, too monocausal. Such an approach to suffering will rarely, if ever, suffice. This does not mean that preachers need to offer a robust record of every possible cause from the pulpit: "Now today we might suffer from x, or y, or z—did I mention x^2, $y^3 + \pi$, and $\sqrt{z}$?" That kind of all-encompassing rhetoric can be as distancing as it is inclusive, if only because it dies the death of a thousand qualifications. It is enough, in my judgment, to acknowledge briefly—maybe even as an aside—that other causes of suffering are possible in life and in the Bible, but *this particular text*, and so *this particular sermon*, focuses on *this particular cause*. Tuck the other causes away; they live in the other texts, after all, and they will assume center stage soon enough in future sermons.

THE IMPORTANCE OF PREACHING HONESTLY

Like preaching honestly about sin, honest preaching about suffering will treat candid texts about suffering as sites and scripts: *sites* where candor about suffering and its complexities are manifest, which also offer us *scripts* to repeat as placeholders or fill-in-the-blanks for our own deep struggles. Honest preaching about suffering must be done because Scripture repeatedly demonstrates that *everything begins in grief* and because we know—early and late—that nonverbalization about suffering leads directly to sickness of soul and body. Conversely, honest disclosure is a primary route to healing. It is important, therefore, whenever preaching candid texts about suffering, which are often so hard to hear, that preachers explicitly note how even the most brutal honesty facilitates healing in us *and also* in Israel. Concerning the latter, it would've taken at most just a phrase or two to have disabused the New Jersey mother of her inaccurate beliefs, beliefs she was all too eager to pass on to her children. Preaching about suffering, therefore, may end up healing a number of wounds, including the wounds of anti-Semitism, an especially unfortunate brand of Christian sin that has caused immense suffering.

✷ Preachers should *preach candid texts about violence, noting how violence belongs to a malevolent matrix* that also includes sin and suffering and how honesty about violence permits recovery from its deleterious effects. Preachers should note the double-sided nature of violence, which is not unlike suffering: violence can be done *to us* and *we ourselves* can be violent. In the first case, trauma must be told and retold as a critical, irreplaceable step in the recovery process. Repeated telling lessens the intensity of the trauma and helps those who have experienced it to somehow organize and manage it. Preachers may be tempted to avoid trauma-filled texts like the imprecatory psalms or the book of Lamentations, but honest preaching about violence knows that only *repeated exposure* to these types of texts provides the way to healing and recovery from what has been done, whether to us, our friends and family, or those we don't personally know, near or far. *Repeated exposure* in this case means, of course, *repeated preaching*. Surely the perennial availability of traumatic texts for purposes of retelling is partly what the canonical process achieves; it may also explain why such texts were canonized in the first place: for the very purpose(s) of rereading, retelling, recovery. Censoring these texts will only serve to stymie our own recovery and thwart our compassion toward others who are also in recovery.

Preaching honestly about violence should admit our own proclivities to violence and somehow offer, in the process, ways to contain our violence. That can be done in a whole host of ways, with the Psalms demonstrating the way of prayer and liturgy, practices with which preachers are already deeply familiar. Public prayer can, just as various psalms did millennia ago, honestly include violent sentiments and leave them where they belong: at God's feet. And the liturgy has ways to accentuate and attenuate violence, not to mention transform it (Eucharist!). Whatever the method, preachers must again be fully honest about the real world out there, so rife with violence, and also the real world within us, so as to avoid giving congregants Band-Aids when only deep-tissue sutures will do. To ignore the violence of the world or of ourselves in the pulpit, glossing over all that with syrupy platitudes about an easy ethic of love, is nothing less than dope dealing, with preachers the drug dealers in question, pushing Karl Marx's religion-as-opium, narcoticizing and numbing the church to a world in pain—and to a church and Christians in pain . . . and in rage. Preaching honestly about violence must recognize, therefore, the sheer pervasiveness of violence, not neglecting the violence *within us*—our bloodlust for it, our dread fascination with it, our great expenditure of money and time for more and more and more of it, even for fun. Preachers must preach candid texts about violence to combat seriously negative outcomes: a thinning of the gospel to praise songs and a mild sense of (temporary!) relief, on the one hand, and, on the other, a profound desensitization to a world of violence *out there* and also *in here*, within us. Avoiding preaching honestly about violence will lead only to projection and a *lack* of recovery.

There are still other difficulties to navigate in preaching honestly about violence. One of these concerns those individuals who are *far too comfortable* with religious violence, whether back then or here and now, *a bit too eager* to use that as justification for present-day action. Preaching honestly about violent texts must therefore recognize the severely limiting conditions placed on religious violence in Scripture *that disallow biblical violence to be replicated or imitated now*. The canonical boundaries alone, not to mention other factors, mark a firm and final divide between ancient Israel and the early church and our own, more recent, hyperviolent days. Scripture still has much to teach us about matters of violence—clearly!—but what it does *not* do is teach us how to repeat and enact violence. Those days are over; thus says the canon and thus says the canonical constraints on violence. Scripture's ultimate accent is on limitation and constraint, containment and critique of violence—the end of violence! The canon does this by managing and controlling violence within narratives and poetry containing violence, showing us in these texts and in yet other stories and songs different, nonviolent, and better ways of being in the world and with our enemies. At this point, as also in the case of sin and suffering, preaching about violence will put Israel's (and the early church's) honesty to the best possible use, not as a tool to punish our ancestors in the faith, who were so generously transparent, but as a way to situate our own violence (done to us and/or performed by us) amid the great cloud of witnesses and their truthful testimonies—the whole truth, even about violence. Israel's honesty is a schoolmaster for us to recover from violence. We have this teaching, "written for our instruction" and "for our sake" (Rom 15:4; 1 Cor 9:10), only because of the truth the Old Testament repeatedly demonstrates:

And then Israel writes it all down, telling us all about it, in detail, for posterity, forever.

In sum, preachers can and should follow Israel's honest testimonies about sin, suffering, and violence as entry points into our own struggles with sin, suffering, and violence. The candor offered in these texts, activated in us who hear, read, and preach them now, can unmask our own problems, uncover our own cover-ups, expose our own sickly secrets. These acts of "revelation" are not and must not be pursued for purposes of shaming and discarding—"canceling," in today's parlance—not with reference to the original truth tellers in Israel, nor with reference to those of us who follow in their wake now. Rather and instead, the exposure of secrets that cannot and will not be hid is for the endgame of forgiveness and reconciliation, healing and recovery. There is no shame here, no canceling; instead, there is redemption and new life, a re-upping to service and relationship with God and for God in the world.

> Remember: Israel *so unfaithful* on its wedding night!
> Remember: Israel *so obedient* with the tabernacle!
> Remember: David, *adulterer* and *murderer*!
> Remember: David, *forgiven* and *restored*!

I am aware that the suggestions offered above are less specific how-tos than they are gestures toward a more general strategy or disposition to adopt toward Israel's candid texts. But a general strategy underwrites any and every how-to method. Once the disposition recommended here is in place as a foundation, that is, the how-to can and will vary. For the sake of clarity, the disposition or strategy of approach that I have been arguing for is encapsulated in the two points offered at the very start of this book: (1) the Old Testament is full of Israel's honesty about a vast number of topics, and (2) that honesty should be emulated in Christian discourse and practice, including from the pulpit. Israel's honesty, our homiletic. When these two points (and their proper sequencing) are fully grasped, any honest text from Scripture—and they're *all* honest!—can be preached with the results both beneficial and benevolent to all who hear.

Honest to God Preaching, Part 2: Honest Discourse *about* God

There is another way to construe the notion of *honest to God preaching*, and that is to understand it as honest discourse *about* God. Two agents are at work in honest disclosure: the one who utters honest testimony and the Secret-Knowing Lord. Most of what I've said in this and the previous chapters concerns the former, human agent, whether that be Israel in the Old Testament or us, more recently, now. But the second agent should not be neglected, especially as this is the God from whom no secrets are hid. What can be said, what must be said, honestly, *about* this God with reference to the dread topics of sin, suffering, and violence?

Quite a lot, no doubt, and, once again, more than I can say here. I cannot begin to cover all that might be said about the Divine Subject on these serious subjects. What I offer here, then, is but a sampling. Gifted preachers who are interested in honest preaching about God will be able to follow further scriptural paths on their own. Before taking up the three topics in order, it should be noted that this second angle on honest preaching as candor *about* God is very important because it demonstrates that Israel's honesty is not finally about the self alone. There is much more to talk about, especially when the topic is preaching Scripture, than our own personal (let alone petty) honesties. There is another, very important, far more interesting Subject to consider.

Sin

Scripture is clear that honest confession of sin facilitates reconciliation with God, who is often the aggrieved party who is nevertheless, after confession, "faithful and just to forgive us our sins and cleanse us from everything we've done wrong" (1 John 1:9). But honest preaching about God and sin must also acknowledge that, according to Israel's testimony, confession is occasionally *not always* prerequisite to reconciliation. In some cases, the path to reconciliation does not depend, finally or ultimately, on the confessor or the confession alone, perhaps because that would assign too much significance to the human agent. Confession is crucial, to be sure—that is the dominant accent in Israel's honest disclosure about sin—but there is more to say at those times when human confession proves too little and too late, or at those times when it is absent altogether. That "something more" is that God can forgive *even without honest confession.* Two brief textual explorations illustrate this claim.

Exploration 1: The Structure of Exilic Preaching

As Thomas Raitt and others have shown, the prophets of the exilic period reveal an unexpected and sudden switch in God's attitude toward Israel before and after the destruction of Jerusalem.[10] Before that decisive moment, prophetic preaching of judgment abounds and is even radicalized when Israel proves consistently unrepentant. (How honest is that last bit?) But after the fall of the city, things change. The threatened destruction has taken place. There is no need to go on and on about judgment anymore. To use the key verbs from Jeremiah's call, "to dig up and pull down, to destroy and demolish" has happened; so now it is time "to build and plant" (see Jer 1:10). But this shift is not explainable only because the threats of judgment have finally come about; it is also evidently due to a change within the very heart of God, which now moves decisively toward mercy. The swift and surprising nature of this shift is nicely captured in the following passage from Jeremiah:

> ¹²This is what the Lord says:
> Your injury is incurable;
> > your illness is grave.
> ¹³No one comes to your aid;
> > no one attends to your wound;
> > your disease is incurable.
> ¹⁴All your lovers disregard you;
> > they write you off as a lost cause,
> > because I have dealt harshly with you as an enemy
> > > would,
> > because your guilt is great and your sins are many.
> ¹⁵Why cry out for relief from your pain?
> > Your wound is incurable.
> I have done these things to you,
> > because your guilt is great
> > and your sins are many.
> ¹⁶Yet all who ravage you will be ravaged;
> > all who oppress you will go into exile.
> Those who rob you will be robbed,
> > and all who plunder you will be plundered.
> ¹⁷I will restore your health,
> > and I will heal your wounds, declares the Lord,
> > because you were labeled an outcast, "Zion, the
> > > lost cause."

> ¹⁸The Lord proclaims:
>   I will restore Jacob's tents and have pity on their
>   birthplace.
>   Their city will be rebuilt on its ruins and the palace
>   in its rightful place.
> ¹⁹There will be laughter and songs of thanks.
>   I will add to their numbers so they don't dwindle
>   away.
>   I will honor them so they aren't humiliated.
> ²⁰Their children will thrive as they did long ago,
>   and their community will be established before me.
>   I will punish their oppressors.
> ²¹They will have their own leader;
>   their ruler will come from among them.
> I will let him approach me, and he will draw near.
>   Who would dare approach me unless I let them
>   come? declares the Lord.
> ²²You will be my people,
>   and I will be your God. (Jer 30:12–22)

Everything pivots in the space between verses 15 and 16.[11] In verse 15, God takes sole responsibility for what has been done to judged-and-decimated Israel and offers a morbid prognosis to boot: "I have done these things to you" and "your wound is incurable." Then, in verse 16, everything changes: it is now *Israel's enemies*, not Israel, who will be recompensed, and what was an untreatable affliction becomes healable after all (v. 17). This drastic change of affairs comes about not simply because of what has transpired, which is referred to in terms of being ravaged, oppressed, robbed, and plundered (v. 16). The sudden change is *especially* because (*kî*, v. 17) all that has happened has been grossly misinterpreted by others who assumed that Zion is now forever cast off and permanently hopeless. Not so! Not even for a verse! The Lord's dread punishment has been enacted, the long-delayed judgment finally experienced, and so now God decides to do a new thing, do we not perceive it? Now there is divine restoration, health, rebuilding, laughter, thanksgiving, singing, flourishing, and more—all of which culminates in nothing less than the formal statement of covenant: "You will be my people and I will be your God."[12]

The book of Ezekiel attests to this same shift as it moves from the most devastating of blows, the death of Ezekiel's wife and the destruction of Jerusalem in chapter 24, to a pronounced change in the chapters that follow.[13] What is not to be missed about these texts from Jeremiah and Ezekiel is that they *do not* report Israel to have confessed its sin prior to the marked shift that takes place, but God forgives and moves toward reconciliation *nevertheless*.

Exploration 2: The Day of Reconciliation (Leviticus 16)
The second exploration is perhaps a bit trickier. The text is Leviticus 16, which recounts the rituals for Yom Kippur, the great "Day of Reconciliation" (CEB) or "Day of Atonement" (NRSV) during which all the Israelites are regularly forgiven all their sins. The rites are several, complex, and not entirely clear in every detail, but unmistakable is the repeated sentiment, running like a refrain throughout the chapter, that speaks of Aaron's priestly actions during this highest of holy days. For example:

* In this way, he will make reconciliation [*kipper*] for the inner holy area because of the pollution of the Israelites

and because of their rebellious sins, as well as for all their other sins. (v. 16a)
* He will make reconciliation [*kipper*] for himself, for his household, and for the whole assembly of Israel. (v. 17b)
* In this way, he will make reconciliation [*kipper*] for himself and for the people. (v. 24b)

After this refrain dealing with the priestly work of reconciliation, it is no wonder that the chapter concludes on two high notes. First, the text affirms the efficacy of all this activity:

On that day reconciliation will be made [*yĕkappēr*, from *kipper*] for you in order to cleanse you. You will be clean before the Lord from all your sins. (v. 30)

Second, the importance of this day and the forgiveness it effects is twice underscored by the assertion that its performance is "a permanent rule" (*ḥuqqat 'ôlām*; vv. 31, 34a) "in order to make reconciliation [*lĕkappēr*, from *kipper*] for the Israelites from all their sins once a year" (v. 34b). And that's exactly what happened: "It was done just as the Lord commanded Moses" (v. 34c).

For present purposes, it is important to observe that the Day of Reconciliation functions *effectively* ("*all* your sins") and *automatically* ("a permanent rule . . . once a year"), quite apart from explicit confession of every single sin on the part of each individual Israelite. The ritual itself, of course, could be seen as a kind of confession, and that is no doubt correct; but, even so, such an interpretation is at some remove from how we tend to think of reconciliation now, as involving *personal and intentional* confession made by one person to another. The Day of Reconciliation operates *without* that kind of individual acknowledgment of wrongdoing . . . and it works! The Day of Reconciliation truly *reconciles*!

Astute readers of Leviticus will notice that I have omitted a key verse from the previous discussion: Leviticus 16:21, where Aaron interacts with one of the two male goats involved in the ceremony:

> Aaron will press both his hands on its head and *confess* over it all the Israelites' offenses and all their rebellious sins, as well as all their other sins, putting all these on the goat's head. (v. 21a; emphasis added)

Doesn't this verse make reconciliation with God dependent on confession? The answer is not exactly straightforward; it's a bit of yes and no. *Yes*, insofar as Aaron is explicitly instructed to *confess* "offenses," "rebellious sins," and "all . . . other sins."[14] If that listing sounds a bit like a catchall, that is probably because it is, since the list captures three of the most important words for wrongdoing in Israel's lexicon (*ʿāwōn*, *pešaʿ*, and *ḥaṭṭāʾt*). In his confession, therefore, Aaron confesses *everything* (*kol*, "all," three times!). Furthermore, Aaron's confession occurs near the center of Leviticus 16, which culminates in the climax found in verse 30: "You will be clean . . . from all your sins." But also *no*; not even Aaron's confession can completely obviate the point made earlier that the Day of Reconciliation functions effectively, year after year quite apart from every single Israelite confessing every single one of their individual *ʿāwōn*s, *pešaʿ*s, and *ḥaṭṭāʾt*s in thought, word, and deed—whether against God, their offended neighbors, or their estranged enemies. God can forgive offenses, even big-ticket items in catchall categories like "*all* offenses . . . *all* rebellious sins . . . *all* other sins . . . *all* your sins," sometimes, it seems, even before people have admitted to or become aware of those offenses. And by *sometimes*, Leviticus means *at least once a year*!

To be sure, Aaron's role remains crucial and of great significance for contemporary "priests," whatever their denominational affiliation. In our own, much belated, priestly contexts, it is likely that some of the sinners we serve (including us!) will not yet have confessed for themselves. But no matter, "Aaron" will confess for them—and that will suffice. That will do the trick! They will be clean before the Lord from all their sins (Lev 16:30). Preachers, that is, can easily see in Aaron's vicarious actions a model for their own, not only liturgically, *but also homiletically*. Indeed, what Aaron does in his *confession on behalf of* in the Day of Reconciliation ceremony is exactly what Israel as a whole does throughout the Old Testament, everywhere and anywhere it is candid about sin. It *confesses on behalf of*—on behalf of us, now, who follow in its footsteps, emulating its example. Part of Israel's honest disclosure is how God is reconciled to sinners and forgives them *when they confess*. Another part of that candor is how God can *also* be reconciled to sinners *in other ways*, through yearly rituals, for example, "intercessory confession," and/or because God simply wants to. Saint Paul echoes the point much later when he writes that "while we were still sinners Christ died for us" (Rom 5:8). Long before the apostle, the great prophet Ezekiel experienced the same when he stood up alongside the Chebar River in Babylon and rubbed his eyes because he was sure they were deceiving him. But they weren't. No, there it was: God's mobile throne on its way, coming into exile too, exactly where it was least expected but precisely where it was needed most. God, after all, is "rich in mercy"; even when "we were dead as a result of those things that we did wrong," God "brought us to life with Christ . . . because of the great love that he has for us" (Eph 2:4–5).[15] Preachers who are considerably younger than Paul and Ezekiel can nevertheless follow their examples—and Aaron's and Israel's—in recognizing and enacting confession *on behalf of*, with reconciliation happening at God's initiative because God so wills, irrespective, at least at times, of the wrongdoings involved. François de La Rochefoucauld said that "nothing is so contagious as an example," whether that be of "great good or great evil."[16] The "great good" exemplified by Aaron or Israel or by a preacher in the pulpit with regard to confession and reconciliation should, with any luck, bring about "more of the same on the part of others."[17] "Sharing a secret can be contagious," noted Frank Warren, in light of his PostSecret project.[18] *Confessing* one can do the same. But, Israel adds, honesty *about* God and sin requires one to also say, with full candor, not to mention with deep gratitude, that God can forgive even in the absence of confession, vicarious or otherwise. It remains a very real, very open question if we can ever do the same. Then again, there is Jesus on the cross (Luke 23:34) and there is Stephen at his stoning (Acts 7:60)—both forgiving others without hearing their confession.

Suffering

What has been said about sin applies equally to Israel's honest testimony about God and suffering. In addition to the usual scenario, whereby Israel moves to healing via honest disclosure about suffering, there is another option. Especially when the suffering in question is due to Israel's own sin, God can sometimes move Israel toward healing, even without waiting for its confession. This is but a variation on the theme sounded above.

A different note is heard in the cursing psalms, however, which are quite intriguing to consider with reference to honesty *about* God and the topic of suffering. In these psalms, and other texts like them, God proves patient and attentive to Israel in all its articulations of pain and grief. There is no divine judgment expressed that the psalmist has somehow misspoken or overstepped or sinned with her lips (cf. Job 2:10). Instead, space is made available for the full articulation of the painful utterance, and we are evidently to imagine that God's ears take all of that in. Building on what I suggested in chapter 4, perhaps it isn't going too far to say that God's body—not just God's ears—absorbs the rage, anger, disappointment, and sorrow that these extremely honest texts express. If so, that is of great significance, if only because our enemies' and our neighbors' bodies (and ears) simply cannot do the same. Honest speech about God and suffering, in this light, indicates that *precisely via the biblical texts* the Lord provides a way to articulate, yes, but also to listen, remember, see, and know human suffering. In this process, God is the equivalent of an empathetic parent, fully attuned to God's children, mirroring back to them what needs to be received and recognized. By means of this process, the children maintain good attachment to God.[19] And still more: in this process, God, too, somehow experiences firsthand the suffering of these children, carrying their pain by experiencing it—absorbing it—in prayer, story, and song.[20] As the old hymn puts it,

> What a Friend we have in Jesus,
>   All our sins and griefs to bear!
> What a privilege to carry
>   Everything to God in prayer![21]

Violence

What, finally, of honesty about God and violence? This is an especially difficult topic, since, as noted in chapter 4, the "hard part" of Israel's candor about its participation in violence includes God's own participation in the same.[22] Of course, chapter 4 also noted that the divine origin of some (perhaps even much?) of the Bible's violence is, in actuality, a profoundly limiting condition. That said, we must nevertheless admit that divine violence is something that causes great concern for a decent number of contemporary readers—and not without good reason. It is important, in the face of such offense, to emphasize the "two-testamented" nature of this problem. The divine violence of the book of Revelation, for example, rivals, and likely surpasses, anything found in the Old Testament. Violence is not, and never was, an *Old Testament only* kind of problem. It is equally important to emphasize, however—again at the canonical level, for both Testaments—the connections and constraints of divine violence. To speak of *connections* is to recall how God's punitive actions are intertwined with notions like divine judgment and wrath, both of which are typically focused on specific instances of sin and injustice. When those are remedied, God's wrath and judgment dissipate, and there is no more need for punishment.[23] Even when divine wrath is not forgone altogether by human repentance beforehand (see, e.g., Jonah 3:10), God's judgment can be transcended nevertheless, as in the cases of Jeremiah and Ezekiel, even as a matter of course, as in the case of Leviticus 16 (see above). To speak of *constraints* is not entirely unrelated to these connections. Once again, there are several, very real limitations placed on divine violence. It is restricted to particular moments, particular situations, and for particular reasons.

Further, it is in service to divine justice and, once the record is set straight, is no longer operational or necessary. Such contextual or circumstantial considerations further restrict the already severely limited condition of violence with a divine origin.

The limitations just outlined are all *after the fact*, whether after threats of judgment or after the actual experience of punishment. But in many ways, the constraint of divine violence is present *from the very beginning*, as, for example, when God creates the cosmos *non*violently and commends (and commands!) similar practices for the created world.[24] Among other things that might be mentioned here is the fact that all animals, human or otherwise, are to be strictly vegetarian "in the beginning" (Gen 1:29–30), and the very first homicide is speedily judged by God (with mercy!).[25] Even the conquest, the most warlike section of Joshua, begins—*before* any battle has begun—with a not-so-chance encounter between Joshua and a strange figure:

> When Joshua was near Jericho, he looked up. He caught sight of a man standing in front of him with his sword drawn. Joshua went up and said to him, "Are you on our side or that of our enemies?" He said, "Neither! I'm the commander of the Lord's heavenly force. Now I have arrived!" (Josh 5:13–14a)

"Neither!" Let the record show that the heavenly commander said *neither*: not Joshua's side and not Jericho's side. The commander of the divine armies is decidedly neutral, downright Swiss. This passage from Joshua, *even this one word alone*, if known and emulated, might have prevented countless atrocities made by many, over the centuries, who have not been very honest about their own violence, preferring to mask it as God's own.

The limitations are also *in the midst* and *in the fray*. Walter Brueggemann has provocatively spoken of God being "in recovery," because the biblical God "is deeply enmeshed in violence."[26] That assessment may be a bit *too* honest for some preachers to handle, or for congregants to receive, but it is certainly a possible reading of the literature qua literature with God a literary character therein. But important caveats should immediately be entered. It is crucial to stress that in God's case, there is no "history of prior violence." God's primordial past is quite otherwise—decidedly *non*violent, according to the first few chapters of Genesis. Furthermore, God proves fully capable of reconciliation and resolution *internally*, as it were, without the standard requirements of confession and repentance (see above). These two considerations nuance Brueggemann's assessment, at least to some degree. To his credit, and not surprisingly, Brueggemann himself is aware of both points. He notes the presence of the latter, for example, in Hosea 11, where, after venting great rage at Israel, God moves to a new resolve, "in effect recalibrating the way" God will act:[27]

> How can I give you up, Ephraim?
>   How can I hand you over, Israel?
> How can I make you like Admah?
>   How can I treat you like Zeboiim?
> My heart winces within me;
>   my compassion grows warm and tender.
> I won't act on the heat of my anger;
>   I won't return to destroy Ephraim;
> for I am God and not a human being,
>   the holy one in your midst;
> I won't come in harsh judgment. (Hos 11:8–9)

This recalibration is entirely comparable to what was observed earlier from Jeremiah and Ezekiel concerning the destruction of Jerusalem. The superscription of Hosea, however, would locate this type of divine shift considerably earlier, already in the eighth century, among the very earliest of Israel's writing prophets (see Hos 1:1).[28] Furthermore, it is significant that Hosea 11 presents this divine shift by means of a parent-child metaphor, as that relationship can be highly fraught but is usually dominated, ultimately, by compassionate care.[29] But note: in the case of Hosea 11, it is precisely God's *nonhumanity*—this parent is *not human* (v. 9)—that tips the divine balance toward *nonanger, nondestruction,* and *nonjudgment.*

Brueggemann has noted another factor in God's turning away from violence—a further limitation, as it were. It is the presence of brave interlocutors who intercede with God on behalf of Israel at critical moments. The preeminent example is Moses in Exodus 32 and Numbers 14. In both passages, God's fierce anger is allayed, leading Brueggemann to suggest that God's "recovery" depends in part "on bold human agents who will dare to challenge God's intent and summon God to alternative behavior."[30] Perhaps so. Moses's skills in prayer should not be gainsaid; they provide another aspirational example for preachers. But as Gary Anderson has argued, courageous intercessors like Moses in the Torah, Abraham in Genesis 18, or Amos in Amos 7:1–6 have been taken by God into the divine confidence. This means that

> when Moses and God go head to head in Exod. 32–34, the identity of God is not represented solely by what the character marked "God" says in the dialogue. *The identity is fleshed out by the combination of the two voices. Through the prophets, God has invited Israel into his own person.*[31]

If Anderson is right, we see yet one more way that divine violence is constrained *internally*. Being honest about God and violence, therefore, must include the fact that, whenever Israel (or we ourselves) is tempted to violence, it (and we) is caught up into a larger theological context in which God's own self contains, limits, and finally departs from violence. If God *is* in recovery, these texts urge us "to be about the same recovery," especially when we so often are not.[32] Perhaps we can do that because God has taken us into the divine confidence precisely through this honest Scripture bequeathed to us by Israel.

The mention of "a larger theological context" provides one more angle from which to consider the phrase *honest to God preaching*. This additional angle suggests that our honesty transpires *within the presence of God*. On the one hand, this is easy to imagine given the divine epithet that asserts that God already knows all that might be said and all that might be held back and kept secret. In one sense, therefore, honesty *within the presence of God* sounds much like honesty *before God*. On the other hand, the theological context of our honesty, when understood as taking place amid a divine audience, adds nuance, especially when we recognize how hard it can be to be honest with others and how easy it is to deceive ourselves.[33] We can all recall times when it has been profoundly difficult to be honest with someone, especially in admitting our own wrongdoing or in acknowledging pain we have caused. Alternatively, we can all think of times when we have dissembled with others and ourselves, becoming guilty of projection, perhaps, or simply of keeping some secret hidden, all the while trying to convince ourselves that it can stay in the dark indefinitely. Even if "we" can't remember such things (perhaps I shouldn't speak for the reader), God knows

I can—and I use the phrase "God knows" in that admission quite intentionally. Here is my honest confession! The "theological context of honesty" means that honest disclosure, even my own just now, takes place in, with, and under the presence of God, where everything that might be said *and* everything that might be held back is already fully known. It can safely be uttered to God, because God already knows it. And with God's help, perhaps it can also be uttered to others. In whatever form it takes, honesty *in the presence of God*—and the preaching that manifests it—can transform and better us.

Way Too Honest? "The Preacher" Weighs In

It is time to invite an unusual conversation partner to join this discussion. When the topic is truth telling, especially to others in proclamatory modes, we could easily appeal to the prophets. But other texts deserve equal attention, if only because they are so frequently overlooked and undervalued, particularly in the pulpit. The book of Ecclesiastes is one such text. As noted earlier in this chapter, the Hebrew title for the book was understood by Luther as signaling that the somewhat cranky persona who speaks in the book was a preacher. Luther's interpretation draws on the fact that the Hebrew word *qōheleth* derives from the same root used for the "assembly" or "congregation" of Israel (*qāhāl*). The English title for the book, which comes to us from the Greek via the Latin, does the same thing: this person named "Ecclesiastes" (*Ekklēsiastēs*) is a member of the *ekklesia*, the term that the New Testament authors regularly use for "church." In the case of Qoheleth, this isn't just any old church member, however, but a leader and wise teacher, one who

> constantly taught the people knowledge. He listened
> and investigated. He composed many proverbs. The
> Teacher [Hebrew: *Qoheleth*, Greek: *Ekklēsiastēs*, Latin:
> *Ecclesiastes*] searched for pleasing words, and he wrote
> truthful words honestly. (Eccl 12:9–10)

This testimony, which comes at the very end of the book, suggests that, cranky or not, Qoheleth is worth listening to. In fact, given this testimony—especially the last phrase—it seems that Qoheleth could be an important resource for honest to God preaching.

That suspicion receives further confirmation in light of our own propensities to self-deception and the fact that God already knows the whole truth and nothing but it.[34] With reference to *self-deception*, Qoheleth is quite sober about the limits to all human knowledge:

> No one can grasp what happens under the sun. Those
> who strive to know can't grasp it. Even the wise who are
> set on knowing are unable to grasp it. (Eccl 8:17b)

With regard to *divine knowledge*, Qoheleth is quite fond of asking "Who knows?" (2:19; 3:21; 6:12; 8:1; cf. 10:14)—a question that seems to imply that *God*, at least, does.[35] Self-deception and divine knowledge seem to be two sides of a single coin for Qoheleth, at least in some instances and in the case of certain topics. In other words and once again, we are often sick on our secrets, but no secret is hidden from God.

According to most accounts, Ecclesiastes is a strange book—a rather odd inclusion in what is already a rather diverse canon—with its preacher something of an odd bird as a result. Yes, he is honest, not only according to the testimony of Ecclesiastes

THE IMPORTANCE OF PREACHING HONESTLY

12:9–10, but also according to the specific content of the "sermon" he preaches. But readers may well wonder if Qoheleth is at times a wee bit *too* honest. It's not that Preacher Qoheleth is shockingly candid about sin, suffering, or violence, nor is it a case of his oversharing; instead, it's simply that Qoheleth appears rather skeptical, if not thoroughly cynical. And this is not yet to mention that Qoheleth's sermon seems highly convoluted and contradictory.[36] Finally, there is the relationship between this peculiar preacher and his God. It's complicated, to say the least. Elias Bickerman memorably remarked that the "fear of God" idea in Ecclesiastes means nothing less than "to be on guard against *Elohim*"![37] These factors duly acknowledged, Qoheleth remains nothing if not an honest to God preacher. That means it's worth listening to what "the Preacher" (*Qōheleth*) has to say about honest proclamation to the faithful congregation (*qāhāl*).

The summary of Qoheleth's work cited earlier isn't a bad place to start (Eccl 12:9–10). In the canonical process, Israel (and the Christian church) recognized in this cranky skeptic someone with gifts and graces for ministry, for teaching, and even for preaching. Note the high points on Qoheleth's résumé, which earn him high marks:

* he was *wise*;
* he *constantly taught* people;
* what he taught was *knowledge*;
* he *listened*;
* he *investigated*;
* he *composed many sayings* encapsulating *wisdom in memorable ways*;
* he looked for just *the right words*—ones that were *aesthetically engaging*;

- he wrote *truthful words*; and
- he wrote them *honestly*.

Not a bad list for any preacher! Contemporary readers of Ecclesiastes may be forgiven if they occasionally struggle to find all of these qualities in clear evidence at every turn in the book as we now have it. Maybe that is proof that Qoheleth's preaching ministry was far more extensive than what has been preserved in the book that bears his name. That is entirely speculative, of course; what is not speculative in the least, however, and immediately at hand, is Qoheleth's book, including its final, remarkable, and rather unexpected commendation of crabby ole Qoheleth. That encomium begins with this crotchety preacher's *wisdom* and ends with his *honesty*. Once again, not bad for any preacher! And, regardless of the other items of his résumé, it isn't hard at all to trace wisdom and honesty in Ecclesiastes—especially honesty.

In Qoheleth's case, the honesty in question concerns the world and the self. Qoheleth's is a sober take but also a personalized one, as evidenced by how often he uses first-person verb phrases, like "I saw," "I said," "I considered," "I turned," "I know" (e.g., Eccl 1:14, 16; 2:2, 11, 12, 13, 15, 20; 3:10, 12, 14). This interface between the world and the self, leavened with all due candor, means that Qoheleth frequently expresses great uncertainty. Hence his fondness for "Who knows?" There are real limitations on what we can and cannot know. Thus spake Qoheleth. That judgment is very honest as well as highly accurate. And Qoheleth isn't done: he extends the limitations of human knowledge to include God and human speech about God. Honest to God preaching should do the same if it wishes to be wise like Qoheleth.

THE IMPORTANCE OF PREACHING HONESTLY

To illustrate matters, the earlier citation from 8:17 was only partial. The full verse is revealing:

> I observed all the work of God—that no one can grasp what happens under the sun. Those who strive to know can't grasp it. Even the wise who are set on knowing are unable to grasp it. (Eccl 8:17)

The limitations on human knowledge have to do with God, God's work. Now Qoheleth is surely overstating things when he says he has observed "*all* the work of God." Let's chalk that up to "preacher's license." Regardless, Qoheleth's conclusion is what is so striking: not even the wise, those who really want and try to know, can grasp what is happening down here on earth, "under the sun." Make no mistake about it—this conclusion is a devastating critique of the wisdom project, one that Qoheleth himself, so wise according to chapter 12, was deeply involved with. That means that Qoheleth is engaged here in a form of *self-criticism*. The Preacher is offering strong words of caution to other preachers: beware self-deception, *especially* when it comes to any self that makes a living speaking about the work of God![38] This point is driven home earlier in Ecclesiastes 5 by a verse that deserves to be printed on every pulpit (or at least imprinted on every pulpiteer's frontal cortex): "God is in heaven, but you are on earth. Therefore, let your words be few" (5:2b).[39]

God is something of a real mystery in Qoheleth's "sermon." Honest preachers know the same. Not everything can be said about God—certainly not correctly and certainly not briefly—in a fifteen- or even forty-five-minute sermon. Honest to God preaching knows this, with honest to God preachers taking some comfort in the fact that the problem doesn't lie solely with them.

God has revealed *and* concealed, which makes it possible to say *something* but impossible to say *everything*:

> God has made everything fitting in its time, but has also placed eternity in their [humanity's] hearts, without enabling them to discover what God has done from beginning to end. (Eccl 3:11)

Or, in the words of Second Isaiah,

> Truly, you are a God who hides himself, O God of Israel, the Savior. (Isa 45:15 NRSV)

Even the best, most honest preachers can only be *so* forthcoming, not because they don't want to say more, but because they simply *can't* in the face of the Great Mystery of God.[40]

Now, it would be wrong to leave the impression that Qoheleth's sermon is nothing but a bunch of crabby realism. While this particular preacher repeatedly shows that preaching the "good news" must not be solipsistic and simplistic, he is also not unacquainted with the glories of (quotidian) life and the (small) gifts of God. Peppered throughout Ecclesiastes are passages that commend enjoyment of life's simple pleasures (2:24–26; 3:12–13; 3:22; 5:18–20; 8:15; 9:7–10; 11:7–10; see also 7:14). These are apparently strategically deployed, leading one biblical scholar to call Qoheleth a "preacher of joy."[41] If that seems a bit overstated, perhaps it is because we aren't sufficiently honest about how joy in life is often far less triumphant than we are prone to pronounce from the pulpit.[42] Indeed, when it comes to self-deception, those of us who ascend the pulpit may be true masters of mendacity.[43] Much pressure is exerted on us to *not* tell the truth, to avoid it at all costs, whether that truth is about us, our world, or our God. Budgets have to be made, after all, and people need to be pleased, not to mention comforted or pacified or placated—or all of the above. Why not put a good face on it all, maybe even for good reasons, because of our compassion and care—our *love*—for those we serve?⁴⁴

Qoheleth's own countenance frowns back at us at this point, with his book reminding us that a sad face, not a stupidly happy one, is what is good for the heart (7:3) and that what is most important is *wisdom*—words that may be memorable, even aesthetically pleasing, but can often end up stinging "like iron-tipped prods" (12:11). His prophetic colleague, Jeremiah, would no doubt concur, when he weighs in heavily against prophets and priests (preachers, that is!) who "treat the wound of my people as if it were nothing: 'All is well, all is well,' they insist, when in fact nothing is well" (Jer 6:14; 8:11). For Qoheleth, what matters in the end is writing and saying *truthful* words *honestly*.⁴⁵ Among other things, that means—at least for Qoheleth's sermon as now canonized in Scripture—that the ethics must be *attainable*.⁴⁶ Qoheleth's joy is "to scale." He does not preach as if all of us will end up like Moses (or Paul or Mother Theresa or Martin Luther King Jr.) because, well, we *won't*. That's God's honest truth. Time to rescale the rhetoric. Time to honestly assess what we can and cannot achieve, what we are and aren't capable of. Comprehensive mastery of the mysterious work of God? Nope. Unthinkable. Not even the folks who think they are wise (one thinks, perhaps, of seminary professors) can pull that off. Complete and total joy? Nope, not possible, despite so much Christianly efforts to the contrary.⁴⁷ Easy emulation of divine love in every exchange? Nope. Not even close. Give me a break! But enjoyment of what God has given—things like food, drink, friends, spouses, even work—at least on occasion, now and then, here and there? Well, yes, that, it seems, *can* be done, if and when God so wills (see Eccl 5:19). These are small glories, but they, too, are the gifts of God for the people of God. Thanks be to God!

Qoheleth's sermon about life with God under the sun may not be spectacular—your best life now! always! especially on Fridays at 5 p.m.!—but it is honest and real nevertheless; it is *attainable*. It is also not without profound *ethical import*. It has feet that will walk to work on Monday, to the beach on Saturday, and to church again on Sunday (Eccl 5:1; 9:10). It has hands that will hold others' hands and arms that will embrace (3:5bα; 9:9). It has a mouth that will eat and drink with a merry heart (9:7) and lips that will talk and smile and smack delightfully after a delicious dinner (2:24; 5:18; 8:15). Honest preaching that attends to the "glory of the ordinary" might help us realize, in turn, that "small righteousnesses," while not everything, can be significant.[48] They can also, sometimes, be *enough*.

And God in all this? As I noted earlier, Qoheleth seems somewhat cool toward God. Let's be honest: preachers, even the most stalwart of them, also feel the same way sometimes, if not worse. Sometimes a clerical collar can feel like a noose, according to one of the PostSecrets collected by Frank Warren.[49] But despite the coolness, maybe even distance, Qoheleth can't escape God and can't get around talking about God. Although he doesn't use the same terms, it's not hard to picture him feeling what Jeremiah felt:

> If I say, "I will not mention him [God],
>   or speak any more in his name,"
> then within me there is something like a burning fire
>   shut up in my bones;

THE IMPORTANCE OF PREACHING HONESTLY

> I am weary with holding it in,
>   and I cannot. (Jer 20:9 NRSV)

Similarly, honest to God preaching can never forget the "to God" part, and from both of the angles discussed above, honest preaching *before* God and honest preaching *about* God, despite and in spite of the very real limitations that everyone who would speak of God faces. Israel's honesty and the honesty of its great teachers like Qoheleth, some of whom are occasionally stupefied by the task, light our way, even if sometimes our way seems dim.[50]

In Place of a Conclusion

At the end of the day—and the end of this book—it seems we should acknowledge once more that, in its fullest articulation, Israel's honesty in the Old Testament is not only arresting but also and not infrequently *off-putting*, especially to some modern sensibilities according to which certain things are not topics for polite discussion (though binge-watching them is quite another story). It seems that we are often caught in a curious conundrum between cover-up and voyeurism. Within that bind, Israel's honesty comes to us as a great gift, not a cause for alarm. Israel's honesty helps us avoid both cover-up and voyeurism by bringing sin, suffering, and violence out in the open, in the light of the God from whom no secrets are hid, in the process freeing us from the secrets that make us sick, but only insofar as we continue to hide them. The secret things that belong to God (cf. Deut 29:29; Mark 4:11), which are brought to light in Israel's practices of disclosure, are not wallowed in, despairingly, but are revealed for transformation, for the sake of reconciliation, healing, and recovery.

What's not to like about that? Precious little, it seems, unless we are committed to enmity, sickness, and vindictiveness. And if we are committed to those things, that is likely due to the fact that we have failed to follow Israel's pattern of unstinting, unremitting honesty that can change us for the better. And why wouldn't we follow that pattern? Because of sin, probably, and suffering and violence—especially of the *undisclosed* variety. In some twisted way, it is far easier to scoff at the honest confession of others than to emulate it. *Preacher beware.*

Rather than try to wrap everything up in a perfect bow, which I candidly confess seems beyond me, I have chosen to end with some quotations that might inspire us to greater honesty in preaching—an honesty that would recognize the profundity of Israel's testimony and imitate it, that would avoid centuries of stupidity and duplicity in the pulpit (and worse), and that would transform God's people for the sake of God's world. So let the preacher *understand* what follows. And let the preacher also *preach . . . honestly . . . to God.*

The novelist Franz Kafka:

If the book we are reading does not wake us, as with a fist hammering on our skull, why then do we read it? So that it shall make us happy? Good God, we would also be happy if we had no books, and such books as make us happy we could, if need be, write ourselves. But what we must have are those books which come upon us like ill-fortune, and distress us deeply, like the death of one we love better than ourselves, like suicide.

THE IMPORTANCE OF PREACHING HONESTLY

A book must be an ice-axe to break the sea frozen inside us.[51]

The poet Richard Wilbur:
One of the jobs of poetry is to make the unbearable bearable, not by falsehood but by clear, precise confrontation. Even the most cheerful poet has to cope with pain as part of the human lot; what he shouldn't do is to complain, and dwell on his personal mischance.[52]

The philosopher Harry G. Frankfurt:
One of the most salient features of our culture is that there is so much bullshit. Everyone knows this. Each of us contributes his share. . . . There is nothing in theory, and certainly nothing in experience, to support the extraordinary judgment that it is the truth about himself that is the easiest for a person to know. . . . And insofar as this is the case, [merely personal] sincerity . . . is bullshit.[53]

The philosopher Sissela Bok:
In an imperfect world, [the practices of deception] cannot be wiped out altogether; but surely they can be reduced and counteracted. . . . They can disguise and fuel all other wrongs. Trust and integrity are precious resources, easily squandered, hard to regain. They can thrive only on a foundation of respect for veracity.[54]

Daniel in Babylon, according to the book of Daniel:
God's name be praised from age to eternal age!
    Wisdom and might are his!
God is the one who changes times and eras,
    who dethrones one king, only to establish another,
    who grants wisdom to the wise and knowledge to
        those with insight.
God is the one who uncovers what lies deeply hidden;
    he knows what hides in darkness;
    light lives with him! (Dan 2:20–22)

King David, according to Psalm 51:
And yes, you want truth in the most hidden places;
you teach me wisdom in the most secret space.
    (Ps 51:6)

Jesus, according to the Gospels:
Therefore, don't be afraid of those people because nothing is hidden that won't be revealed, and nothing secret that won't be brought out into the open. (Matt 10:26; cf. Mark 4:22; Luke 8:17; 12:2)

Whoever has ears to listen should pay attention! (Mark 4:23)

The Secret-Knowing Lord God of
Israel, according to Psalm 81:
In distress you called, and I rescued you;
    I answered you in the secret place of thunder.
        (Ps 81:7a NRSV)

NOTES

Preface

1 Brent A. Strawn, *Lies My Preacher Told Me: An Honest Look at the Old Testament* (Louisville: Westminster John Knox, 2021).

Chapter 1

1 It is important to observe that the part about "hating your enemy" in the "you have heard it said [before]" saying is not to be found as such in the Old Testament, and so it is unclear where exactly it comes from. It may be a reference to a contemporary (non-Scriptural) saying, some sort of interpretive deduction on the basis of prior written and/or oral traditions or a rhetorical innovation (even flair?) within Matthew. See, e.g., Ulrich Luz, *Matthew 1–7: A Commentary*, ed. Helmut Koester, trans. James E. Crouch (Minneapolis: Fortress, 2007), 285–88; also Amy-Jill Levine, "Matthew and Anti-Judaism," *Currents in Theology and Mission* 34 (2007): 409–16, esp. 410–11.

2 By this more generous formulation I mean to signal that I do not believe the subject matter of this book is restricted solely to preachers or only to the preaching task. Teaching, too, can be honest (or otherwise), and as I will argue below and in the other chapters, the practices of honest disclosure have benefits at individual and communal levels beyond (but certainly including) the preaching and teaching arts.

3 In this book, I use "Israel" to refer to the community of faith that lies behind, produced and passed on, and is the primary protagonist within

the sacred literature of Scripture. It should be obvious that I use this term in synchronic fashion as a convenient way to refer to the people of God reflected throughout the pages of the Old Testament, no matter what period in Israelite history those pages happen to come from.

4. It is all too easy to let this happen, as Amy-Jill Levine rightly notes: "Homilists need to be alert for the slippage that sometimes occurs between what the texts say and the impression that can be conveyed to the congregation." Levine, *The Misunderstood Jew: The Church and the Scandal of the Jewish Jesus* (San Francisco: HarperSanFrancisco, 2006), 222.

5. See Norbert Lohfink, *The Covenant Never Revoked: Biblical Reflections on Christian-Jewish Dialogue* (New York: Paulist, 1991); also, and more technically, J. Ross Wagner, *Heralds of the Good News: Isaiah and Paul in Concert in the Letter to the Romans* (Boston: Brill, 2003).

6. Here and throughout, translations are taken from the Common English Bible (CEB) unless otherwise noted.

7. The forgiveness of all sin, confessed or otherwise, intentional or unintentional, is the burden of the Day of Atonement (Yom Kippur) ritual found in Lev 16. See further chapter 5.

8. For more on projection, see Brent A. Strawn, "Scripture, Guns, and Psychology: Projecting on Joshua," in *God and Guns: The Bible against American Gun Culture*, ed. Christopher B. Hays and C. L. Crouch (Louisville: Westminster John Knox, 2021); and see chapter 4.

9. See, e.g., Jeremy Cohen, ed., *Essential Papers on Judaism and Christianity in Conflict: From Late Antiquity to the Reformation* (New York: New York University Press, 1991).

10. See the wonderful essay by Paul Rorem, "Empathy and Evaluation in Medieval Church History and Pastoral Ministry: A Lutheran Reading of Pseudo-Dionysius," *Princeton Seminary Bulletin* 19 (1998): 99–115.

11. In *Lying: Moral Choice in Public and Private Life*, 2nd ed. (New York: Vintage, 1999), xix–xx, Sissela Bok cites François de La Rochefoucauld's (1613–80) well-known maxim "Nothing is so contagious as an example. We never do great good or great evil without bringing about more of the same on the part of others."

12 As chapters 2–4 will show, there is a good bit of overlap or relationship between these three topics, though they can also be distinguished.
13 Ellen F. Davis, *Getting Involved with God: Rediscovering the Old Testament* (Cambridge, MA: Cowley, 2001), 8.
14 For some thoughtful ways of linking, especially homiletically, the Psalms and narrative portions of the Bible in preaching, see Ellen F. Davis, *Wondrous Depth: Preaching the Old Testament* (Louisville: Westminster John Knox, 2005).
15 The literature is now quite vast and, within Christian theology, begins as early as Saint Augustine's treatises "On Lying" and "Against Lying." See, inter alia, the literature cited in Bok, *Lying*, esp. 250–88; and in Sissela Bok, *Secrets: On the Ethics of Concealment and Revelation* (New York: Vintage, 1989). See further below and chapters 2–4.
16 Much of what follows is adapted from Brent A. Strawn, "The Psalms and the Practice of Disclosure," in Walter Brueggemann, *From Whom No Secrets Are Hid: Introducing the Psalms*, ed. Brent A. Strawn (Louisville: Westminster John Knox, 2014), xiii–xxiv.
17 *The Book of Common Prayer and Administration of the Sacraments and Other Rites and Ceremonies of the Church: Together with the Psalter or Psalms of David According to the Use of the Episcopal Church* (New York: Seabury, 1979), 323 (Rite One); cf., 355 (Rite Two).
18 Cf. Bok, *Secrets*, 77, 81.
19 On Scripture reading as prayer, and vice versa, see especially Mariano Magrassi, *Praying the Bible: An Introduction to Lectio Divina*, trans. Edward Hagman (Collegeville, MN: Liturgical, 1998). On "reperformance" and the Psalms, see Brueggemann, *From Whom*.
20 To illustrate one of these "other things," this one more positive on the face of it, we might note that Scripture's candid praise of God, too, can be a point of embarrassment for modern readers and for a number of reasons (see Rolf Jacobson, "The Costly Loss of Praise," *Theology Today* 57 [2000]: 375–85). But in the case of doxology, the problems have less to do—or so it seems to me—with readers' lack of honesty than with an apparently deficient *theology*: belief in God's existence, God's actions, and so forth, which indicate *there is*, in fact,

a God to be praised in the first place and that this God is, in fact, praiseworthy.

21 See Frank Warren, *PostSecret: Extraordinary Confessions from Ordinary Lives* (New York: Regan, 2005); Warren, *My Secret: A PostSecret Book* (New York: Regan, 2006); Warren, *A Lifetime of Secrets: A PostSecret Book* (New York: William Morrow, 2007); Warren, *The Secret Lives of Men and Women: A PostSecret Book* (New York: William Morrow, 2007); Warren, *PostSecret: Confessions on Life, Death, and God* (New York: William Morrow, 2009); and Warren, *The World of PostSecret* (New York: William Morrow, 2014). Warren's project was featured in the music video for the song "Dirty Little Secret," by the band The All-American Rejects, from their album *Move Along* (2005).

22 All of the following come from Warren, *Secret Lives of Men and Women*, which does not use page numbers.

23 Warren, *PostSecret: Confessions*, vii.

24 Warren, *Secret Lives of Men and Women*, n.p.

25 Warren, introduction to *My Secret*, n.p.

26 Warren, *PostSecret: Extraordinary Confessions*, 3.

27 Warren, introduction to *Lifetime of Secrets*, n.p. See note 11 above and Judith Lewis Herman, *Trauma and Recovery* (New York: Basic, 1997), 140: "trauma is contagious" (see further chapter 4 below). Cf. Warren, *Secret Lives of Men and Women*, where, in response to the question "What have you learned from all the secrets you have seen?" he writes, "Courage can be more important than training or technique in creating meaningful art" (n.p.).

28 Warren's response to the question "Do you think all the secrets are true?" seems somehow instructive at this point. He tells the story of someone who sent in a faked secret that was partially lost in the mail from damage. After the partial form was posted, the original author wrote Warren and said, "The new altered meaning of the secret on the card is true to me." Warren concludes, "I think the postcards work like art. So to ask me if the postcards are true or false is like asking if a painting or sculpture in a museum is fiction or nonfiction" (*Secret Lives of Men and Women*, n.p.).

29 See Reese Butler's foreword in Warren, *My Secret*.
30 Warren, *Secret Lives of Men and Women*, n.p.
31 Warren, *Lifetime of Secrets*, n.p.
32 Warren, *Secret Lives of Men and Women*, n.p. (emphasis in original).
33 See Sigmund Freud, *Five Lectures on Psycho-Analysis* (New York: W. W. Norton, 1989), 8; Sigmund Freud and Josef Breuer, *Studies in Hysteria*, trans. Nicola Luckhurst (London: Penguin, 2004), 34–35, 44, 49–50; and the comments by Rachel Bowlby, "Introduction: Never Done, Never to Return," in Freud and Breuer, *Studies*, vii, ix–xi, xiv, xxix–xxxi.
34 See Stephen A. Mitchell and Margaret J. Black, *Freud and Beyond: A History of Modern Psychoanalytic Thought* (New York: Basic, 1995).
35 James W. Pennebaker, *Opening Up: The Healing Power of Expressing Emotions*, rev. ed. (New York: Guilford, 1997), originally published as *Opening Up: The Healing Power of Confiding in Others* (New York: William Morrow, 1990). Citations come from the revised edition from Guilford Press. Although presented as a new edition, the later volume by James W. Pennebaker and Joshua M. Smyth, *Opening Up by Writing It Down: How Expressive Writing Improves Health and Eases Emotional Pain*, 3rd ed. (New York: Guilford, 2016), has a good number of differences from the earlier works authored solely by Pennebaker himself.
36 Alice Miller, *The Body Never Lies: The Lingering Effects of Hurtful Parenting* (New York: Norton, 2006).
37 See also Herman, *Trauma and Recovery*, 238, for physiological changes due to trauma, including "lasting alterations in the endocrine, autonomic, and central nervous systems," with the same holding true for certain areas of the brain, "particularly the amygdala and the hippocampus, brain structures that create a link between fear and memory." In Herman's opinion, various investigations "validate the century-old insight that traumatized people relive in their bodies the moments of terror that they cannot describe in words" (239).
38 Pennebaker, *Opening Up*, 2.
39 Pennebaker, 2 (emphasis added). See, from a different angle, the dangers of secrecy described by Bok, *Secrets*, 25–26, citing Lord Acton, that "everything secret degenerates." Bok shows how "secrecy can harm

those who make use of it in several ways," including debilitating our judgment by shutting out criticism and feedback; negatively affecting our character and moral choice; corroding us from within before others can be of use or help us; and lowering our resistance to things pathological and irrational—all of this made worse by the tendency of secrecy to spread. Bok later comments on the connection between keeping secrets for years and going "slightly mad" (283). See further Bok, *Secrets*, 285; and note also Bok's comments on the "near universal urge among human beings to bare personal secrets" (79). In her earlier work on lying, Bok argues that deceptive practices can "fuel all other wrongs" (*Lying* 249).

40 J. Cheryl Exum, *Tragedy and Biblical Narrative* (Cambridge: Cambridge University Press, 1992), 152.
41 Exum, 152.
42 Gerhard von Rad, *God at Work in Israel*, trans. John H. Marks (Nashville: Abingdon, 1980), 16.
43 Von Rad, 16.
44 Von Rad, 16.
45 Anne C. Fisher, "The Most Trusted Stranger in America," in Warren, *PostSecret: Extraordinary Confessions*, viii–ix.
46 Fisher, ix.
47 Fisher, ix (emphasis added).
48 Warren, *PostSecret: Extraordinary Confessions*, 276.
49 Warren, *PostSecret: Confessions*, 275 (emphasis added). Cf. Warren, *Secret Lives of Men and Women*, where he writes, "In some cases, the postcards are so soulful and painstakingly crafted that the cards might hold deep symbolic value to the sender, *perhaps a search for grace*" (n.p.; emphasis added).
50 Warren, *PostSecret: Confessions*, vii (emphasis added).
51 Fisher, "Most Trusted Stranger," ix. Elsewhere, in response to the question "Why do you think people continue to mail their secrets to you?" Warren has written, "I believe the motives are as raw and complicated as the secrets themselves. . . . I have tried to create a nonjudgmental 'place' where every secret is treated respectfully. In this safe environment

where there is no social cost for exposing a guarded secret to millions, it might be easier for someone to confess an embarrassing story, hidden act of kindness, or sexual taboo. . . . People have told me that facing their secret on a postcard and releasing it to a stranger have allowed them to uncover passions, experiences, hopes, regrets, and fears that have been too painful to otherwise acknowledge" (*Secret Lives of Men and Women*, n.p.).

52 See, e.g., God's looking in Amos 9:8; cf. Pss 14:2; 33:13–15; 53:2. God's watchfulness is nevertheless a resource for those in distress to call upon (see, e.g., Sus 1:42).

53 See, inter alia, Howard Clark Kee and Irvin J. Borowsky, eds., *Removing Anti-Judaism from the Pulpit* (New York: Continuum, 1996); Marilyn J. Salmon, *Preaching without Contempt: Overcoming Unintended Anti-Judaism* (Minneapolis: Fortress, 2006); Clark M. Williamson and Ronald J. Allen, *Interpreting Difficult Texts: Anti-Judaism and Christian Preaching* (London: SCM, 2012); George M. Smiga, *The Gospel of John Set Free: Preaching without Anti-Judaism* (New York: Paulist, 2008); and Donald J. Harrington, *The Synoptic Gospels Set Free: Preaching without Anti-Judaism* (New York: Paulist, 2009).

54 Cf. J. G. McConville's remarks with reference to Israel's honesty in Deuteronomy: "The portrayal of Israel's moral shortcomings is not intended to vilify Israel, but rather stresses both the grace of God in their life and the moral nature of the project. . . . It is essential that [Israel] is characterized first as ill-equipped for its role. This is done, not by mere calumny, but by setting the portrayal within a story" (*God and Earthly Power: An Old Testament Political Theology* [London: T&T Clark, 2008], 80–81).

55 I echo here, and take inspiration from, Will Willimon: "I write in subservience to a relentlessly redemptive God, who wrenches good out of bad through a weapon called preaching" (*Who Lynched Willie Earle? Preaching to Confront Racism* [Nashville: Abingdon, 2017], xiv).

56 Frederic W. Farrar, *History of Interpretation* (1886; repr., Grand Rapids, MI: Baker, 1961), 4.

57 Cf. Fred B. Craddock, *Preaching* (Nashville: Abingdon, 2010).

58 See chapter 5 for more on the preacher's *own* disclosure, which should not, to borrow from Bok's terms, be confused with "indiscriminate self-revelation" (*Secrets*, 82), which can actually be injurious.
59 See above and, further, chapter 3 for the toll inhibition takes. See also Pennebaker, *Opening Up*, passim. In the case of the Psalms, see Walter Brueggemann, "The Costly Loss of Lament," *Journal for the Study of the Old Testament* 36 (1986): 57–71.
60 Warren, introduction to *PostSecret: Confessions*, 2.

Chapter 2

1 For more on projection, see chapter 4.
2 The latter reading, referring to God's meeting of Israel, not Moses's, is probably to be preferred. The difference is very slight in Hebrew (*daʿtî* for Moses vs. *daʿtô* for God), with the early versions of the Old Testament aligning variously. See Brent A. Strawn, "Slaves and Rebels: Inscription, Identity, and Time in the Rhetoric of Deuteronomy," in *Sepher Torath Mosheh: Studies in the Composition and Interpretation of Deuteronomy*, ed. Daniel I. Block and Richard M. Schultz (Peabody, MA: Hendrickson, 2017), 161–91, esp. 173n32.
3 Cf. McConville, *God and Earthly Power*, 80–81.
4 See Norbert Lohfink, "Reading Deuteronomy 5 as Narrative," in *A God So Near: Essays on Old Testament Theology in Honor of Patrick D. Miller*, ed. Brent A. Strawn and Nancy R. Bowen (Winona Lake, IN: Eisenbrauns, 2003), 261–81.
5 See, e.g., Deut 1:8, 35; 4:31, 37; 6:10, 18, 23; 10:15; 30:9.
6 R. W. L. Moberly, "Exodus, Book of," in *Dictionary for Theological Interpretation of the Bible*, ed. Kevin J. Vanhoozer (Grand Rapids, MI: Baker Academic, 2005), 211–16 (214); similarly, Moberly, *Old Testament Theology: Reading the Hebrew Bible as Christian Scripture* (Grand Rapids, MI: Baker Academic, 2013), 192: "could be seen as an equivalent to committing adultery on one's wedding night." Moberly quickly adds that the specific intent of the people "is open to various less-heinous construals" ("Exodus, Book of," 214).

7 The singular rendering of Exod 32:4 in NJPSV ("This is your god, O Israel") is therefore somewhat odd, despite the explanation offered by Nahum M. Sarna, who deems the Hebrew text to be either a plural form used "in a monotheistic context" or "a scribal device to emphasize the unacceptable nature of the object" (*Exodus* שמות: *The Traditional Hebrew Text with the New JPS Translation*, JPS Torah Commentary [Philadelphia: Jewish Publication Society, 5751/1991], 204, see also 261n15; see also the previous note about other possible understandings). Of course, the plural form in the Hebrew text is also odd, since Aaron is said to make *only one* calf (see further below). For a recent, accessible discussion of this unit and the various issues involved, see Nathan MacDonald, "The Golden Calf: A Post-exilic Message of Forgiveness," The Torah, accessed July 28, 2021, https://tinyurl.com/y3n32dum.
8 Note that the modifier here, *ʾăḥērîm* ("other"), is plural, securing that the *ʾĕlōhîm* in question are also plural.
9 See, inter alia, Sharon Moughtin-Mumby, *Sexual and Marital Metaphors in Hosea, Jeremiah, Isaiah, and Ezekiel* (Oxford: Oxford University Press, 2008).
10 See W. L. Moran, "The Scandal of the 'Great Sin' at Ugarit," *JNES* 18 (1959): 280–81. The calf is called a great sin (*ḥăṭāʾāh gĕdōlāh*; CEB: "terrible sin") three times in Exodus (32:21, 30, 31). The only other instance of this phrase is found in Gen 20:9, where Abimelech laments Abraham's duplicity regarding his wife, Sarah, and where the context has to do with marital infidelity.
11 See, e.g., Patrick D. Miller, "The Good Neighborhood: Identity and Community through the Commandments," in *The Character of Scripture: Moral Formation, Community, and Biblical Interpretation*, ed. William P. Brown (Grand Rapids, MI: Eerdmans, 2002), 55–72.
12 See chapter 3 for more on the important verb *zāʿaq* ("to cry out"). A useful study is Richard Nelson Boyce, *The Cry to God in the Old Testament*, SBLDS 103 (Atlanta: Scholars Press, 1988).
13 The treatment of 2 Sam 11–12 and Ps 51 found below depends in part on Brent A. Strawn, "David and Bathsheba: Commentary on 2 Samuel 12:1–9; Psalm 51:1–9," Working Preacher, October 19, 2014, https://

tinyurl.com/n4xnebab. Of the many good commentaries on 2 Samuel, see especially Walter Brueggemann, *First and Second Samuel*, Interpretation (Louisville: John Knox, 1990).

14 Cf. J. Gerald Janzen, *Exodus* (Louisville: Westminster John Knox, 1997), 152; and, further, John C. Holbert, *The Ten Commandments: A Preaching Commentary* (Nashville: Abingdon, 2002).

15 The adultery in question is David's, not Bathsheba's. Note that Bathsheba is never addressed by Nathan in a condemnatory way. How could she be? She was *taken* by David and in more than one way. He, then, is the one guilty of wrongdoing, not Bathsheba, who is presented as nothing but an object of David's abusive power.

16 The judgment that David will not die (*lō' tāmût*) for his sin might be seen as one more (and final) installment in the two-word phrases that drive the plot. Although the words are not adjacent in the same way as the other phrases, the two verbs that begin the account "he sent . . . and he took her" (*wayyišlaḥ . . . wayyiqqāḥehā*; 2 Sam 11:4; my translation) are also crucial to the series.

17 For the enduring consequences of sin, see Mark E. Biddle, *Missing the Mark: Sin and Its Consequences in Biblical Theology* (Nashville: Abingdon, 2005).

18 Confession out loud, in public, has, of course, had a long tradition in Christian circles. It was only at the Council of Trent (1551) that the Catholic Church recommended that confession should be secret (Bok, *Secrets*, 77–78, 78n*). Prior to that point, public confession was the norm, as was public penance. In the eighteenth century, the Methodist movement started by the Wesley brothers (John and Charles) urged communal consultation on things that might be sin. Raymond Brown has suggested that the confession spoken of in 1 John (Greek: *homologeō*) was public (*The Epistles of John: Translated with Introduction, Notes, and Commentary*, Anchor Bible 30 [New York: Doubleday, 1982], 207–8).

19 Walter Brueggemann, *The Message of the Psalms: A Theological Commentary* (Minneapolis: Augsburg, 1984), 95. Interestingly enough, this approach to the problems discussed in the Psalter is a minor key. Brueggemann speaks of the penitential psalms as part of a "second

opinion" on what most (and primarily) ails the psalmists (88–106). Patrick D. Miller has noted that the problem of sin is rather muted in the Psalter: "None of the texts that ask the question 'What is a human being?' answer by identifying human existence as sinful. That is not the first answer or the dominant answer to the question as far as the Psalter is concerned. In fact, it could be argued that the Psalter does not see sin as a large issue for human life, that is, if one looks at the expressions of confession and repentance" ("The Sinful and Trusting Creature: The Anthropology of the Psalter II," in *The Way of the Lord: Essays in Old Testament Theology* [Tübingen, Germany: Mohr Siebeck, 2004], 237–49 [237]). Miller's qualification about confession and repentance is important, since one might view at least some of what troubles the psalmist, especially as that comes from enemies, as a result of their opponents' sin. See further in chapter 3.

20 Karl Menninger, *Whatever Became of Sin?* (New York: Hawthorn, 1973). For a more recent, thoughtful treatment of sin language, see Barbara Brown Taylor, *Speaking of Sin: The Lost Language of Salvation* (Cambridge, MA: Cowley, 2000).
21 MacDonald, "Golden Calf" (emphasis in original).
22 The notion of sin as a curving in on oneself (*incurvatus in se*) goes back to Augustine, though it is often credited to Luther. See Matt Jenson, *The Gravity of Sin: Augustine, Luther, and Barth on* homo incurvatus in se (London: T&T Clark, 2006).
23 This written confession toward reconciliation recalls a poem by Linda Pastan, "What Does Poetry Save You From?" where one of her answers is, "From my worst sins. / From the failure of any other absolution" (*Queen of a Rainy Country: Poems* [New York: W. W. Norton, 2006], 39).
24 I owe this phrase to L. Gregory Jones, *Embodying Forgiveness: A Theological Analysis* (Grand Rapids, MI: Eerdmans, 1995), which he defines as "the ongoing and ever-deepening process of unlearning sin through forgiveness and learning, through specific habits and practices, to live in communion—with the Triune God, with one another, and with the whole Creation" (xii). See further pp. 207–39; and earlier, L. Gregory Jones, "The Craft of Forgiveness," *Theology Today* 50 (1993): 345–57.

25 The centerpiece of Leviticus, furthermore, is the yearly Day of Reconciliation/Atonement (Yom Kippur) ritual found in chapter 16, in which all are forgiven all their sins. For further discussion of this text, see chapter 5.

26 Cf. Prayer of Azariah 1:16: "Yet with a contrite heart and a humble spirit may we be accepted" (NRSV).

27 Cf. MacDonald, "Golden Calf": "The fact that even the grossest transgression in Israel's history can receive God's forgiveness provides grounds for hope that the subsequent failures of Israel and Judah can also be forgiven."

28 Carol Tavris and Elliot Aronson, *Mistakes Were Made (but Not by Me): Why We Justify Foolish Beliefs, Bad Decisions, and Hurtful Acts* (Orlando: Harcourt, 2007), 9–10.

29 Among other things, Tavris and Aronson cite hospital studies that have found that "patients are actually less likely to sue when doctors admit and apologize for mistakes, and when changes are implemented so that future patients will not be harmed in the same way" (*Mistakes Were Made*, 219). See also Bok, *Lying*, xxviii: "Honesty from health professionals matters more to patients than almost everything else that they experience when ill."

30 A case of dissembling, in marked contrast to David, can be seen at several points in the life of King Saul. See discussions in Bill T. Arnold, *1 & 2 Samuel*, NIVAC (Grand Rapids, MI: Zondervan, 2014); and Stephen B. Chapman, *1 Samuel as Christian Scripture: A Theological Commentary* (Grand Rapids, MI: Eerdmans, 2016).

31 Tavris and Aronson, *Mistakes Were Made*, 222; they go on to cite the playwright Lillian Hellman, who says, "It is considered unhealthy in America to remember mistakes, neurotic to think about them, psychotic to dwell upon them" (229).

32 Tavris and Aronson, 216–17.

33 Taylor, *Speaking of Sin*, 41–67, has spoken of sin as "our only hope," though, in my judgment, it is better to speak of honest confession of sin, which moves to reconciliation, as the hope in question.

34 See Desmond Tutu, *No Future without Forgiveness* (New York: Image, 2000); see also Antjie Krog, *Country of My Skull* (Johannesburg: Random House, 1998); and Tavris and Aronson, *Mistakes Were Made*, 210–12.

Chapter 3

1. On bloodshed, see chapter 4 and, further, Matthew J. Lynch, *Portraying Violence in the Hebrew Bible: A Literary and Cultural Study* (Cambridge: Cambridge University Press, 2020), 213–15, 271–72.
2. Typically in the Piel (intensive) stem, with this meaning.
3. Hagar's own mistreatment of Sarai is also important to note (see Gen 16:4–5). On the Hagar texts, see esp. Phyllis Trible, *Texts of Terror: Literary-Feminist Readings of Biblical Narratives*, Overtures to Biblical Theology (Philadelphia: Fortress, 1984), 9–35.
4. See, e.g., Gen 21:16, where Hagar "cried out in grief, and wept." See further below.
5. See, e.g., Pamela Barmash, "Amnesty and Reform Texts," in *The Oxford Encyclopedia of the Bible and Law*, ed. Brent A. Strawn et al., 2 vols. (Oxford: Oxford University Press, 2015), 1:9–13.
6. See further chapters 4–5 for more on these points, especially with reference to homiletics.
7. See Job 19:7; Hab 1:2; cf. Jer 20:8; also Lynch, *Portraying Violence*, 151, 270–71; and Patrick D. Miller, *They Cried to the Lord: The Form and Theology of Biblical Prayer* (Minneapolis: Fortress, 1994), 45.
8. The use of "crying out" language in 1 Sam 8:18 with reference to Israel's own native king (see chapter 2) takes on greater significance in the light of this background from Exodus, as does 1 Sam 8:17, which says that the Israelites will become their own king's slaves. See further chapter 4.
9. See, e.g., Walter Brueggemann, *The Prophetic Imagination*, 40th anniversary ed. (Minneapolis: Fortress, 2018), 11.
10. See Exod 13:3, 14; 20:2; Deut 5:6; 6:12; 7:8; 8:14; 13:5, 10; Josh 24:17; Judg 6:8; Jer 34:13; Mic 6:4.

11 See, inter alia, Cornelis Houtman, *Exodus*, vol. 1, Historical Commentary on the Old Testament (Kampen, Netherlands: Kok, 1993), 190–212 and 212–18, respectively. See also Alastair J. Roberts and Andrew Wilson, *Echoes of Exodus: Tracing Themes of Redemption through Scripture* (Wheaton, IL: Crossway, 2018). A particularly intriguing example in the New Testament is Luke's account of the transfiguration where Jesus speaks with Moses and Elijah about his "exodus" (Luke 9:31: *tēn exodon autou*; CEB: "departure"). See Roberts and Wilson, *Echoes of Exodus*, 131–36.

12 See, e.g., Walter J. Harrelson, *The Ten Commandments and Human Rights*, rev. ed. (Macon, GA: Mercer University Press, 1997), 40.

13 "Because of their broken spirit [*miqqōṣer rûaḥ*]" may perhaps be translated as "because of their shortness of breath." Israel can't even catch its breath due to its hard labor (cf. CEB: "complete exhaustion"). See further below.

14 Katie M. Heffelfinger, *I Am Large, I Contain Multitudes: Lyric Cohesion and Conflict in Second Isaiah*, BIS 105 (Leiden, Netherlands: Brill, 2011), has traced this dynamic in a profound way in Isa 40–55.

15 The underlying grammatical constructions that follow are not identical, though most are either verbless clauses (with their tense derived from context) or constructions with the verb "to be," which, in certain forms, could be rendered as either "I am" or "I will be." Exod 20:6 is a participial clause that is translated differently in NRSV and NJPSV.

16 Cf. also Lev 21:15, 23; 22:9, 16, where God is the one who makes the priests or offerings holy.

17 Perhaps, at this point, we should add that the forty years of wilderness wandering, provoked by Israel's faithlessness in the spy debacle (honestly disclosed in Num 13–14) is, at best, a blink of an eye when compared to four hundred years of enslavement. Furthermore, every year that passed in the wanderings took Israel further from Pharaoh and brought it closer to promise.

18 See further chapter 5.

19 See note 11 above.

20 On this text, and more generally, see Terence E. Fretheim, "'I Was Only a Little Angry': Divine Violence in the Prophets," in *What Kind of God? Collected Essays of Terence E. Fretheim*, ed. Michael J. Chan and Brent A. Strawn, Siphrut 14 (Winona Lake, IN: Eisenbrauns, 2015), 172–84.
21 See Brueggemann, *Message of the Psalms*, 88–106.
22 Cf. Miller, "Sinful and Trusting Creature," 237–49, esp. 237: "The Psalter does not see sin as a large issue for human life . . . if one looks at the expressions of confession and repentance." It is, of course, easy enough to see a great deal of what troubles the psalmist as a result of their enemies' sin.
23 Gert Kwakkel, *According to My Righteousness: Upright Behaviour as Grounds for Deliverance in Psalms 7, 17, 18, 26, and 44* (Leiden, Netherlands: Brill, 2002).
24 See also Pss 18:21–25; 35:13–14; 38:21; 44:18–22; 86:2.
25 Kwakkel's explication of these psalms demonstrates that the poetic speaker is facing dire straits. The psalmist's claim to upright behavior, therefore, is appropriately "described as a claim to loyalty to God" (*According to My Righteousness*, 296), *not* as a claim to moral perfection. Rather, the "issue at stake was whether they as righteous people were really on YHWH's side, and were faithful and respected his will. Such loyalty to God, then, is exactly what is claimed in the claims to righteous behaviour in all of the psalms discussed in this study" (303). In the end, then, Kwakkel concludes that "instead of self-righteousness, Psalms 7, 17, 18, 26, and 44 bear witness to the firm belief that YHWH must show himself a righteous God. The petitions . . . are all motivated by the idea that his righteousness is at stake if he fails to deliver those who have a right to expect the life due to the righteous" (304). Much resonates here with the dynamics at work in the imprecatory psalms, discussed in chapter 4 (see there), but equally related seems to be what is described earlier in the present chapter—namely, that God must prove faithful to an Israel that is healing ever so slowly. As in Exodus, so also in the Psalms.
26 See M. Craig Barnes, *The Pastor as Minor Poet: Texts and Subtexts in the Ministerial Life* (Grand Rapids, MI: Eerdmans, 2009).

27 In the consonantal text, the word for "distress" here (*mṣrym* > *měṣārîm*) is spelled identically to the consonants that make up the word "Egypt" (also *mṣrym* > *misrayim*).
28 A thoughtful treatment of this issue, and how it is especially accomplished by means of the poetic form and poetry of Lamentations, may be found in F. W. Dobbs-Allsopp, *Lamentations*, Interpretation (Louisville: John Knox, 2002).
29 Note the acknowledgment of deserved suffering in Prayer of Azariah 1:5.
30 See the insightful interpretations in Dobbs-Allsopp, *Lamentations*; and Kathleen M. O'Connor, *Lamentations and the Tears of the World* (Maryknoll, NY: Orbis, 2006).
31 Only Psalm 119 goes one better with its eightfold acrostic poem that encompasses 176 verses.
32 See Psalms 9–10, 25, 34, 37, 111, 112, 119, 145; Prov 31:10–31; Nah 1:2–8; and, more generally, David Noel Freedman with Jeffrey C. Geoghegan and Andrew Welch, *Psalm 119: The Exaltation of Torah* (Winona Lake, IN: Eisenbrauns, 1999).
33 It was published in the *New York Times* on September 6, 2002 (p. A23), and not again until Billy Collins, *Aimless Love: New and Selected Poems* (New York: Random House, 2014), 254–56. It is also widely available on the web.
34 Collins, 256.
35 Walter Brueggemann, "The Formfulness of Grief," in *The Psalms and the Life of Faith*, ed. Patrick D. Miller (Minneapolis: Fortress, 1995), 84–97.
36 Elisabeth Kübler-Ross, *On Death and Dying: What the Dying Have to Teach Doctors, Nurses, Clergy, and Their Own Families*, 50th anniversary ed. (New York: Scribner, 2014).
37 Gerard Manley Hopkins, *The Major Works* (Oxford: Oxford University Press, 2002), 168, and widely available on the web.
38 See further below on the work of James Pennebaker. Note esp. his *Opening Up*, 185: "Writing, then, organizes traumas."

39 The Hebrew text, esp. the construction in v. 22, is complicated. See the discussions in R. B. Salters, *A Critical and Exegetical Commentary on Lamentation* (London: T&T Clark, 2010), 373–75; Dobbs-Allsopp, *Lamentations*, 148–49. The idea that v. 22 ends with an ellipsis is to be found in Tod Linafelt, *Surviving Lamentations* (Chicago: University of Chicago Press, 2000), 60–61; and Linafelt, "The Refusal of a Conclusion in the Book of Lamentations," *Journal of Biblical Literature* 120 (2001): 340–43.
40 Cf. Dobbs-Allsopp, *Lamentations*, 149: "Voiced hurt already contains the seeds of life revived and resurrected. . . . Lamentations' closing anxious plaint . . . contains within its very vocality the bequest of life . . . an inheritance bestowed ritually, lyrically upon readers each time they encounter and reutter for themselves the words of this poetry."
41 See, again, Brueggemann, "Formfulness of Grief"; also Claus Westermann, *Praise and Lament in the Psalms*, trans. Keith R. Crim and Richard N. Soulen (Atlanta: John Knox, 1981), esp. 165–73, 181–94, 259–80. Important nuances have been offered by Federico G. Villanueva, *The "Un*cer*tainty of a Hearing": A Study of the Sudden Change of Mood in the Psalms of Lament* (Leiden, Netherlands: Brill, 2008).
42 See Villanueva, Un*certainty of a Hearing*, and the literature cited therein; see also Eo Kon Kim, *The Rapid Change of Mood in the Lament Psalms: A Matrix for the Establishment of a Psalm Theology* (Seoul: Korea Theological Study Institute, 1985).
43 See Brent A. Strawn, "The Psalms: Types, Functions, and Poetics for Proclamation," in *Psalms for Preaching and Worship: A Lectionary Commentary*, ed. Roger Van Harn and Brent A. Strawn (Grand Rapids, MI: Eerdmans, 2009), 3–40, esp. 11–12; and Strawn, "The Triumph of Life: Towards a Biblical Theology of Happiness," in *The Bible and the Pursuit of Happiness: What the Old and New Testaments Teach Us about the Good Life*, ed. Brent A. Strawn (Oxford: Oxford University Press, 2012), 287–322, esp. 290–300.
44 A profound reflection, which takes its title from Psalm 88, is found in Kathryn Greene-McCreight, *Darkness Is My Only Companion: A*

Christian Response to Mental Illness, rev. ed. (Grand Rapids, MI: Brazos, 2015).

45 What follows depends in part on Strawn, "Psalms and the Practice of Disclosure," xiii–xxiv; and Strawn, "Trauma, Psalmic Disclosure, and Authentic Happiness," in *Bible through the Lens of Trauma*, ed. Elizabeth Boase and Christopher G. Frechette, Semeia Studies 86 (Atlanta: Society of Biblical Literature, 2016), 143–60; see also chapter 1 in the present volume. The main work by Pennebaker is *Opening Up* (see note 38 above). See also Pennebaker, "Writing about Emotional Experiences as a Therapeutic Process," *Psychological Science* 8 (1997): 162–66; Pennebaker, "The Effects of Traumatic Disclosure on Physical and Mental Health: The Values of Writing and Talking about Upsetting Events," *International Journal of Emergency Mental Health* 1 (1999): 9–18; Pennebaker, "Telling Stories: The Health Benefits of Narrative," *Literature and Medicine* 19 (2000): 3–18; and Pennebaker, "The Social, Linguistic, and Health Consequences of Emotional Disclosure," in *Social Psychological Foundations of Health and Illness*, ed. Jerry Suls and Kenneth A. Wallston (Malden, MA: Blackwell, 2003), 288–313. Note also Pennebaker's many multiauthored works—for example, James W. Pennebaker and Robin C. O'Heeron, "Confiding in Others and Illness Rates among Spouses of Suicide and Accidental Death," *Journal of Abnormal Psychology* 93 (1984): 473–76; James W. Pennebaker, Cheryl F. Hughes, and Robin C. O'Heeron, "The Psychophysiology of Confession: Linking Inhibitory and Psychosomatic Processes," *Journal of Personality and Social Psychology* 52 (1987): 781–93; James W. Pennebaker and Joan R. Susman, "Disclosure of Traumas and Psychosomatic Processes," *Social Science and Medicine* 26 (1988): 327–32; Larry Vandecreek et al., "Praying about Difficult Experiences as Self-Disclosure to God," *International Journal for the Psychology of Religion* 12 (2002): 29–39. These and other publications can be found on Pennebaker's faculty page: https://liberalarts.utexas.edu/psychology/faculty/pennebak.

46 Pennebaker, *Opening Up*, 2.

47 Pennebaker, 2.

48 Pennebaker, 5 (emphasis added).
49 Pennebaker, 9.
50 Pennebaker, 10.
51 Pennebaker, 10.
52 Pennebaker, 19.
53 Pennebaker, 19.
54 Pennebaker, 22.
55 Pennebaker, 23. Cf. George A. Bonanno, *The Other Side of Sadness: What the New Science of Bereavement Tells Us about Life after Loss* (New York: Basic, 2009), 74, who speaks of "avoidance and distraction."
56 Pennebaker, *Opening Up*, 23.
57 Pennebaker, 26–42, 185–97; and esp. Pennebaker and Smyth, *Opening Up by Writing*. See also Eva-Maria Gortner, Stephanie S. Rude, and James W. Pennebaker, "Benefits of Expressive Writing in Lowering Rumination and Depressive Symptoms," *Behavior Therapy* 37 (2006): 292–303; James W. Pennebaker and Cindy K. Chung, "Expressive Writing, Emotional Upheavals, and Health," in *Foundations of Health Psychology*, ed. Howard S. Friedman and Roxane Cohen Silver (New York: Oxford University Press, 2007), 263–84; and the items cited in note 45 above.
58 Pennebaker, *Opening Up*, 185.
59 Pennebaker, 34; and further, 35–42. Health benefits—specifically "heightened immune function"—persisted for up to six weeks after writing, according to Pennebaker's findings (37).
60 Pennebaker, 37.
61 In light of Israel's candid admission of sin early in its covenantal relationship with God, indeed from night one, as it were (see chapter 2), the following from Pennebaker, *Opening Up*, seems significant: "Early childhood traumas that are not disclosed may be bad for your health as an adult" (20). Israel is honest early on and consistently thereafter—an indicator, in Pennebaker's categories, of good health, not to mention good attachment. For the latter, see Brent A. Strawn, "Poetic Attachment: Psychology, Psycholinguistics, and the Psalms," in *The Oxford Handbook of the Psalms*, ed. William P. Brown (Oxford: Oxford University Press, 2014), 404–23.

62 Pennebaker, *Opening Up*, 24. For other therapeutic aspects of prayer, see Bernard Spilka and Kevin L. Ladd, *The Psychology of Prayer: A Scientific Approach* (New York: Guilford, 2013), 22, 88–138, esp. 107, 136.
63 See James H. Cone, *The Spirituals and the Blues: An Interpretation* (Maryknoll, NY: Orbis, 1991).

Chapter 4

1 Astute readers will note the difference between the first two letters of the words ṣāʿaq, in Gen 4, and zāʿaq, in Exod 2. The two consonants are phonologically related, with the two roots apparently by-forms or dialectical variants. See the standard Hebrew dictionaries for discussion. The important instance of the cry to God in 1 Sam 8:18 also employs (a form of) zāʿaq: "When that day comes, you will cry out [zĕʿaqtem] because of the king you chose for yourselves, but on that day the Lord won't answer you." See the next note.
2 This point makes the last part of 1 Sam 8:18 particularly poignant: God will not listen to Israel's cries caused by its monarch(s).
3 See chapter 3.
4 See further Lynch, *Portraying Violence*, 213–15.
5 For dām/dāmîm, see Lynch, 271–72 and 272n17, who notes that there is debate over whether "the plural of dispersion" is deployed consistently in the Old Testament. Even so, Lynch writes, the plural form dāmîm "in general . . . refers to bloodshed or bloodguilt," and cites Exod 22:2; Deut 19:10; 1 Sam 25:26, 33; Isa 1:15 (Lynch, 272).
6 See Lynch, 4, 270, 272. Lynch points out that the "biblical writers are careful to dissociate Yhwh from associations with 'shedding blood' because of its unlawful connotations" (272).
7 See, e.g., the presentations in William Day Crockett, *A Harmony of Samuel, Kings, and Chronicles* (1897; repr., Grand Rapids, MI: Baker, 1985); and Abba Bendavid, *The Twice-Told Tale: Parallels in the Bible* (Jerusalem: Carta, 2017). It is well known that the story about Uriah and Bathsheba goes completely unmentioned in the book of Chronicles, which offers a highly sanitized portrait of King David.

8 See chapter 2.
9 See Herman, *Trauma and Recovery*. For a thoughtful treatment of healing versus curing, see Kristin M. Swenson, *Living through Pain: Psalms and the Search for Wholeness* (Waco, TX: Baylor University Press, 2005).
10 Lynch points out that *violence* is a concept that exhibits a certain kind of "plasticity" (*Portraying Violence*, 2; see further there, including 3n11, for working definitions). For *recovery*, see especially the works of Herman and Swenson cited in the previous note.
11 A minimal listing would likely include Psalms 58, 69, 79, 83, 94, 109, and 137, but others could be added. See further below and the important treatment by Erich Zenger, *A God of Vengeance? Understanding the Psalms of Divine Wrath* (Louisville: Westminster John Knox, 1996). More briefly, see Brent A. Strawn, "Imprecation," in *Dictionary of the Old Testament: Wisdom, Poetry and Writings*, ed. Tremper Longman III and Peter Enns (Downers Grove, IL: IVP Academic, 2008), 314–20.
12 Also in Pss 57, 59, and 75. This phrase also occurs in Deut 9:26; cf. 1 Sam 26:9.
13 See, e.g., Hans-Joachim Kraus, *Psalms 1–59: A Commentary*, trans. Hilton C. Oswald (Minneapolis: Augsburg, 1988), 529, who thinks it is "probably the name of the tune according to which Psalm 57 [and Psalms 58, 59, and 75] is to be intoned." Cf. John Goldingay, *Psalms*, vol. 2, *Psalms 42–89* (Grand Rapids, MI: Baker Academic, 2007), 698, who thinks it may also be "an exhortation not to destroy the psalm, which is designed to stand as a written testimony." Goldingay depends here upon Patrick D. Miller, *Israelite Religion and Biblical Theology: Collected Essays* (Sheffield, UK: Sheffield Academic, 2000), 210–32.
14 C. S. Lewis, *Reflections on the Psalms* (San Francisco: HarperCollins, 2017), 25.
15 For discussion of some of the problems modern readers have with the Old Testament, see Strawn, *Lies My Preacher Told Me*.
16 Lewis, *Reflections*, 23.
17 Babylon is called "you destroyer" in v. 8, but the Hebrew form is passive: "(you who are) destroyed." Interpreters vary on the significance and

meaning of this form, with many translations opting for a passive understanding: contrast NRSV ("devastator") and NJPSV ("predator"). For more on precise payback, see Lynch, *Portraying Violence*, 178–83, 266.
18 Herman, *Trauma and Recovery*, 1 (emphasis in original). The work of James Pennebaker, discussed in the previous chapter, is also important at this point: the psalmist of Psalm 137 does not inhibit or nonverbalize. See further below.
19 Herman, 240 and 280n15. Research has continued to progress since the publication of Herman's book (1997), along with the development of new techniques such as cognitive processing therapy (CPT), prolonged exposure therapy (PE), and eye movement desensitization and reprocessing (EMDR). See, inter alia, Bessel van der Kolk, *The Body Keeps the Score: Brain, Mind, and Body in the Healing of Trauma* (New York: Penguin, 2014); and Peter A. Levine, *Healing Trauma: A Pioneering Program for Restoring the Wisdom of Your Body* (Boulder, CO: Sounds True, 2008). Note also Rachel Yehuda, Charles W. Hoge, Alexander C. McFarlane et al., "Post-traumatic Stress Disorder," *Nature Reviews Disease Primers* 1 (2015): 1–22, https://doi.org/10.1038/nrdp.2015.57. I am grateful to Warren Kinghorn for bringing these resources to my attention and for his kind assistance and insight.
20 Herman, *Trauma and Recovery*, 1.
21 Herman, 1 (emphasis added). Cf. Pennebaker, *Opening Up*, 9–10, on how disclosure helps people understand and assimilate their traumatic experiences.
22 Herman, *Trauma and Recovery*, 1.
23 Herman, 1.
24 Herman, 1.
25 See, provisionally, Brent A. Strawn, "Psalm 137," in Van Harn and Strawn, *Psalms for Preaching and Worship*, 345–53. I take up this line of inquiry more fully in "The Art of Poetry in Psalm 137: Movement, Reticence, Cursing," in *The Incomparable God: Essays in Biblical Exegesis and Theology*, ed. Collin Cornell and Justin Walker (Grand Rapids, MI: Eerdmans, 2022).

26 Emily Dickinson, "Tell all the Truth but tell it slant (1129)," in *The Complete Poems of Emily Dickinson*, ed. Thomas H. Johnson (Boston: Back Bay, 1976), 506.
27 Herman, *Trauma and Recovery*, 155; cf. 133: "The first principle of recovery is the empowerment of the survivor." Note how Psalm 137 speaks of intentional resistance on the part of the exiles in verses 2–3: they hung up their lyres *because* the Babylonians requested songs from them.
28 Herman, 175.
29 Herman, 196.
30 Herman, 140. Expressions of trauma often mention other people and frequently include others, even if that is only in an imaginative sense or in the context of therapy. Perhaps the flipside of this point is another—namely, that "recovery can take place only within the context of relationships; it cannot occur in isolation. In her renewed connections with other people, the survivor recreates the psychological faculties that were damaged or deformed by the traumatic experience. These faculties include the basic capacities for trust, autonomy, initiative, competence, identity, and intimacy. Just as these capabilities are originally formed in relationships with other people, they must be reformed in such relationships" (133).
31 Herman, 195.
32 Herman, 195. Worry or concern over forgetting one's trauma appears to be present in Ps 137:5–6.
33 Herman, 189.
34 Herman, 189.
35 Herman, 189.
36 Cf., e.g., Exod 32:13; Lev 26:45; Num 10:9; Deut 9:27; 2 Chr 6:42; Neh 13:14, 22. See further Strawn, "Art of Poetry."
37 Herman, *Trauma and Recovery*, 104 (emphasis added).
38 Herman, 230.
39 Herman, 230.
40 The only thing the poet resists is her tormentors (see note 27 above).

41 See Strawn, "Art of Poetry"; and, more generally, Trevor W. Thompson, "Punishment and Restitution," in Strawn et al., eds., *Oxford Encyclopedia of the Bible and Law*, 2:183-84.
42 Note that these last two verses are not directly addressed to God; perhaps the poet realizes the danger of such a formulation. See further Strawn, "Imprecation"; and Strawn, "Art of Poetry."
43 See, e.g., Moshe Weinfeld, *Social Justice in Ancient Israel and in the Ancient Near East* (Jerusalem: Magnes, 1995), 179–214; and Enrique Nardoni, *Rise Up, O Judge: A Study of Justice in the Biblical World*, trans. Seán Charles Martin (Peabody, MA: Hendrickson, 2004), passim, but esp. 42–67, 86, 124.
44 See Zenger, *God of Vengeance*; cf. Davis, *Getting Involved with God*, 27: "No personal vendetta is authorized" in these psalms, "no pouring sugar in the gas tank, no picking up a gun or hiring one. On the contrary, the validity of any punishing action that may occur depends entirely on its being God's action, not ours."
45 See further there and, more generally, Walter Brueggemann, *The Psalms and the Life of Faith*, ed. Patrick D. Miller (Minneapolis: Fortress, 1995), 3–32.
46 Later post-traumatic growth, even flourishing, is in no small way dependent on disclosure. See Bonanno, *Other Side of Sadness*. See further below for more discussion of how the imprecatory psalms allow one to unburden the self of rage.
47 For what follows, see further Strawn, "Trauma, Psalmic Disclosure, Authentic Happiness," 143–60, esp. 155–58. See also Strawn, "Poetic Attachment," 404–23.
48 Walter Brueggemann has also spoken of the psalms as scripts, and I have no doubt that I first came across that language in his work. See esp. Brueggemann, *From Whom*.
49 Davis, *Getting Involved with God*, 20.
50 Strawn, "Trauma, Psalmic Disclosure, Authentic Happiness," 158: "The psalmists somehow knew these truths, although perhaps not in the way we know or articulate them today, and so disclosed their traumas; the Psalter as a whole now does the same. In so doing, both the

psalmists and the book of Psalms offer us models for how we might begin the long and hard process of recovery from our own similar difficulties."

51 Frank Warren, *Secret Lives of Men and Women*, n.p. (emphasis added).
52 See briefly Strawn, *Lies My Preacher Told Me*, 41–53.
53 See, among others, Shelly Matthews and E. Leigh Gibson, eds., *Violence in the New Testament* (New York: T&T Clark, 2005); Pieter G. R. de Villiers and Jan Willem van Henten, eds., *Coping with Violence in the New Testament* (Leiden, Netherlands: Brill, 2012); and Jerome F. D. Creach, *Violence in Scripture*, Interpretation (Louisville: Westminster John Knox, 2013), 217–39. Critics of Christianity have not always missed the fact that the New Testament suffers from some of the same problems as the Old—see, e.g., Christopher Hitchens's chapter "The 'New' Testament Exceeds the Evil of the 'Old' One," in his *God Is Not Great: How Religion Poisons Everything* (New York: Twelve, 2007), 109–22.
54 See, among many others, the following (which often vary quite profoundly among themselves): Lynch, *Portraying Violence*; Paul Copan, *Is God a Moral Monster? Making Sense of the Old Testament God* (Grand Rapids, MI: Baker, 2011); Copan, *Did God Really Command Genocide? Coming to Terms with the Justice of God* (Grand Rapids, MI: Baker, 2014); Creach, *Violence in Scripture*; Creach, *The Violence of Scripture: Overcoming the Old Testament's Troubling Legacy* (Minneapolis: Fortress, 2012); Eric A. Seibert, *Disturbing Divine Behavior: Troubling Old Testament Images of God* (Minneapolis: Fortress, 2009); Christian Hofreiter, *Making Sense of Old Testament Genocide: Christian Interpretations of Herem Passages* (Oxford: Oxford University Press, 2018); Gregory A. Boyd, *Crucifixion of the Warrior God: Interpreting the Old Testament's Violent Portraits of God in Light of the Cross*, 2 vols. (Minneapolis: Fortress, 2017); and L. Daniel Hawk, *The Violence of the Biblical God: Canonical Narrative and Christian Faith* (Grand Rapids, MI: Eerdmans, 2019). This is just a sampling. In my judgment, one of the best treatments is, happily, also much shorter than these others: Stephen B. Chapman, "Martial Memory, Peaceable Vision: Divine War in the Old

Testament," in *Holy War in the Bible: Christian Morality and an Old Testament Problem*, ed. Heath Thomas, Jeremy Evans, and Paul Copan (Downers Grove, IL: IVP Academic, 2013), 47–67.

55 For this first point, see esp. Lynch, *Portraying Violence*, passim, but esp. 4, 8–9.
56 I have discussed some of what follows in other places, including Strawn, *Lies My Preacher Told Me*, 31–53; Strawn, "Canaan and Canaanites," in *The Oxford Encyclopedia of the Bible and Theology*, 2 vols., ed. Samuel E. Balentine et al. (Oxford: Oxford University Press, 2015), 1:104–11; Strawn, "Scripture, Guns, and Psychology"; and Strawn, "Who's Afraid of the Old Testament? Tough Texts for Rough Times," in *The Oxford Handbook of the Bible in Orthodox Christianity*, ed. Eugen J. Pentiuc (Oxford: Oxford University Press, in press).
57 I am indebted to Lynch, *Portraying Violence*, 214, for this phrasing.
58 Solomon's formal request for wisdom doesn't come until 1 Kgs 3, suggesting that, at this point in the story, Solomon's wisdom "consisted primarily of political savvy" (Lynch, *Portraying Violence*, 214).
59 Lynch, 214.
60 Lynch, 215.
61 It would appear that David sets Solomon an unfortunate example: Solomon, too, proves unfaithful at the very end of his life (1 Kgs 11:1–13).
62 Violent speech is not exactly the same as violent action, but both are arenas in which violence can take place. See Lynch, *Portraying Violence*, 95–143, for a treatment of how "certain biblical writers describe violence as a problem that manifests in the form of deceitful and arrogant speech, and thus threatens the community that depends on reliable, or wise, speech. Violence is said to be 'under the tongue' or 'behind the lips' of the wicked. In these portrayals, deceitful and arrogant speech is not just an accompaniment to violence, but is a form of violence itself" (11). Obviously, Lynch is not speaking here of the violent speech of the psalmists when that is considered righteous (for various reasons; see the earlier discussion in this chapter), but the dynamics of *speech-into-violence* and/or *violence-into-speech* in both scenarios are comparable and something to worry about and consider carefully.

63 Miller, *Way of the Lord*, 200. This quotation is pulled from a chapter entitled "The Hermeneutics of Imprecation" (193–202), which is, in my judgment, the single best article-length treatment of the imprecatory psalms.
64 Miller, 200.
65 Miller, 201.
66 Warren, *Secret Lives of Men and Women*, n.p. (emphasis added).
67 Davis, *Getting Involved with God*, 27 (emphasis added).
68 Millard Lind, *Yahweh Is a Warrior: The Theology of Warfare in Ancient Israel* (Scottdale, PA: Herald, 1980), has argued that divine action is in fact the ultimate warrant for human pacifism.
69 See Strawn, "Canaan and Canaanites," 1:109; Chapman, "Martial Memory, Peaceable Vision," 47–61, esp. 56, 61; Creach, *Violence in Scripture*, 110, 123–24; and Norbert Lohfink, "חרם *ḥāram*," in *Theological Dictionary of the Old Testament*, ed. G. Johannes Botterweck and Helmer Ringgren, trans. David E. Green (Grand Rapids, MI: Eerdmans, 1986), 5:180–99, esp. 197.
70 See, e.g., Dennis T. Olson, *Deuteronomy and the Death of Moses: A Theological Reading*, Overtures to Biblical Theology (Minneapolis: Fortress, 1994).
71 See Brent A. Strawn, "Commentary on Esther 7:1–6, 9–10; 9:20–22," Working Preacher, September 27, 2009, https://tinyurl.com/5td66snn.
72 But see Lawson G. Stone, "Ethical and Apologetic Tendencies in the Redaction of the Book of Joshua," *Catholic Biblical Quarterly* 52 (1991): 25–36, who has convincingly demonstrated that most of the battles in Joshua are also *defensive* ones.
73 See the useful discussion in Geoffrey Parsons Miller, "Property," in Strawn et al., *Oxford Encyclopedia of Bible, Law*, 2:175–82.
74 Chapman, "Marital Memory, Peaceable Vision," 64.
75 Note Strawn, "Canaan and Canaanites," 1:105: "For all intents and purposes," references to the Canaanites "cease after Judges (the only exceptions being 2 Sam 24:7; and 1 Kgs 9:16)." Here, as throughout the present volume, I am, of course, speaking about biblical Israel (see chapter 1, note 3) and not the modern nation-state of Israel. For those

who are interested in contemporary land issues in Israel/Palestine, see (among others) Walter Brueggemann, *Chosen? Reading the Bible amid the Israeli-Palestinian Conflict* (Louisville: Westminster John Knox, 2015).

76 What follows depends in part on Strawn, "Scripture, Guns, and Psychology."
77 Andrew M. Colman, *A Dictionary of Psychology*, 2nd ed. (Oxford: Oxford University Press, 2006), 606.
78 Colman, 268.
79 Mitchell and Black, *Freud and Beyond*, 27. Colman provides a different example, "when a child converts unconscious angry or aggressive impulses into a fear of monsters or demons in the dark" (*Dictionary of Psychology*, 268).
80 Anna Freud, *The Ego and the Mechanisms of Defense*, rev. ed. (New York: International Universities Press, 1966). See also Joseph Sandler with Anna Freud, *The Analysis of Defense: The Ego and the Mechanisms of the Self Revisited* (New York: International Universities Press, 1985). Colman, *Dictionary of Psychology*, 606–7, delineates various "projective tests" such as the Rorschach test, word-association test, and sentence completion test that some have thought provide "X-ray images of the unconscious mind."
81 Nancy McWilliams, *Psychoanalytic Diagnosis: Understanding Personality Structure in the Clinical Process*, 2nd ed. (New York: Guilford, 2011), 103 (emphasis in original).
82 McWilliams, 101. Different schools of thought have emphasized different reasons for such behavior: ego psychologists have emphasized *anxiety*, object relations theorists *grief*, and self psychologists *a strong sense of self* (McWilliams, 101). See Mitchell and Black, *Freud and Beyond*, 70, for Harry Stack Sullivan's idea that anxiety-minimizing processes express the need for security.
83 For another positive understanding of externalizing things, see Fisher, "Most Trusted Stranger," viii–ix (cited in chapter 1, note 45).
84 McWilliams, *Psychoanalytic Diagnosis*, 111.
85 McWilliams, 111.
86 McWilliams, 111.

87 André LaCocque, "A Psychological Approach to the Book of Jonah," in *Psychology and the Bible: A New Way to Read the Scriptures*, 4 vols., ed. J. Harold Ellens and Wayne G. Rollins (Westport, CT: Greenwood-Praeger, 2004), 2:83–92 (85).
88 Denise Levertov, "Life at War," in *Selected Poems*, ed. Paul A. Lacey (New York: New Directions, 2002), 64–65 (64).
89 Levertov, 64.
90 Levertov, 65.
91 Walter Brueggemann, *Praying the Psalms: Engaging Scripture and the Life of the Spirit*, 2nd ed. (Eugene, OR: Cascade, 2007), 64, 80–81 (emphasis added).
92 Richard B. Hays, *The Moral Vision of the New Testament: Community, Cross, New Creation: A Contemporary Introduction to New Testament Ethics* (San Francisco: HarperSanFrancisco, 1996), 343.
93 I owe this connection to Rev. Evan Marbury, who shared it in a sermon.
94 Davis, *Getting Involved with God*, 25.
95 See, among others, Erich Zenger, "Psalm 76," in *Psalms 2: A Commentary on Psalms 51–100*, ed. Klaus Baltzer, trans. Linda M. Maloney (Minneapolis: Fortress, 2005), 259, 261; Goldingay, *Psalms 42–89*, 449, 455; Marvin E. Tate, *Psalms 51–100* (Dallas: Word, 1990), 262; and Hans-Joachim Kraus, *Psalms 60–150: A Continental Commentary*, trans. Hilton C. Oswald (Minneapolis: Fortress, 1993), 108. The essay by J. A. Emerton, "A Neglected Solution of a Problem in Psalm lxxvi 11," *Vetus Testamentum* 24 (1974): 136–46, is of special note. Emerton's work with the Hebrew text produces the following translation: "Surely thou dost crush the wrath of man: / Thou dost restrain the remnant of wrath" (145).

Chapter 5

1 Oscar Wilde, *The Importance of Being Earnest and Other Plays* (Oxford: Oxford University Press, 1998), 307.
2 The term "truth dumping" was coined by the psychiatrist Will Gaylin to convey "the harm that brutal, needless, or uncaring truth-telling can

wreak." See the discussion in Bok, *Lying*, xxii, who goes on to speak of the importance of discretion (see further below).
3 *Oxford English Dictionary*, 3rd ed. (March 2015); cited online (latest version published December 2020).
4 John Carey, *A Little History of Poetry* (New Haven, CT: Yale University Press, 2020), 262–68.
5 Bok, *Lying*, xxiii, describes *discretion* as "the ability to discern what is and is not intrusive and injurious while navigating in and between the worlds of personal and shared experience." See further below and, more extensively, Bok, *Secrets*.
6 Carey, *Little History of Poetry*, 264. See Bok, *Secrets*, 26, for "the safety valve between the inner and shared worlds" as well as "the pathologies of prying into the private spheres of others, and of losing all protection for one's own: voyeurism and the corresponding hunger for self-exposure that destroy the capacity to discriminate and choose." See further there on how a discloser must "consider the degree to which his revelations might burden or manipulate the person to whom he speaks" (84). The risks that accompany self-revelation delineated by Bok (88) are instructive, though, in my judgment, Israel's own honesty is not of the kind she describes and thus doesn't run those risks.
7 It is worth recalling that in contrast to such public displays, Jesus thrice calls attention to "your Father who sees [what is done] in secret" (6:4, 6, 18) and twice identifies that Father as the one "who is present in that secret place" (6:6, 18).
8 See, inter alia, Carl Dennis, *Poetry as Persuasion* (Athens: University of Georgia Press, 2001).
9 See chapter 2, note 34, and especially Tutu, *No Future without Forgiveness*.
10 See Thomas M. Raitt, *A Theology of Exile: Judgment/Deliverance in Jeremiah and Ezekiel* (Philadelphia: Fortress, 1977); as well as Walter Brueggemann, *The Theology of the Book of Jeremiah*, Old Testament Theology, ed. Brent A. Strawn and Patrick D. Miller (Cambridge: Cambridge University Press, 2007), 40, 127.

11 Cf. Brent A. Strawn, "Pivots in Scripture," in Walter Brueggemann, *Delivered out of Empire: Pivotal Moments in the Book of Exodus, Part One*, Pivotal Moments in the Old Testament, ed. Brent A. Strawn (Louisville: Westminster John Knox, 2021), ix–xiii.
12 See Rolf Rendtorff, *The Covenant Formula: An Exegetical and Theological Investigation*, trans. Margaret Kohl (Edinburgh: T&T Clark, 1998).
13 First, in oracles against the nations (chaps. 25–32), before turning to promises of salvation (chaps. 33–39) and a vision for a restored Israel (chaps. 40–48).
14 The verb is *yādāh*, often used for praise in the Hiphil stem but appearing here in the Hithpael (*wĕhitwaddāh*) with the meaning "to confess sin," as also in Lev 5:5; 26:40; Num 5:7; and so on.
15 Cf. Luke 6:35b: God "is kind to ungrateful and wicked people." Perhaps to be considered here are the remarkable texts where God appears to be reconciled with some of Israel's most hated enemies. See, e.g., Isa 19:23–25; Amos 9:7; and Ps 87. Ezek 32:31–32 also deserves mention; though, in this text, it appears that Pharaoh repents—in Sheol!
16 Cited in Bok, *Lying*, xix–xx. See chapter 1, note 11.
17 La Rochefoucauld, cited in Bok, xx; see previous note.
18 Warren, *Lifetime of Secrets*, n.p.
19 See further Strawn, "Poetic Attachment," 404–23; and Strawn, "Trauma, Psalmic Disclosure, Authentic Happiness," 143–60.
20 For more on the suffering of God, see esp. Terence E. Fretheim, *The Suffering of God: An Old Testament Perspective*, Overtures to Biblical Theology (Philadelphia: Fortress, 1984).
21 Joseph Medlicott Scriven, "What a Friend We Have in Jesus" (1855).
22 Chapman, "Martial Memory, Peaceable Vision," 64: "God was not able, given the violence of the world, to preserve Israel purely nonviolently." See also chapter 4, notes 54 and 69.
23 The best treatment of the issues is found in Abraham Joshua Heschel, *The Prophets* (New York: HarperCollins, 2001), 358–92. See also the thorough exploration in Dale Patrick, *Redeeming Judgment* (Eugene, OR: Pickwick, 2012).

24 See further Strawn, *Lies My Preacher Told Me*, 43, also 31–40; as well as Lynch, *Portraying Violence*, 273–74, for ways the biblical authors worked to make clear that "God was not an agent of violence or unjustified acts of bodily harm."

25 Cf. Chapman, "Martial Memory, Peaceable Vision," 64: "Someone . . . might ask, 'Couldn't God design a world in which war wasn't necessary?' The appropriate theological response is that God in fact did so (Gen 1–2), but human sinfulness spoiled it precisely by generating violence (Gen 6:11–13)." See further Brent A. Strawn, "From *Imago* to *Imagines*: The Image(s) of God in Genesis," in *The Cambridge Companion to Genesis*, ed. Bill T. Arnold (Cambridge: Cambridge University Press, 2021).

26 Walter Brueggemann, "God in Recovery," originally posted on the Center for Biblical Studies's website (thecenterforbiblicalstudies.org), on July 21, 2012, but no longer available. Other online sources reprint parts of the original blog post or summarize it. A fuller treatment is found in Walter Brueggemann, "The Recovering God of Hosea," *Horizons in Biblical Theology* 30 (2008): 5–20. See also Walter Brueggemann and Clover Reuter Beal, *An On-Going Imagination: A Conversation about Scripture, Faith, and the Thickness of Relationship*, ed. Timothy Beal (Louisville: Westminster John Knox, 2019), 63–68.

27 Brueggemann, "Recovering God of Hosea," 17.

28 Commentators, of course, frequently fillet the prophetic texts into multiple strata and sources such that not everything from the book of Hosea can with certainty be traced back to an eighth-century context.

29 For some reflections, see Brent A. Strawn, "'Israel, My Child': The Ethics of a Biblical Metaphor," in *The Child in the Bible*, ed. Marcia Bunge, Terence E. Fretheim, and Beverly R. Gaventa (Grand Rapids, MI: Eerdmans, 2008), 103–40.

30 Brueggemann, "God in Recovery."

31 Gary A. Anderson, *Christian Doctrine and the Old Testament: Theology in the Service of Biblical Exegesis* (Grand Rapids, MI: Baker Academic, 2017), 37 (emphasis added).

32 Brueggemann, "Recovering God of Hosea," 20.

33 On self-deception, see David McRaney, *You Are Not So Smart: Why You Have Too Many Friends on Facebook, Why Your Memory Is Mostly Fiction, and 46 Other Ways You're Deluding Yourself* (New York: Gotham, 2011); and Bok, *Secrets*, 59–72, 81, 86. Within the pastoral realm, see also Dayton Hartman, *Lies Pastors Believe: Seven Ways to Elevate Yourself, Subvert the Gospel, and Undermine the Church* (Bellingham, WA: Lexham, 2017).

34 See the previous note on self-deception, and cf. Jer 17:9: "The heart is devious above all else; it is perverse—who can understand it?" (NRSV), as well as 1 John 3:20: "Even if our hearts condemn us, God is greater than our hearts and knows all things."

35 See James L. Crenshaw, "The Expression *mî yôdēa'* in the Hebrew Bible," *Vetus Testamentum* 36 (1986): 274–88; reprinted in Crenshaw, *Urgent Advice and Probing Questions: Collected Writings on Old Testament Wisdom* (Macon, GA: Mercer University Press, 1995), 279–91. See also Brent A. Strawn, "Who Indeed? A Reconsideration of מי יודע in the Hebrew Bible" (forthcoming).

36 A helpful exploration of the latter item, in particular, is found in Michael V. Fox, *Qohelet and His Contradictions* (Decatur, GA: Almond, 1989), which appeared in revised and expanded form as *A Time to Tear Down and a Time to Build Up: A Rereading of Ecclesiastes* (Grand Rapids, MI: Eerdmans, 1999).

37 Elias Bickerman, *Four Strange Books of the Bible: Jonah, Daniel, Koheleth, Esther* (New York: Schocken, 1967), 149.

38 Of course, Scripture as a whole offers the same counsel. If Israel's testimony is not in service, ultimately, to *self-honesty* (see above), it is at the very least a strong antidote to *self-deception*.

39 Simplistic words that claim to know too much, therefore, are to be studiously avoided. The (to my mind) thoroughly unhelpful expression "Everything happens for a reason" must surely head the list of such words. "How would anyone even know that?" Qoheleth would derisively ask in reply to that phrase.

40 Cf. Barbara Brown Taylor, *When God Is Silent: The 1997 Lyman Beecher Lectures on Preaching* (Cambridge, MA: Cowley, 1998), 121, on "why

we did not say more . . . than we did" with reference to why preachers serve up on Sunday: "It was not that we didn't [want to]. It was that we couldn't." See also Taylor, 117.

41 R. N. Whybray, "Qoheleth, Preacher of Joy," *Journal for the Study of the Old Testament* 23 (1982): 87–98. See further, and more recently, Eunny P. Lee, *The Vitality of Enjoyment in Qohelet's Theological Rhetoric* (Berlin: De Gruyter, 2005); T. A. Perry, *The Book of Ecclesiastes (Qohelet) and the Path to Joyous Living* (Cambridge: Cambridge University Press, 2015); and Jerome N. Douglas, *A Polemical Preacher of Joy: An Anti-apocalyptic Genre for Qoheleth's Message of Joy* (Eugene, OR: Pickwick, 2014).

42 Cf. Thomas G. Long, *Preaching from Memory to Hope* (Louisville: Westminster John Knox, 2009), 20: "Preacher stories that always yield the right moral lesson or end up in triumph without struggle are a damned lie about human life and Christian faith."

43 See the previous note and Taylor, *When God Is Silent*, 107, for lying in the pulpit. Bok, *Lying*, 242, comments on how easy it is to deceive and the wide range of tools available to us to do so: clearly intended lies, evasion, euphemism, and exaggeration, among others. For more on lying in the context of preaching, see Frank G. Honeycutt, *The Truth Shall Make You Odd: Speaking with Pastoral Integrity in Awkward Situations* (Grand Rapids, MI: Brazos, 2011), passim, but especially xiv, 55–81; and Walter Brueggemann, *Truth-Telling as Subversive Obedience*, ed. K. C. Hanson (Eugene, OR: Cascade, 2011), 68–80. Cf. also the epigraph to the present volume from Farrar, *History of Interpretation*, 4–5, which states that interpreters must be people of "invincible honesty" if they wish to "avoid the misleading influences of [their] own *a priori* convictions."

44 Some would say, with David Bartlett, that we tell the truth in preaching because "there is no better way to love a congregation than to preach truth to them" ("Preaching the Truth," in *But Is It All True? The Bible and the Question of Truth*, ed. Alan G. Padgett and Patrick R. Keifert [Grand Rapids, MI: Eerdmans, 2006], 129). But honesty requires that we admit that love can also encourage duplicity in the

pulpit. See Bok, *Lying*, 244, for the many powerful social incentives to deceive, with controls against such deception often very weak. Her judgments apply equally to the society of the church. My own experience running a Doctor of Ministry (DMin) program for five years taught me how truly scared most ministers were to say anything that mattered—in other words, how frightened they were to tell the whole and real truth.

45 And for more than one reason. According to Bok, "to be given false information about important choices" in life "is to be rendered powerless" (*Lying*, xxix). For the importance of *writing* honest truth, see the work of Pennebaker discussed in chapters 1 and 3.

46 I owe this language to Tom Long, whom I first heard use it in a lecture.

47 Eric G. Wilson, *Against Happiness: In Praise of Melancholy* (New York: Farrar, Straus & Giroux, 2008), 20, has called Christian denominations "basically happiness companies." He didn't mean it as a compliment.

48 The language of "glory of the ordinary" comes from William P. Brown, *Ecclesiastes*, Interpretation (Louisville: John Knox, 2000). As an example of a "small righteousness" that has profound impact, see Jan Karon's children's book, *Miss Fannie's Hat* (New York: Puffin, 2001). Even more powerfully, note the Mishnah, which asserts that saving one life is equivalent to saving the whole world (*m. Sanh.* 4:5).

49 See chapter 1.

50 Bok, *Lying*, 244, notes that, absent controls, it is "wishful thinking . . . to expect individuals [including preachers!] to bring about major changes in the collective practices of deceit by themselves. Public and private institutions, with their enormous power to affect personal choice, must help alter the existing pressures and incentives." It seems to me that Israel's testimony to candor in the Old Testament, so often (potentially, at least) found in the preached text on any given Sunday, provides exactly such pressure. Bok goes on to note how institutional leaders "have to be the first to be held to such standards" (244). Her further reflections on how to develop people who are less prone to duplicity are instructive (244–49) and include educational institutions. Here one might think analogically (and profitably) of the church as a

kind of school of honesty with preachers "the first to be held to such standards."

51 Cited in George Steiner, *Language and Silence: Essays on Language, Literature, and the Inhuman* (New Haven, CT: Yale University Press, 1998), 67, who adds, "students of English literature, of any literature, must ask those who teach them, as they must ask themselves, whether they know, and not in their minds alone, what Kafka meant."

52 Richard Wilbur in Robert Bagg and Mary Bagg, *Let Us Watch Richard Wilbur: A Biographical Study* (Amherst: University of Massachusetts Press, 2017), 223.

53 Harry G. Frankfurt, *On Bullshit* (Princeton, NJ: Princeton University Press, 2005), 1, 66–67. See further Gary L. Hardcastle and George A. Reisch, eds., *Bullshit and Philosophy: Guaranteed to Get Perfect Results Every Time* (Chicago: Open Court, 2006).

54 Bok, *Lying*, 248–49.

AUTHOR INDEX

Allen, Ronald J., 187
Anderson, Gary A., 167, 212
Arnold, Bill T., 192, 212
Aronson, Elliot, 56–58, 192–93

Bagg, Mary, 216
Bagg, Robert, 216
Balentine, Samuel E., 206
Baltzer, Klaus, 209
Barmash, Pamela, 193
Barnes, M. Craig, 76, 195
Bartlett, David, 214
Beal, Clover Reuter, 212
Beal, Timothy, 212
Bendavid, Abba, 200
Berryman, John, 142
Bickerman, Elias, 171, 213
Biddle, Mark E., 190
Black, Margaret J., 185, 208
Block, Daniel I., 188
Boase, Elizabeth, 198
Bok, Sissela, 179, 182–83, 185–86, 188, 190, 192, 210–11, 213–16
Bonaano, George A., 199, 204

Borowsky, Irvin J., 187
Botterweck, G. Johannes, 207
Bowen, Nancy R., 188
Bowlby, Rachel, 185
Boyce, Richard Nelson, 189
Boyd, Gregory, A., 205
Breuer, Josef, 185
Brown, Raymond, 190
Brown, William P., 189, 199, 215
Brueggemann, Walter, 66, 83, 135, 166–67, 183, 188, 190, 193, 195–97, 204, 208–12, 214
Bunge, Marcia, 212
Butler, Reese, 185

Carey, John, 210
Chan, Michael J., 195
Chapman, Stephen B., 129, 192, 205, 207, 211–12
Chung, Cindy K., 199
Cohen, Jeremy, 182
Collins, Billie, 82–83, 196
Colman, Andrew M., 208
Cone, James H., 200

217

AUTHOR INDEX

Copan, Paul, 205-6
Cornell, Collin, 202
Craddock, Fred B., 187
Creach, Jerome F. D., 205, 207
Crenshaw, James L., 213
Crockett, William Day, 200
Crouch, C. L., 182

Davis, Ellen F., 6, 118, 126, 183, 204, 206, 209
Dennis, Carl, 210
Dickinson, Emily, 111, 143, 203
Dobbs-Allsopp, F. W., 196-97
Douglas, Jerome N., 214

Ellens, J. Harold, 209
Emerton, J. A., 209
Enns, Peter, 201
Evans, Paul, 206
Exum, J. Cheryl, xiii, 19-20, 186

Farrar, Frederic W., xiii, 25-26, 187, 214
Fisher, Anne C., 20-23, 186-87, 208
Fox, Michael V., 213
Frankfurt, Harry G., 179, 216
Frechette, Christopher G., 198
Freedman, David Noel, 196
Fretheim, Terence E., 195, 211-12
Freud, Anna, 131, 208
Freud, Sigmund, 18, 185
Friedman, Howard S., 199

Gaventa, Beverly Roberts, 212
Gaylin, Will, 209-10
Geoghegan, Jeffrey C., 196
Gibson, E. Leigh, 205
Goldingay, John, 201, 209
Gortner, Eva-Maria, 199
Greene-McCreight, Kathryn, 197

Hanson, K. C., 214
Hardcastle, Gary L., 216
Harrelson, Walter J., 194
Harrington, Donald J., 187
Hartman, Dayton, 213
Hawk, L. Daniel, 205
Hays, Christopher B., 182
Hays, Richard B., 136, 209
Heffelfinger, Katie M., 194
Hellman, Lillian, 192
Herman, Judith Lewis, 109-10, 112-15, 117-18, 132, 184-85, 201-3
Heschel, Abraham Joshua, 211
Hitchens, Christopher, 205
Hofreiter, Christian, 205
Hoge, Charles W., 202
Holbert, John C., 190
Honeycutt, Frank G., 214
Hopkins, Gerard Manley, 83-84, 196
Houtman, Cornelis, 194
Hughes, Cheryl F., 198

AUTHOR INDEX

Jacobson, Rolf, 183
Janzen, J. Gerald, 190
Jenson, Matt, 191
Johnson, Thomas H., 203
Jones, L. Gregory, 191

Kafka, Franz, 178
Karon, Jan, 215
Kee, Howard Clark, 187
Keifert, Patrick R., 214
Kim, Eo Kon, 197
Koester, Helmut, 181
Kolk, Bessel van der, 202
Kraus, Hans-Joachim, 201, 209
Krog, Antjie, 193
Kübler-Ross, Elisabeth, 83, 196
Kwakkel, Gert, 195

LaCocque, André, 133, 209
Ladd, Kevin L., 200
La Rochefoucauld, François de, 162, 182, 211
Lee, Eunny P., 214
Levertov, Denise, 134, 209
Levine, Amy-Jill, 181-82
Levine, Peter A., 202
Lewis, C. S., 106-7, 201
Linafelt, Tod, 197
Lind, Millard, 207
Lohfink, Norbert, 182, 188, 207
Long, Thomas G., 214-15
Longman, Tremper III, 201
Lowell, Robert, 142

Luther, Martin, 141, 169, 191
Luz, Ulrich, 181
Lynch, Matthew J., 123, 193, 200-202, 205-6, 212

MacDonald, Nathan, 52, 189, 191-92
Magrassi, Mariano, 183
Marbury, Evan, 209
Marx, Karl, 151
Matthews, Shelly, 205
McConville, J. G., 187-88
McFarlane, Alexander C., 202
McRaney, David, 213
McWilliams, Nancy, 131-32, 208
Menninger, Karl, 50, 191
Miller, Alice, 19, 185
Miller, Geoffrey Parsons, 207
Miller, Patrick D., 124-25, 127, 189, 191, 193, 195-96, 201, 204, 207, 210
Mitchell, Stephen A., 185, 208
Moberly, R. W. L., 35, 38, 188
Moran, W. L., 189
Moughtin-Mumby, Sharon, 189
Nardoni, Enrique, 204

O'Connor, Kathleen M., 196
O'Heeron, Robin C., 198
Olson, Dennis T., 207

Padgett, Alan G., 214
Pastan, Linda, 191

AUTHOR INDEX

Patrick, Dale, 211
Pennebaker, James, 18–19, 91–95, 97, 113, 125, 132, 185, 188, 196, 198–200, 202, 215
Pentiuc, Eugen J., 206
Perry, T. A., 214

Rad, Gerhard von, xiv, 20, 186
Raitt, Thomas, 155, 210
Reisch, George A., 216
Rendtorff, Rolf, 211
Ringgren, Helmer, 207
Roberts, Alastair J., 194
Rollins, Wayne G., 209
Rorem, Paul, 182
Rude, Stephanie S., 199

Salmon, Marilyn J., 187
Salters, R. B., 197
Sandler, Joseph, 208
Sarna, Nahum M., 189
Schultz, Richard M., 188
Scriven, Joseph Medlicott, 211
Seibert, Eric A., 205
Sexton, Anne, 142
Silver, Roxane Cohen, 199
Smiga, George M., 187
Smyth, Joshua M., 185, 199
Spilka, Bernard, 200
Steiner, George, 216
Stone, Lawson G., 207
Strawn, Brent A., 181–83, 188–89, 193, 195, 197–99, 201–8, 211–13

Sullivan, Henry Stack, 208
Suls, Jerry, 198
Susman, Joan R., 198
Swenson, Kristin M., 201

Tate, Marvin E., 209
Tavis, Carol, 56–58, 192
Taylor, Barbara Brown, 191–93, 213–14
Thomas, Heath, 206
Thompson, Trevor W., 204
Trible, Phyllis, 193
Tutu, Desmond, 58, 193, 210

Vandecreek, Larry, 198
Van Harn, Roger, 197, 202
Van Henten, Jan Willem, 205
Vanhoozer, Kevin J., 188
Villanueva, Federico G., 197
Villiers, Pieter G. R. de, 205

Wagner, J. Ross, 182
Walker, Justin, 202
Wallston, Kenneth A., 198
Warren, Frank, 13, 15–16, 18, 20–24, 27, 94, 162, 176, 184–86, 188, 205–6, 211
Weinfeld, Moshe, 204
Welch, Andrew, 196
Westermann, Claus, 197
Whybray, R. N., 214
Wilbur, Richard, 179, 216
Wilde, Oscar, 139–41, 209

AUTHOR INDEX

Williamson, Clark M., 187
Willimon, Will, 187
Wilson, Andrew, 194
Wilson, Eric G., 215

Yehuda, Rachel, 202

Zenger, Erich, 116, 201, 204, 209

SCRIPTURE INDEX

Genesis
1–2 212
1:1 36
1:29–30 165
2:25 28
4 . . . . 100, 200
4:7 . . . . 99, 125
4:10 99
6:11–13 212
15 . . . . 61–62, 67, 71
15:1 71
15:7 128
15:12–16 128
15:13 62
16 61
16:4–5 193
16:6 61
17:8 128
18 167
20:9 189
21:6 61
21:16 193

Exodus
1:1–7 62
1:8 62
1:10 62
1:11–14 63
1:12a 63
1:12b 63
1:15–22 63
2 . . . . 100, 200
2:23–25 100
2:23a 64
2:23b 64–65
2:24–25 . . . . 65, 125
2:24 64
3:6 69
3:12 69
3:14 70
4:30–31 68
5:21 68
5:22–23 68
6:6 70
6:9 69
7:5 72

SCRIPTURE INDEX

7:17 72
11:4 72
12:12 72
12:23 72
12:29–32 71
13:3 193
13:14 193
14:4 71–72
14:17 72
14:18 72
14:19 72
15:16 72
15:26 70
19:5 72
19:8 38
20:2 . . . . 37, 67, 70, 193
20:3 36
20:4–5a 37
20:4b-5a. 38
20:4b 37
20:6 . . . . 70, 194
22:2 200
22:27 70
24:7 38
31:18 52
32–34 167
32 167
32:1 35–36
32:4 . . . . 36, 189
32:4b 37
32:8 37
32:11–14 53
32:13 203
32:14 147
32:21 189
32:30 189
32:31 189
33:12–34:9 53
33:14 147
33:17 147
34:1 53
34:6–7 147
34:10–28 53
40:33b-38 54

Leviticus
5:5 211
10:3 70
11:44–45 70
11:45 70
16 . . . . 158, 160, 164,
                              182, 192
16:16a 158–59
16:17b 159
16:21 160
16:21a 160
16:24b 159
16:30 160–61
16:31 159
16:34a 159
16:34b 159
16:34c 159
19:2 70
20:8 70
21:8 70
21:15 194

SCRIPTURE INDEX

21:23 194
22:9 194
22:16 194
22:32 70
22:33 70
25:23 128
25:38 70
26:13 70–71
26:40 211
26:45 203

Numbers
5:7 211
10:9 203
13–14 194
14 167
18:20 71

Deuteronomy
1:8 188
1:35 188
4:20 66
4:31 188
4:37 188
5:6 193
5:15 69
6:10 188
6:12 193
6:18 188
6:23 188
7:8 193
8:14 193
9:4–24 32–33

9:4–5 35
9:8 35
9:26 201
9:27 203
10:5 188
10:12–13 33–34
11:1 34
11:8–9 34
13:5 193
13:10 193
19:10 200
29:29 177
30:9 188
32:35–36a 119
32:35 125
32:39 71

Joshua
5:13–14a 165
6:25 129
9:1–27 129
13:13 129
15:63 129
16:10 129
17:12 129
24:17 193

Judges
6:8 193

1 Samuel
1 88
1:16 87

SCRIPTURE INDEX

1:17 87
8 45
8:5 39
8:9 39
8:11–17 39–40
8:11a 40
8:17 193
8:18 . . . . 40, 193, 200
8:19–20 40
13:14 53
25:26 200
25:33 200
26:9 201

2 Samuel
7 46
11–12 44–46
11:1 39
11:1a 39
11:1b 39
11:2–4a 41
11:4 . . . . 43–44, 190
11:4a 43
11:4b 42
11:5b 42
11:11 44
11:24 44
11:27 50
11:27b 42
12 . . . . 48, 50–51, 102
12:1–4 50
12:3a 43
12:3b 43
12:4 43–44
12:6 43–44
12:7–10 50
12:7a 42–43
12:9 44
12:10 45
12:11 59
12:11a 45
12:11b 45
12:12 . . . . 42, 45
12:13 . . . . 50, 147
12:13a 42, 46
12:13b 47
12:14 47
16:7–8 . . . . 60, 101, 103
16:11b-12a 60
18:33 60
24:7 207

1 Kings
2:1–4 123
2:5–6 123
2:6 123
2:8 123
2:9 123
2:36–37 123
2:38 123
2:39–46 123
3 206
9:16 207
11:1–13 206

SCRIPTURE INDEX

2 Kings
17:22–23 60–61
25:21b 61

1 Chronicles
22. 102
22:8 101

2 Chronicles
6:42 203

Nehemiah
13:14 203
13:22 203

Esther
7:1–6 207
7:9–10 207
9:20–22 207

Job
2:10 163
19:7 193

Psalms
6. 49
7. . . . . 76, 195
7:1–2 102
7:3–5 75
7:8 75
7:11 137
9–10. 196
10:11 10

10:14 10
13. 86–87
13:1–4 87
13:4 88
13:5–6 87–88
14:2 187
17. . . . . 76, 195
17:3 75
17:5 75
17:8–12 102
18. 195
18:21–25 195
22. 87
22:21 87
25. 196
26. . . . . 76, 195
26:1 75–76
26:3–6b 76
26:11 76
30:5 69
32. . . . . 49, 97
32:3–7 97–98
33:13–15 187
34. 196
35:4 102
35:13–14 195
37. 196
38. 9, 49
38:9 9
38:21 195
44. . . . . 9, 195
44:18–22 195
44:20–21 9

SCRIPTURE INDEX

51. . . . . 48–51, 59, 74, 102–3
51:1–4 49
51:3 60
51:4 50
51:4b 60
51:6 . . . . 55, 180
51:8 60
51:10–13 58
51:14 102–3
51:17 . . . . 55, 147
53:2 187
57. 201
58. . . . . 104, 201
58:6–8 104
59. 201
64:5 10
69. . . . . 9, 136, 201
69:5 9
75. 201
76. 137
76:8 137
76:9a 137
76:9b 137
76:10 137
76:11–12 138
79. 201
81:7a 180
83. 201
86:2 195
87. 211
88. 88–90
88:1a 88
88:1b-2 88
88:3–12 88
88:4 90
88:13 89
88:14–18 89
89. 90
89:52 90
90. . . . . 9, 90
90:8 . . . . 9, 27, 42, 45
90:12 90
94. 201
94:1 116
94:7 10
102. 49
103. 31
103:10–12 30
109. 201
111. 196
112. 196
119. 196
130. 49
130:1 89
130:7 57
137. . . . . 73–74, 76, 107–12,
    114–17, 124, 143, 201–3
137:1–9 107–8
137:1–6 107
137:1–4 73
137:1 110
137:2–3 203
137:5–6 . . . . 110, 203
137:7 . . . . 108–10, 114, 125
137:8–9 115–16
137:8 . . . . 111, 114, 201

137:8a 108
137:9 . . . . 108, 111, 114
139. 105–6
139:19–24 105–6
139:19–22 106
139:22 106
139:23–24 106
143. 49
145. 196
150:6 90

Proverbs
31:10–31 196

Ecclesiastes
1:14 172
1:16 172
2:2 172
2:11 172
2:12 172
2:13 172
2:15 172
2:19 170
2:20 172
2:24–26 174
2:24 176
3:5bα 176
3:10 172
3:11 173
3:12–13 174
3:12 172
3:14 172
3:21 170
3:22 174
5. 173
5:1 176
5:2b 173
5:18–20 174
5:18 176
5:19 176
6:12 170
7:3 175
7:14 174
8:1 170
8:15 174–75
8:17 173
8:17b 170
9:7–10 174
9:7 176
9:9 176
9:10 176
10:14 170
11:7–10 174
12. 173
12:9–10 169–71
12:11 175

Isaiah
1:15 200
6:5 133
19:23–25 211
40:1–2 86
45:15 173

Jeremiah
1:10 156

SCRIPTURE INDEX

6:14 175
8:11 175
11:4 66
17:9 213
20:8 193
20:9 176–77
30:12–22 156–57
30:15 156
30:16 156
30:17 156
31:8–14 86
34:13 193
52:27 61

Lamentations
1–4 84
1 84
1:1 77
1:2 77–78
1:3 77
1:8 78
1:8a 78
1:10 78
1:14 78
1:15 78
1:16 78
1:20b 78
1:21–22 106
1:21b-22 78
2 84
2:11–12 77
2:16–17 84
2:19–20 77

3 . . . . 79–81, 84
3:21–33 79
3:21 78
3:24 78
3:41–51 78
3:42–45 80
3:46–51 84
3:56–58 78
3:64–66 . . . . 78, 106
4–5 80
4 84
4:2–4 77
4:10 77
4:16–17 84
4:21–22 . . . . 78, 106
5 84
5:19–22 84
5:21–22 80
5:21 . . . . 80–81, 85
5:22 . . . . 80–81, 85, 197

Ezekiel
24 158
25–32 211
32:31–32 211
33–39 211
40–48 211

Daniel
2:20–22 180

Hosea
1:1 167

SCRIPTURE INDEX

11 166
11:8–9 166
11:9 167

Amos
7:1–6 167
7:11 61
7:17 61
9:7 211
9:8 187

Obadiah
1 75

Jonah
3:10 164

Micah
6:4 193

Nahum
1:2–8 196

Habakkuk
1:2 193

Zechariah
1 75
1:14–17 74

Prayer of Azariah
1:5 196
1:16 192
1:21 78

Susanna
1:42 187

Prayer of Manasseh
1 49
1:13–15 147
1:13 57

Matthew
5:21–22 1
5:27–28 1
5:31–32 1
5:33–34 1
5:38–39 1
5:43–44 1
5:43 2
6:2–6 142
6:2 142
6:4 . . . . 26, 210
6:5 142
6:6 . . . . 26, 210
6:16–18 142
6:16 142
6:18 . . . . 26, 210
6:60 33
7:3–5 31
7:4 136
10:26 . . . . 26–27, 180
15:22–28 129
28:16–17 52
28:20 71

SCRIPTURE INDEX

Mark
4:11 177
4:22 . . . . 27, 180
4:23 180

Luke
6:35b 211
8:17 . . . . 27, 180
9:31 194
12:2 . . . . 27, 180
23:33–34a 126
23:34 162

John
5. 3
5:7 4
6:35 71
6:41 71
6:48 71
6:51 71
8:12 71
9:5 71
10:7 71
10:9 71
10:11 71
10:14 71
11:25 71
14:6 71
15:1 71
15:5 71

Acts
7:59–60 127
7:60 162

Romans
2:16 27
5:8 161
11:29 3
12:18–21 125
12:19 119
15:3 136
15:4 . . . . 136, 152

1 Corinthians
5:7a-8 xiv
9:10 152
11:31 55
11:32 55

Ephesians
2:4–5 161–62
2:4 48
6:12 128

Hebrews
4:12 127
4:13 10
10:30 119

1 John
1:8–9 . . . . 31, 48
1:9 155
1:10 31
3:20 213

Revelation
6:10 . . . . 116, 136

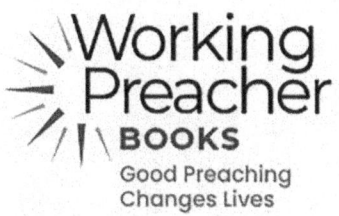

Working Preacher Books is a partnership between Luther Seminary, WorkingPreacher.org, and Fortress Press.

Books in the Series

Preaching from the Old Testament by Walter Brueggemann

Leading with the Sermon by William H. Willimon

The Gospel People Don't Want to Hear: Preaching Challenging Sermons by Lisa Cressman

A Lay Preacher's Guide: How to Craft a Faithful Sermon by Karoline M. Lewis

Preaching Jeremiah: Announcing God's Restorative Passion by Walter Brueggemann

Preaching the Headlines: Pitfalls and Possibilities by Lisa L. Thompson

Honest to God Preaching: Talking Sin, Suffering, and Violence by Brent A. Strawn

Writing for the Ear, Preaching from the Heart by Donna Giver-Johnston

The Peoples' Sermon: Preaching as a Ministry of the Whole Congregation by Shauna K. Hannan